Paul Odoeme

Human Rights and the Mission of the Church in Nigeria

Tübinger Perspektiven zur Pastoraltheologie und Religionspädagogik

herausgegeben von

Ottmar Fuchs, Albert Biesinger, Reinhold Boschki

Band 46

LIT

Paul Odoeme

Human Rights and the Mission of the Church in Nigeria

LIT

Printed with support of Weltkirche, Hilfswerk der Diözese Rottenburg-Stuttgart and Stiftung Landesbank Baden-Württemberg.

Bibliographic information published by the Deutsche Nationalbibliothek
The Deutsche Nationalbibliothek lists this publication in the Deutsche Nationalbibliografie; detailed bibliographic data are available in the Internet at http://dnb.d-nb.de.

ISBN 978-3-643-90199-6
Zugl.: Tübingen, Univ., Diss., 2011

A catalogue record for this book is available from the British Library

Klosbachstr. 107
CH-8032 Zürich
Tel. +41 (0) 44-251 75 05
Fax +41 (0) 44-251 75 06
E-Mail: zuerich@lit-verlag.ch
http://www.lit-verlag.ch

LIT VERLAG Dr. W. Hopf
Berlin 2013
Fresnostr. 2
D-48159 Münster
Tel. +49 (0) 2 51-62 03 20
Fax +49 (0) 2 51-23 19 72
E-Mail: lit@lit-verlag.de
http://www.lit-verlag.de

Distribution:
In Germany: LIT Verlag Fresnostr. 2, D-48159 Münster
Tel. +49 (0) 2 51-620 32 22, Fax +49 (0) 2 51-922 60 99, E-mail: vertrieb@lit-verlag.de

In Austria: Medienlogistik Pichler-ÖBZ, e-mail: mlo@medien-logistik.at
In Switzerland: B + M Buch- und Medienvertrieb, e-mail: order@buch-medien.ch
In the UK: Global Book Marketing, e-mail: mo@centralbooks.com
In North America: International Specialized Book Services, e-mail: orders@isbs.com
e-books are available at www.litwebshop.de

Contents

Acknowledgements....................v

GENERAL INTRODUCTION....................1

CHAPTER ONE....................6

HUMAN RIGHTS IN NIGERIA....................6

Introduction....................6

1.1 A BRIEF HISTORY OF HUMAN RIGHTS IN NIGERIA....................7

1.2 THE NIGERIAN CONSTITUTION....................14

1.2.1 Origin and history....................14

1.2.1.1 Structure and contents of the 1999 Nigerian Constitution....................19

1.2.2 African Commission on Human and Peoples' Rights....................22

1.2.3 The African Charter on Human and Peoples' Rights and the Universal Declaration on Human Rights: Similarities and Differences....................25

1.2.4 National Human Rights Commission of Nigeria....................26

1.3 THE NIGERIAN CONSTITUTION AND THE ISLAMIC SHARIA LAW....................27

1.4 THE NIGERIAN CONSTITUTION AND HUMAN RIGHTS....................32

1.5 CURRENT TRENDS IN HUMAN RIGHTS QUESTION IN NIGERIA....................34

1.5.1 Civil and Political Rights....................37

1.5.1.1 Right to Life....................37

1.5.1.2 Right to Freedom of Religion....................41

1.5.1.3 Right to freedom from discrimination....................44

1.5.1.4 Right to Freedom of Expression....................48

1.5.1.5 Right to Freedom of Association....................50

1.5.2 Judicial Rights....................52

Equal judicial rights for all....................52

1.5.3 Socio-economic Rights....................57

1.5.3.1 Rights to decent standard of living and equal employment opportunities....................57

1.5.3.2 Rights of women and children....................61

1.5.4 Environmental Rights....................65

Right to healthy environment, and nature preservation....................65

Summary....................69

CHAPTER TWO....................72

CULTURAL AND RELIGIOUS TRADITIONS IN NIGERIA AND HUMAN RIGHTS....................72

Introduction....................72

2.1 NIGERIAN CULTURAL TRADITIONS AND HUMAN RIGHTS....................74

2.1.1 The Hausa cultural tradition 74
2.1.2 The Yoruba cultural tradition 75
2.1.3 The Igbo cultural tradition 75
2.1.4 Common values of the Nigerian cultural traditions and the Human Rights Question 77
2.1.4.1 The value of Communalism: 77
2.1.4.2 The value of human relations: 78
2.1.4.3 The value of the sacredness of life 79
2.1.4.4 The value of religion 80
2.1.5 Human rights violations in Nigerian cultural contexts 81
2.1.5.1 Right to life 82
2.1.5.2 Right to freedom from discrimination 83
2.1.5.3 Rights of women 84
2.1.5.3.1 Women as victims of violence 84
2.1.5.3.2 The Traditional bride price 85
2.1.5.3.3 Right of inheritance 85
2.1.5.3.4 The traditional widowhood rites 86
2.1.5.3.5 Female Genital Mutilation (FGM) 88
2.1.5.3.6 Child marriages 91
2.2 RELIGIOUS TRADITIONS IN NIGERIA AND HUMAN RIGHTS 93
2.2.1 Islam and human rights in Nigeria 94
2.2.1.1 Right to Equality in Islam 96
2.2.1.2 Rights of Women in Islam 100
2.2.1.3 Right to Freedom of Religion in Islam 102
2.2.1.4 Right to protection of life in Islam 104
2.2.2 Christianity and human rights in Nigeria 107
2.2.2.1 Right to Equality in Christianity 110
2.2.2.2 Right to Freedom from discrimination in Christianity 111
Summary 114
CHAPTER THREE 115
THE MISSION OF THE CHURCH FROM THE PERSPECTIVE OF THE MISSION OF CHRIST 115
Introduction 115
3.1 BIBLICAL SOURCES OF CHRIST'S MISSION 116
3.2. THE MISSION OF THE CHURCH TODAY 121
3.2.1. The Church's Mission as Liberation-oriented 126
3.3. HUMAN RIGHTS: AN ELABORATION OF THE CHURCH'S MISSION OF LIBERATION 131

3.3.1. Legitimation of the Church's Involvement in Human Rights Question 132
3.3.1.1. Pre-Vatican II Council Official Publications and Human Rights....... 133
Papal Encyclicals and Apostolic Letters 133
3.3.1.2 Conciliar and Post Conciliar Documents and Human Rights.......... 136
3.3.1.3 Post-Vatican II Council Official Publications and Human Rights 138
3.4 THE CHURCH'S MISSION OF DIALOGUE....................... 143
Summary 146
CHAPTER FOUR...148
EMPIRICAL RESEARCH IN RELIGION AND HUMAN RIGHTS IN NIGERIA 148
Introduction 148
4.1 FUNDAMENTAL CLARIFICATION TO SOME OF THE RESEARCH QUESTIONS AND ATTITUDES.................................... 149
4.1.1 Theoretical conceptualization and empirical methods 158
4.2 ATTITUDES TOWARDS THE CHURCH (RELIGION)................. 161
4.2.1. The Church in Nigeria and Human Rights 161
4.2.1.1. Positive Effects on Human Rights 162
4.2.1.2. Negative Effects on Human Rights 163
4.2.1.3. Zero Effects on Human Rights................................ 166
4.2.2 Theoretical Perspective.. 167
4.2.3 Empirical Perspective.. 169
4.2.3.1 Attitudes towards the Church: Empirical Perspective................ 171
4.2.3.1.1RELIGIOUS PRACTICES (q18): 171
4.2.3.1.2 RELIGIOUS CONVICTIONS:................................ 172
4.2.3.1.2.1 God (q25):... 172
4.2.3.1.2.2 Jesus (q27): 174
4.2.3.1.2.3 Mohammed (q28):... 177
4.2.3.1.3 CULTURAL OPENNESS: Religious Communities (q29) 180
4.2.3.1.4 DEMOCRATIC OPENNESS: Religious Communities (q29)........ 181
4.2.4 Interpretation 182
4.3 ATTITUDES TOWARDS HUMAN RIGHTS 184
(i) First Generation Rights 185
(ii) Second Generation Rights 186
(iii) Third Generation Rights.. 187
4.3.1 Theoretical Perspective.. 190
4.3.2 Empirical Perspective 191
4.3.2.1 CIVIL RIGHTS 193
4.3.2.2 RIGHT TO LIFE.. 197

4.3.2.3 POLITICAL RIGHTS 200
4.3.2.4 JUDICIAL RIGHTS 202
4.3.2.5 SOCIO-ECONOMIC RIGHTS 204
4.3.2.6 ENVIRONMENTAL RIGHTS 209
4.4 CORRELATIONS BETWEEN ATTITUDES TOWARDS THE CHURCH AND ATTITUDES TOWARDS HUMAN RIGHTS 212
4.4.2 General Analysis 229
CHAPTER FIVE 231
TOWARDS A CHURCH FOR HUMAN RIGHTS IN NIGERIA 231
Introduction 231
5.1 CHURCH'S MISSION IN THE PROMOTION AND PROTECTION OF HUMAN RIGHTS 233
5.1.1 Liberation 233
5.1.1.1 Liberation from Human Rights Violations 234
5.2 THE CHALLENGES OF HUMAN RIGHTS TO THE NIGERIAN CHURCH 236
5.2.1 Carrier of Human Rights Culture 238
5.2.1.1 What is Human Rights Culture? 238
5.2.1.2. Self-examination 242
5.2.1.3. Liberation from Within 244
5.2.1.4. Prophetic Option 246
5.2.1.5. Commitment to the Marginalized 249
5.2.1.5.1. Agenda for the Emancipation and Empowerment of Women 250
5.2.1.6. Intercultural/ Interreligious Exchange 254
5.2.1.6.1. Dialogue with Islam 260
Summary 263
GENERAL CONCLUSION 265
EPILOGUE: Agents of 'Hope' 268
EINE DEUTSCHE ZUSAMMENFASSUNG 270
Einführung: 270
Motivation: 271
Ziel: 272
Kapitel Eins: 273
Kapitel Zwei: 273
Kapitel Drei: 274
Kapitel Vier: 276
Kapitel Fünf: 279

BIBLIOGRAPHY 281
BOOKS 281
SACRED SCRIPTURES 283
CODE OF CANON LAW AND CATECHISM OF THE CHURCH 283
VATICAN COUNCIL II DOCUMENTS 284
PAPAL ENCYCLICALS AND APOSTOLIC LETTERS 284
CURIAL DOCUMENTS 284
EPISCOPAL CONFERENCE DOCUMENTS 284
JOURNALS AND NEWSPAPERS 285
ENCYCLOPEDIA 285
DECLARATIONS AND CONSTITUTION 285
UNPUBLISHED DOCUMENTS AND PAPERS 285
INTERNET SOURCES 286

Acknowledgements

'Human rights' is a theme that will remain complex, fragile, authentic, existential and equivocal. Consciously or unconsciously it has passed through different ages, centuries and Generations so that it could be regarded to as a 'culture' without any fear of contradiction. The completion of this research work is only the beginning of my proposed long journey into the quest for the promotion, protection and sustainance of the human rights culture.

The hand, says the Igbos of southern Nigeria, makes the drum to sound. I owe a profound gratitude to God for inspiring this work to His own Glory and for the good of humankind. In a special way I also thank my beloved parents Nze & Lolo Jacob and Bernadette Odoeme, who received me into the world and taught me Respect to God and to my fellow human beings. They laid the foundation of this 'quest' in me in the cradle. I specially dedicate this work to them and pray that my beloved Dad, who has passed into eternity, rests in the bossom of God the Father. To all my brothers and sisters I also owe a special gratitude for also contributing immensely to my being. My numerous friends around the globe deserve also my unalloyed thanks for all we share with each other.

My further studies in Europe would not have been possible without the important role of my Bishop Emeritus, the late Rev. Dr. A.E. Ilonu, who released me from my pastoral assighnment in order to pursue this quest. I owe him my special respect and gratitude. I also thank heartily his successor, Most Rev. Dr. S.A. Amatu for his fatherly support and encouragement.

I also gratefully appreciate the efforts of my past Rectors and teachers in the junior and senior seminaries, who contributed immensely towards the academic formulation of this quest. I send my heartfelt thank to the Faculty of Catholic Theology at Catholic University of Nijmegen (now Radboud University of Nijmegen) The Netherlands, where the pursuit of this quest took a more formidable shape. I am specially indepted to my teacher and good friend Prof. Dr. Hans van der Ven of the Radoud University, whose contributions to the successful completion of this work cannot be measured. His motivation while I was in Holland to get along with this quest brought me this far. His professionalism could be felt in the quality of this research, especially the empirical aspect.The Catholic Theological Faculty of the Eberhard-Karls University Tuebingen deserves also my thanks for accepting me to actualize this quest in this form. All the Professors whom I came across in the course of this pursuit left their indelible footprints in this endeavour and in my life. I will remain grateful to them as long as I live. Very profoundly I thank my 'Doctor Father', Prof, Dr, Ottmar Fuchs, without whose fatherly and scholarly motivation, support and encouragement this pursuit could not have been realized up to this level. He is not only a teacher, but a special friend to me. I sincerely send my appreciation to all my colleagues in the 'Ottmar Schule', for their useful insights during our meetings and discussions. My research population, students of the various secondary schools where I conducted my empirical research in Lagos, Abuja, Okigwe and Uturu, deserve too my special thanks. Their honesty and openness in responding to the questions of the questionnaire also contributed immensely to the quality of this research. I express my thanks to the Principals and some of the teachers of these schools for granting me the permission and assisting me conduct the empirical research in a conducive atmosphere.

I also thank in a special way my special 'Duo', Mr. & Mrs. Wolfgang and Gabrielle Dreher-Kohlhase for granting me a serene environment at moments I needed to escape distractions in order to pen down some useful thoughts that made this quest what it is. My colleagues in the Pastoral Team and other co-workers in the Seelsorgeeinheit Oberes Nagoldtal also contributed to this success. Without their understanding, goodwill and loving assistance, I could not have been able to come to this level. My special gratitude also goes to Rev. Dr. Kenneth Kurumeh for reading through the manuscript. I also appreciate the pains-taking efforts of my friend Mr. Ferdinand Creutz in formatting this work.

There are numerous others I cannot mention their names here on account of limited space. To all of you mentioned and unmentioned I owe my immense gratitude. I wish to let you know that the 'heart does not forget'.

GENERAL INTRODUCTION

The church's Pastoral Constitution on the Church in the Modern World, which is considered a very resourceful document of Vatican II Council and published under the title – *Gaudium et Spes*, introduces the church's mission for solidarity with the whole human family in the following words:

> The joy and hope, the grief and anguish of the men *and women* of our time, especially of those who are poor or afflicted in any way, are the joy and hope, the grief and anguish of the followers of Christ as well. Nothing that is genuinely human fails to find an echo in their hearts. ...That is why Christians cherish a feeling of deep solidarity with the human race and its history.[1]

It is this history of human race that has over the centuries recorded various aspects of commitment by humankind to promote and protect its dignity. And this said dignity of the human person is one of the basis for the promotion of human rights in its various ramifications.

Generally speaking, human rights could be said to be those rights all human beings possess on the ground of being human. A riddle has it that human rights are like Armour because they protect us; like rules because they tell us how we can behave; like judges because we can appeal to them. They are also considered to be abstract: like emotions because everyone has them, and they are always in existence. They are like nature because they can be violated. They are like spirit because they cannot be destroyed. They are like time because they treat us all in equal manner. One basic issue about human rights is that people may disagree about their definition, but all recognize them whenever and wherever they are seen.

A 'right' could be taken to be a claim one is justified in making. But 'human rights' are claims with a slight difference, in that they are not dependent on any promise or assurance by another party. Someone's right to life is not dependent on someone else's promise to save him or her: their life may be, but their right to life is not. Their right to life is dependent on only one thing: that they are human. If we are to accept human rights we shall invariably accept that everyone is entitled to make claims based on the fact of being human. Human rights are intrinsic to all human beings

1 Vatican Council II Documents, *Gaudium et Spes*, no. 1, St. Paul's Publication Edition, 1965, p. 794.

and are bound to be respected, promoted and protected. Over the recent past centuries, some remarkable improvement has been recorded about the promotion and protection of the human rights culture in some parts of the globe. Yet regrettably enough, some other parts are yet to make impressive efforts.

One cannot but recall the gory events of our world that expressly portray the violations of human rights over the recent past decades and in the present era of human history; the chilling stories of apartheid regime in South Africa, the shocking incidents in which the personality of the human was ideologically crushed under the communist era, the horrible situations that humans found and still find themselves in dictatorial regimes, instances of lack of religious freedom witnessed and being witnessed still in many parts of the world. The situation of human rights violations in Nigeria do not present to us a different picture; lack of freedom of speech, lack of employment opportunities, the groaning of the ever growing poor masses, the dejected, oppressed and down trodden, and the bizarre sights of gross social injustices being perpetrated.

Naturally, these events constitute a vital link between humankind's rights and the mission of the church to accomplish the integral liberation of humankind. It implies that the sad and regrettable incidents of human rights violations all over the world constantly seek confidence in the deepest heart of the church, and thus compel her by the force of the gospel to fight that prophetic war of human rights' preservation, promotion and protection in words and deeds. This mission of the church, in virtue of the Gospel heritage, is directly rooted in the prophetic and liberative mission of Christ, "whose words and actions are all for the good of *people*, to save, heal, liberate and assist them all".[2]

From this perspective, the church is looked upon as a kind of panacea for a way out as a result of the socio-political dimension of its salvific mission, which inter alia, should involve recognizing, preserving and promoting human rights.

The aim of this project is to answer the general question of how the church can apply her mission towards salvaging the deplorable situation of human

2 The Church and Human Rights: Pontifical Commission *"Justitia et Pax"*, Vatican City, 1978, no 56.

rights violations, especially in the Nigerian context. It has become a clear fact that every other sector has almost failed to salvage the situation. The religious institutions are more or less, looked upon as the "liberators". This mission, however, will be very difficult and probably impossible if the church does not free herself from *intrusive, ethnocentric,* and *triumphalist* tendencies inherent in some of her methods and structures. Such tendencies constantly expose the church to steady allegations of violations of human rights, especially regarding some of her norms and ideologies. It seems an exaggeration and disrespect to speak of violations of human rights within the church, especially when one considers the gravity of human rights violations being recorded in most parts of the world. The general tone of the allegations has it that the church is very foremost in promoting the fundamental rights of human beings to live lives worthy of their nature, but causes an obstacle to its realization by means of her structures.[3] Is it then possible for the church to do this mission of liberation with this type of allegation against her?

It is part of this project to expose means of answering this question, without any claim to be exhaustive in the expositions and suggestions. This will be handled in five chapters of unequal sizes and magnitude.

Chapter One is a preliminary discussion on the situation of human rights in Nigeria, which begins with a brief history of human rights in Nigeria and an overview of the Nigerian Constitution, the African Charter on Human and Peoples' Rights and the Universal Declaration on Human Rights. The African Commission on Human and Peoples' Rights and the National Commission on Human Rights will be referred to in their special relationship to the 1999 Nigerian Constitution. For the purpose of answering the question of human rights situation in Nigeria, it goes further to paint the picture of the various forms of human rights violations in Nigeria, ranging from political, religious, cultural, socio-economic to gender dimensions. This prepares the ground and depicts areas calling for the urgent attention of the church's mission.

Chapter Two brings into the scene the three major cultural and religious traditions in Nigeria: Hausa, Yoruba, Igbo; Natural religion, Islam and

---

3 Stichele, V. C., *Introduction,* In: Stichele, V.C., van Dijk, B., Torfs, R., and Veliscek, S., (eds.), Disciples and Discipline (European Debate on Human Rights Violations in the Roman Catholic Church). 1993, Leuven, p. 8

Christianity. These traditions will be discussed in view of giving attention to areas of their practices, values and beliefs that promote, protect as well as violate human rights. The church exists within these cultural contexts and as such could be influenced by them and, she could also influence them.

Chapter Three puts in a retrospective form the mission of the church from the perspective of the mission of Christ. This chapter is an effort to answer the question why Christianity or rather the church should be engaged in human rights question. Greater emphasis is placed here on liberation as a perspective for the church's mission, based essentially on Christological liberation. This entails mission for freedom, and justice and peace. This chapter is concluded with a proposal for human rights as an elaboration of the church's mission of liberation, taking cognizance of the situation of human rights violations in history and time.

Chapter Four is to go into both theoretical and empirical investigation to find out whether the church contributes effectively towards human rights question. This will be done by pointing out attitudes of Nigerian youths (senior secondary school students) of various religious backgrounds toward the church and also their attitudes toward human rights. For an effective collaboration between the theoretical and empirical perspectives, the results of an empirical research by means of questionnaire carried out among these youth in the three major geographical and geopolitcal zones of Nigeria will be used broadly in this chapter. A correlation that will be made between attitudes towards the church and attitudes towards human rights will tell us whether the attitudes are positive, negative or zero. The theoretical conceptualization and empirical methods that will be employed here are those developed by Johannes van der Ven, et al.

Chapter Five is another core part of the project, which makes a comparison across the previous chapters. For the purpose of finding out what the church should do in relation to human rights, it will stress the fact that it is not only a duty but also an obligation and responsibility of the church in her mission to care for the rights of peoples. She is expected to live up to the liberative and prophetic dimensions of her mission. This chapter will go further to contextualize this mission of the church to the situation of human rights violations in Nigeria, as it challenges the Nigerian church. This aims at depicting the church as a possible carrier of human rights culture, which aims at letting the church pull down all kinds of barrier that are created by the conflicting tendencies in her mission methods and structures mentioned earlier. For the church and her institutions to be carriers of the human rights culture, she ought to be open to all cultures and all persons. A general conclusion will follow thereafter.

Methodologically, the project is to make an extensive use of theoretical and empirical methods. The Church being referred to here is generally the Roman Catholic Church in Nigeria. Other Christian denominations will be mentioned in passing as part of the Christian Association of Nigeria (CAN).

CHAPTER ONE

HUMAN RIGHTS IN NIGERIA

Introduction

This first chapter does not aim at narrating the history of human rights qua tale, but does not either negate some preliminary historical comments. It suffices to begin by describing human rights as a *fluid term*, which widely means different things at different epochs and in different cultures. The history of human rights shows what Micheline R. Ishay calls the "optimism of humankind's aspirations". This optimism is echoed by the epochal historical development of human rights until the present era. Each era is peculiar to its ideas, speculations and events made manifest in its texts, religious and cultural traditions, architecture and arts. The transformations at different epochs carried with them consciously or unconsciously some elements of the former. History shows that each historical epoch of human rights is fraught with ambivalences and contradictions.

Each epoch however experienced and experiences setbacks, but also steady progressions and transformations. The progression and transformation are however said to be propelled by the structural problems, hindrances and contradictions that accompany each epoch. These problems, hindrances and contradictions are what Paul Klee called the "progress" of human rights development. That means the history of human rights is being moved forward, despite structural problems posed by the fore-mentioned elements.

It is therefore the aim of this chapter to analyze the above conceptual description in the Nigerian context. The major focus here is to address some pertinent questions bordering on basic facts of human rights in Nigeria: How did human rights question get into Nigeria? What is the understanding of human rights in the Nigerian context? To what extent are human rights being respected, promoted, neglected or violated in Nigeria?

It is basically necessary to address these questions at this opening stage in order to judge properly the situational developments of human rights in

Nigeria so as to create suitable basis for useful suggestions. The success of this chapter would depend on to what extent the structural problems could assist us to bring out some constructive criticisms that could eventually lead to another progressive step in the history of human rights in Nigeria.

In order to adequately attempt answering these questions, this chapter is sub-divided into four corresponding parts: A brief history of human rights in Nigeria, which is to describe the progression and transformation of human rights in Nigeria from the point of view of its problems, hindrances and contradictions forms the first part (1.1). The part 1.2 describes the Nigerian Constitution, followed by the exposition of the meaning and understanding of the Sharia Law in Nigeria, without overlooking its irresistible influences on the constitution. The final aspect of this part attempts to describe the link between the Nigerian Constitution and human rights. The following part (1.3) attempts to bring into lime light the important link between the *African Commission on Human and Peoples' Rights, African Charter on Human and Peoples' Rights,* and the *National Human Rights Commission of Nigeria.* The last part (1.4) of this chapter attempts a description of the current trends of human rights in Nigeria, with particular mention of the extent the rights are promoted and violated in special connection to the Nigerian Constitution and where necessary, in comparison to the African Charter on Human and Peoples' Rights, and The Universal Declaration on Human Rights (UDHR).

1.1 A BRIEF HISTORY OF HUMAN RIGHTS IN NIGERIA

The above mentioned assumption of human rights as a fluid term opens up the basis for the description of the historical excursion into human rights in Nigeria. Following this assumption, one can also assume that there were no serious discussions or considerations on human rights in Nigeria during the colonial period prior to the 1940s and prior to the United Nations 1948 Universal Declaration of Human Rights. There was no sustained national movement in the name of human rights. There were no non-governmental organizations (NGOs) with a national or patriotic reach to defend its principles. Ignorance and illiteracy in today's perspective reigned in the region. There was no Constitution crafted to protect human rights as such. The nation was not even colonized in view of establishing and protecting human rights, hence there were a lot of selfish interests manifested in the natural resources loot and perpetration of all sorts of violence and oppression on the native population.

History has it that the laws guiding the daily activities then were colonial rulers' laws of the state, traditional laws and religious laws. These laws did not specifically talk about human rights. Some writers argue that the emphasis was rather on human 'duties'; separate duties of man and woman, duties towards the state and communities and religious duties. I categorize these laws under 'duties'[4] based on the current global description of human rights, some of which are totally opposed to what are obtainable today. According to the cultural law in that era, for example, killing of twin children was regarded legal, and all other kinds of inhuman practices such as Female Genital Mutilation (FGM), were commonly acceptable. This question of 'duties' was not based on the concept of human dignity, therefore projecting the argument that an African concept of human rights "is actually a concept of human dignity that defines the inner moral nature and worth of the human person and his or her proper relations with the society".[5] This position therefore suggests the possibility that 'human rights' activists of the time may not have used the concept 'right' in the precise sense of today's usage.[6] A pertinent example worth mentioning is the Aba[7] women's riot of 1929, which ushered in a gradual creation of awareness and recognition of human rights in Nigeria, but not specifically understood from the perspective of today's context. During this period Nigeria ratified the Slavery Convention of 1926.

At the pre-independence period in Nigeria, human rights could be said to have been motivated by both indigenous concerns and external influences and imposition. Human rights question at the time (in the understanding of the concept of 'duties') remained for many decades passive and imita-

4 "Duty" is understood in this sense as 'Obligation' – towards fellow human being, as differentied from 'Rights' as 'Claims'.

5 Ibhawoh, B.: *Imperialism and Human Rights* (State University of New York, 2007), 15.

6 Ibid. 14.

7 Aba is one of the popular cities of Nigeria. It is situated in the north of South-eastern part of Nigeria. It's population is more of Igbos and christians, who are more of traders and hand workers. The riot was conducted by the women of the city as a show of their discontent with colonial rule.

tive, but nevertheless to some extent approached critically and violently. One of the few recorded specific mention of human rights came from the Nigerian elites, who were privileged to study overseas during the colonial era. These privileged elites used the local News Papers to oppose some of the unjust practices perpetrated by the colonial government, such as discrimination against the local people in the civil service, and demanded for more indigenous representation in the administration of the country, and the campaign for civil and political rights of the indigenous peoples.[8] Mbonu Ojike is an example of such elites, who in 1946 demanded from the colonial masters the natural right of Nigerians to rule themselves.[9] These internal influences constrained Nigeria to sign the Convention of the political rights of women in 1953.

Another factor that influenced this era was the introduction of the 'Atlantic Charter'[10] on human rights. A major significance of this Charter was that it partly inspired the formulation of the United Nations and prepared the basis for the Universal Declaration on Human Rights. The Universal character of the Universal Declaration on Human Rights is however strongly challenged because most colonized peoples were not represented at the United Nations and had no opportunity to represent their interests in the formulation of UDHR. Nevertheless, the UDHR was a formidable external influence and imposition that formulated a structure for human rights in Nigeria, thus forming the bedrock for a later external influence on human rights question, which came from the African Charter on Human and Peoples' Rights. With these external influences Nigeria could begin serious discussions on issues about peoples' rights, children's rights, the right to health, even economic and social rights etc. These and other rights that dominate the Nigerian Constitution and human rights discourses in Nigeria became part of the discussion by the end of the 20th century. The

8 Ibid., 71.

9 Cmiel, K., in www.historycooperative.org/journals/ahr/109.1/cmiel.html

10 Atlantic Charter is a joint program of peace aim, enunciated on August 14, 1941 during World War II, by Prime Minister Winston Churchill of Great Britain and President Franklin D. Roosevelt of United States. The Charter supported the following principles and aims: renunciation of territorial aggrandizement; opposition to territorial changes made against the wishes of the people concerned; restoration of sovereign rights and self-government to those forcibly deprived of them; access to raw materials for all nations of the world and easing of trade restrictions; world cooperation to secure improved economic and social conditions for all; freedom from fear and want; freedom of the seas; and abandonment of the use of force, as well as disarmament of aggressor or nations.

external influences in question (as well as the internal factors) contributed immensely to the liberation of Nigeria from the colonial masters into an independent nation in 1960.

Nnamdi Azikiwe, the first president of Nigeria immediately after Independence is said to be the first Nigerian, who reacted to the British position on the "The Atlantic Charter" by urging Africans and other colonized folks to prepare their own blueprints of rights instead of depending on foreigners.[11] To give an example of his call (as a then nationalist leader), he prepared his own blueprint of rights for Nigeria published in 1943, which included "the right to health, education, social equality, material security and even the right to recreation."[12] The political party of Azikiwe, the National Council for Nigeria and the Cameroons (NCNC) adopted in whole this blueprint of rights in their Freedom Charter in the same year. This Freedom Charter is of a historical significance in Nigeria because it accommodated the first comprehensive list of fundamental human rights in Nigeria.[13] The Charter strongly upheld and recommended a wide range of political, economic and social rights for all Nigerians, including the condemnation of slavery, servitude and imperialism.[14]

Following her attempt on changing the concept of 'duties' into 'rights', and her independence, Nigeria became party to several international human rights treaties[15], such as the International Convention on the elimination of all forms of racial discrimination (1966); the Convention Relating to the Status of Refugees (1967) and the Protocol Relating to the Status of Refugees; and the International Convention on the Elimination of All Forms of Discrimination against Women (1977). It is also on record that Nigeria ratified the Slavery Convention of 1926, the Supplementary Convention of the Abolition of Slavery of 1956, and the 1949 Geneva Conventions Relative to the Treatment of Prisoners of War and the Protection of Civilian Persons in Time of War. However, she had not signed the following

---

11 Ibhawoh, B., Ibid. 155.

12 Ibid.

13 Ibid.

14 Ibid.

15 Details of this later part of history of human rights in Nigeria were obtained from: The Library of Congress Country Studies; CIA World Factbook as described in: www.photius.com/countries/nigeria/national_security/nigeria_national_security_human_rights.html

International Conventions: Convention on the Prevention and Punishment of the Crime of Genocide of 1948; the International Covenant on Civil and Political Rights of 1966; the International Covenant on Economic, Social, and Cultural Rights of 1966; and the Convention against Torture and Other Cruel, Inhuman, or Degrading Treatment or Punishment. This era saw Nigeria also as signatory to the United Nations' Standard Minimum Rules for the Treatment of Offenders, and many other Protocols, Conventions and Covenants on human dignity, human liberty and minimum conditions and best practices that must be obtained in the administration of justice for a civilized society in the modern world.

Three years after Independence Nigeria became a republic. Unfortunately this first republic could not last long as a result of the first recorded military coup d'état in 1966. This coup ushered Nigeria into a long history of military dictatorship regimes. A second military dictatorship regime took over power this same 1966 through another coup that eventually led to a civil war (June 1967 to January 1970), between Biafra (in the southeast) and the rest of Nigeria. The war ensued over what many refer to as unequal distribution of the common national patrimony.

The Nigerian government's human rights record was mixed and generally worse during military regimes, when decrees were exempt from legal challenge. Until the late 1970s, when military rulers deprived many citizens of their rights through detention without trial, physical assault, torture, harassment, and intimidation, the issue of human rights was not a major concern. It had taken for granted that having a bill of rights guaranteed human rights. By the early 1970s, as result of military influence, the days of "innocence" in relation to human rights were over. The then military regimes instituted an era of torture and indefinite detention of her critics. This trend of abuse continued under the military regimes of the time and became frequent with the creation of Nigeria Security Organization (NSO) in 1976. This period saw the formation of the Nigerian Council for National Awareness, founded after the death of the military ruler of this time, Murtala Muhammed, to foster a just and humane society.

The return of constitutional government in the Second Republic (1979-83) reduced the violations. Nevertheless, the human rights record remained poor because of the increasing powers of the Police Force and the NSO and the constant harassment of political opponents. Within this period Nigeria signed the International Convention on the suppression and punishment of the crime of Apartheid (1981), and the African Charter on Human and Peoples' rights (1981).

Another military coup (1983) took place and sent the second republic into oblivion. Under this military regime military security was the criteria for judicial action, often in the form of military tribunals. The government not only gave the NSO greater powers but also promulgated decrees that directly violated human rights. The most notable were State Security (Detention of Persons) Decree Number 2 of 1984, which empowered the Chief of Staff at Supreme Headquarters to detain indefinitely without trial anyone suspected of being a security risk, and Decree Number 4, which made the publication of any material, considered embarrassing to any government official a punishable offense. Under Decree Number 2, many people considered "enemies" of the government were detained in NSO cells and allegedly tortured and eventually tried by a special military tribunal. At these tribunals, the accused was assumed guilty until proved innocent instead of the other way round. Journalists and media organizations were regularly harassed by security agents; organized interest groups whose members dared to criticize the government openly or engage in demonstrations or strike actions were proscribed.

Two years on another military coup took place. This regime justified its power take-over on the grounds of the need to restore civil liberties. This new regime prided itself as being a defender of human rights, and many of her initial acts justified her human rights posture. The NSO was scrapped, and its cells were thrown open and replaced with the State Security Service (SSS) and other agencies; most of the political prisoners were granted freedom and the jail terms of those already convicted were reduced; a renowned human rights advocate was appointed as minister of justice and attorney general; Decree Number 4 was scrapped and punishment for drug traffickers was reduced from execution to jail terms; the proscription of "radical" groups was annulled; a plan was persistently followed for the restoration of civilian rule by 1992.

All these acts notwithstanding, human rights remained substantially circumscribed in 1990. Decree Number 2 remained in place, and numerous citizens had been incarcerated under it, although the allowable period of detention without charge was reduced from six months to six weeks in

January 1990. With the aid of this and other decrees that restricted freedom, usually promulgated retrospectively, some radical and outspoken organizations such as the Civil Liberties Organization, the local branches of Amnesty International, the National Association of Nigerian Students (NANS), the Nigeria Bar Association (NBA), the Nigerian Union of Journalists and the Committee for the defense of human rights, criticized and vehemently opposed the government's violations of civil rights and urged remedial measures. These critics of the government were regularly detained. Despite having annulled Decree Number 4, the government had several brushes with media organizations. In 1988 Newswatch media house was proscribed for six months, and journalists, academics, and civil rights activists continued to be harassed, and in some cases murdered by state security agents. Although the notorious NSO was dissolved in 1986, the new security establishment (SSS) in 1990 continued to act arbitrarily and with impunity. The government proscribed radical interest groups like National Association of Nigerian Students NANS and the Academic Staff Union of Universities ASU, the central body of all university professors and lecturers. Several innocent citizens were subjected to physical assault without government reparations.

1993 was a particularly challenging year for human rights in Nigeria. The results of a presidential election, which would have brought Nigeria into the third republic of civilian rule was annulled. An interim government was installed instead. In mid-November that same year this interim government was forced to give up their governance through the nation's seventh recorded coup d'état. This regime banned all political meetings and associations. No program was set for the return to civil rule. Throughout this crisis, the human rights organizations banded together under a coalition called the Campaign for Democracy (CD). All kinds of unrest, disturbances and demonstrations were the order of the time. Hundreds of protesters, activists and journalists were detained, and in some cases some were killed. Human rights abuses this time were widespread. Several media houses were closed down by the government. The human rights history of this regime followed this order until the emergence of another democratic rule, which is still in place till date.

The structure of human rights in Nigeria from around the 1940s till date has not changed much from the above structural description of the history of human rights in Nigeria. The good news today is that democracy in the Fourth Republic (1999) is surviving for the first time in the Nigerian history for more than one decade. The amendment of the Nigerian Constitution, the expansion of human rights talk and the prominence of human rights NGOs are also positive signals of better things to come. Nevertheless, the increasing talk about human rights and number of NGOs do not necessarily mean that fewer people are being detained, tortured or killed, or denied their fundamental rights in Nigeria. Neither has the amendment of the Constitution relieved the burden of the poor and less privileged, who have remained displaced in the law courts and deprived of their fundamental rights. One wonders to what extent the Nigerian Constitution serves as a standard for human rights protection and promotion.

1.2 THE NIGERIAN CONSTITUTION

1.2.1 Origin and history

A nation's Constitution by which the citizens are ruled plays a very important role in the politics, culture and history of that nation. It is also note-worthy that constitutions are made by citizens and their representatives. Such citizens and their representatives are people who are fully engaged in the Constitution-making process and who understand that their future welfare and that of their descendants will be shaped by the Constitution they make. They are citizens who are passionate about certain political principles. There are bound to be agreements, disagreements and compromises among them on certain issues. But it is part of the process.

Just like many other British colonial possessions, Nigeria went through a succession of constitutions, generally taking from the "form of Orders in Council, Letters Patent, Royal Instructions – followed by Acts of the British and Nigerian Parliaments"[16] This commentary points to the sad fact that Nigeria has lived to experience a legal system, where the constitution changes like the "weather cock in climatology"[17] It is part of the colonial

16 Quoted from a Review of the book: *The Constitutional History of Nigeria*, in *African Journal, XXII Ed., 1982,* Cambridge Universtiy Press Ltd, London.

17 An expression used in describing the Nigerian Constitution in a report presented by the Association of Nigerian Scholars for Dialogue to the Constitution Debate Co-ordinating Committee (CDCC), International Conference Centre Abuja, 1998. (www.waado.

history of Nigeria that following the *amalgamation*[18] of the Northern and Southern Protectorates in 1914 by Lord Lugard, Nigeria had the Clifford Constitution of 1922, the Richard Constitution of 1946, the MacPherson Constitution of 1951 and the Federal Constitution (otherwise known as the Littleton Constitution) of 1954. At Independence Nigeria had the 1960 Independence Constitution. At the first Republic in 1963 came the Republican Constitution. After some experience of military regimes, the country returned to a civilian government by the promulgation of the 1979 Constitution of the Federal Republic of Nigeria. The present Constitution is the 1999 Constitution, which promulgated the birth of the fourth and present Nigerian democratic republic.

The above brief narration shows that the earliest Nigerian Constitutions were of British origin as a result of colonialism at the time. They were conceived and delivered in Britain and conveyed to Nigeria to bind and rule Nigerians. The major impacts made by the above mentioned successive Constitutions could be cited in the following ways: The 1922 Constitution made provision, for the first time, for elected members to sit on a Nigerian legislative council, but did not empower them to make laws for the Northern Nigeria. This Constitution also promulgated the election of Nigerian representatives from Lagos and Calabar to the legislative council of Southern Nigeria; they constituted only a small minority, and Nigerians otherwise continued to have no role in the higher levels of government. Sir Arthur Richard's Constitution of 1946 inaugurated Nigeria's regionalism.[19] This Constitution achieved a half-hearted political breakthrough by integrating the North with the South at the legislative level for the first time. The post second world war political awareness and upsurge of nationalism in Africa brought about the Richard's Constitution of 1950. Po-

org/nigerian_schorlars/archive/contents.html). The Association of Nigerian Scholars for Dialogue comprises of intellectuals and academics who are engaged in promoting the well-being of the Nigerian nation by employing their knowledge resources for resolving the nation's problems through dialogue.

18 Following the total conquer of the Northern Nigeria by the British soldiers in the early 20th century; Britain was able to take a complete control of Nigeria by 1906, hence dividing Nigeria into the colony of Lagos, Protectorate of Southern Nigeria and the Protectorate of Northern Nigeria. In 1914 the Protectorates of Southern and Northern Nigeria were amalgamated resulting into the establishment of the Colony and Protectorate of Nigeria.

19 For better administrative reasons, Nigeria was later divided into colony and provinces: colony of Lagos, Northern, Eastern and Western Provinces.

litical parties were formed on regional and ethnic basis, thus resulting into a full scale regionalism. This Constitution was promulgated on account of the denouncement of the 1947 Constitution promulgated in Britain, which gave traditional authorities a greater voice in national affairs to the exclusion of the Western-educated Nigerian elites.

Until 1951, colonial constitution-making was in the form of decrees in which Nigerians had little involvement. The attempt of the Richard's Constitution of 1947 to repeat another imposition led to an expression of outrage and agitations for constitutional reforms that would respect Nigerians' viewpoints. These resulted in important changes in the ways Nigerian constitutional affairs were handled by British colonial officers, hence introducing the McPherson Constitution of 1951, which brought about a greater measure of autonomy granted to the regions with stronger legislatures. But it proved unworkable in 1952, hence leading to the promulgation of the 1954 Constitution, which solidified the division of Nigeria into three regions (Eastern, Western, and Northern) in addition to the Federal Territory of Lagos. The Eastern and Western regions became internally self-governing, and the Northern region attained this status first in 1959. This 1954 Constitution confirmed and formulated the wishes of Nigerian leaders to move and remain as far apart as they possibly could. The choice for a Federal system of government was opted for and supported by the constitution. Following the wave of nationalism, which added tempo to the call for independence, constitutional conferences took place in 1957, 1958, 1959 and 1960 culminating in the granting of independence to Nigeria on 1 October 1960.

The attainment of the Nigerian independence opened a brand new page in the Nigerian history and her constitutional history. The Independence Constitution of 1960 was promulgated, which provided for a parliamentary government and a substantial measure of self-government for the country's three regions. This Constitution is said to be as a result of a compromise between the British colonial power and the ruling bloc which emerged from colonialism.[20] Nevertheless, it ushered Nigeria into a new era. The 1963 Constitution promulgated the first Republic in Nigeria. This first re-

20 This claim was made by Prof. Edwin Madunagu of the University of Calabar, Nigeria, in his article *The Nigerian Constitution*, published at www.infoplease.com/ce6/world/A0860005.html

public could survive only three years and was exterminated by the first military coup d'état in Nigeria in January 1966. The then head of the military government suspended the national and regional constitutions. This move began the sad history of disrespect the Nigerian Constitutions suffered during her long military regimes. Consequent coups plunged Nigeria into her first civil war, which was caused by the declaration of *Biafra*[21] as an independent state by the Igbos of Southeastern Nigeria. Prior to the start of the civil war Nigeria was re-divided into 12 states as a gesture towards avoiding the war. The war nonetheless was fought. Following the end of the war in January 1970, Nigeria set herself back to National reconstruction and reintegration of the Igbo people into national life, and set the plan for a slow return to civilian rule. A constituent assembly was elected in 1977 to draft a new constitution, which was published in 1979. This 1979 Constitution mandated that political parties and cabinet positions reflect the federal character of the nation. Political parties were required to be registered in at least two-thirds of the states, and each state was required to produce at least one cabinet member. The 1979 elections were held under this new constitution, which ushered Nigeria into the second republic.

The second republic was prematurely ended by another military coup during its fourth year of existence in 1983. A counter coup of 1985 worsened the situation and led to the suspension of the 1979 Constitution. This military regime attempted a promulgation of subsequent constitutional drafts of 1990 and 1995, which were not implemented. At this period the already conceived new (third) republic was prematurely aborted, hence plunging Nigeria back into another military era. The 1979 Constitution remained suspended under two successive military regimes until at the verge of the fourth republic in 1999. The military Provisional Ruling Council (PRC) promulgated a new constitution based largely on the suspended 1979 constitution and the 1995 draft constitution. This 1999 constitution included provision for a bicameral legislature, the National Assembly consisting of a 360-member House of Representative and a 109-member Senate. The today's 1999 Constitution has remained the Constitution of the Federal Republic of Nigeria to the present day. The introductory part of this constitution reads:

---

21 The massacre of thousands of Igbos in Northern Nigeria after the second coup led to an increase in strong Igbo secessionist sentiment. As a result of the increasing fears among the Igbos about their position within Nigeria, the Eastern parliament gave the then region's leader the authority to declare the Republic of Biafra as an independent republic.

We the people of the Federal Republic of Nigeria,
having firmly and solemnly resolved to live in unity and harmony
dedicated to the promotion of inter-African solidarity,
world peace, international cooperation and understanding,
and ... on the principles of freedom, equality and justice,
and for the purpose of consolidating the unity of our people;
Do hereby make, enact and give
ourselves the following Constitution: ...

This present constitution is also criticized by Prof. Madunagu as a continuation of that compromise between the British colonial power and the ruling blocs in Nigeria, but with the international community replacing the colonial power. This critique brings me to the conclusion of this sub-section, in which I wish to sadly reiterate that the *anomaly*[22] of the Nigerian political history is that Nigerian Constitutions were approved by the Imperial Government in Britain in 1960 and by a native military Government's Supreme Council in 1979 and 1999, hence faulting the international standard of constitutional-making process. Nigerians rarely had any opportunity for making their own Constitution. Generally speaking, under colonial rule there was reasonable consultation, but under military rule, Constitutions have been treated as privileged documents that only those who are close to authorities will handle.[23] In most cases the military rule suspended those aspects of the constitution with which it felt uncomfortable, retaining only those articles and sections of the constitution that it found useful for its dictatorial purposes. Unfortunately these changes intruded into the military's attitude towards the Constitution and into its approaches to constitution-making, which influenced to a great extent the structures and contents of the present Constitution of the Federal Republic of Nigeria.[24]

22 This anomaly was reflected in the Comments of the Association of Nigerian Scholars for Dialogue. Op. cit.

23 Ibid.

24 Although the present Constitution (1999) of Nigeria was made open to a wide participation by the Nigerian populace, its making process fell below the international standard since it was made within a very limited time of 2 months, and sadly enough approved by the Military Provisional Ruling Council of the then military regime.

1.2.1.1 Structure and contents of the 1999 Nigerian Constitution

The Nigerian Constitution is said to be one of the world's most voluminous constitutions with an unguided verbosity and comprehensive tediousness. Prof. Madunagu described it as "product of efforts by the ruling blocs to accommodate all their major factions."[25] The 1999 Constitution of Nigeria covers eight chapters and seven schedules; there are 320 sections, most of which are further divided into sub-sections and sub-sub-sections. More than 75,000 words were expended in putting the document together. The long nature of its sections makes the sentences complicated and in some cases difficult to comprehend.

The chapter one of the Constitution is constituted of two parts and 12 sections. Its major theme borders on general provisions, which describes extensively the nature of the Federal Republic of Nigeria and the powers of the Federal republic of Nigeria. Part one has three sections while part two has nine sections. The sections of this chapter outline the supremacy of the constitution and the independence of the three powers (Legislative, Executive and Judiciary) of the Federal republic of Nigeria. Furthermore, these sections also outline, among others, mode of altering provisions of the constitution and outrightly prohibited a State religion. Other aspects such as Public order and public security, and implementation of treaties are also highlighted on in this chapter.

The theme of chapter two is on Fundamental Objectives and directive principles of state policy. This chapter has twelve sections emphasizing on fundamental obligation of the government, the relationship between the government and the governed, political, economic, social, educational, foreign and environmental objectives of the nation. The last four sections dwell on directive on Nigerian cultures, obligation of the mass media, national ethics and duties of the citizens towards the State.

Chapter three with its eight sections dwells on different provisions on Citizenship: citizenship by birth, citizenship by registration, citizenship by naturalization, dual citizenship, renunciation of citizenship, deprivation of citizenship, persons deemed to be Nigerian citizens and finally on power to make regulations.

25 Edwin Madunagu, Ibid.

The fourteen sections of chapter four form the central part of the Nigerian Constitution. The fundamental rights of Nigerian citizens are elaborately outlined in this chapter: right to life, right to dignity of human persons, right to fair hearing, right to private and family life, right to freedom of thought, conscience and religion, right to freedom of expression and the press, right to peaceful assembly and association, right to freedom of movement, right to freedom from discrimination, right to acquire and own immovable property. Other related aspects include: compulsory acquisition of property, restriction on and derogation from fundamental human rights, special jurisdiction of High Court and Legal aid.

Chapter five is divided into two parts and 83 sections. The major concern of this chapter is on the Legislature. The part one borders on the National assembly, describing the composition and staff of the National Assembly; procedure for summoning and dissolution of National Assembly; qualifications for membership of National Assembly and right of attendance; elections to National Assembly; and powers and control over public funds. The part two dwells on the House of Assembly, with emphasis on composition and staff of House of Assembly; procedure for summoning and dissolution of House of Assembly; qualification for membership of House of Assembly and right of attendance; elections to a House of Assembly and powers and control over public funds.

Chapter six is divided into three parts and one hundred sections. The Executive branch of the government forms the major theme of this chapter. Part one borders on the Federal Executive with emphasis on matters relating to the president of the federation, establishment of certain federal executive bodies, public revenue, and the public service of the federation. Part two dwells on the State Executive with particular references to state governor, establishment of certain state executive bodies, and public service of state. Part three has the title Supplemental. This theme goes about other aspects of governmental bodies such as the National population census, the Nigerian Police Force, armed forces of the federation, and political parties.

The chapter seven is devoted to the Judiciary arm of the government. It has four parts and sixty-seven sections. This chapter is very sensitive because of its relations to the different courts in Nigeria. Part one has special emphasis on provisions on the federal courts: the supreme court of Nigeria, the court of appeal, the federal high court, the high court of the federal capital territory Abuja, the Sharia court of appeal of the federal capital territory Abuja, and the customary court of appeal of the federal capital territory Abuja. Part two is devoted to provisions on State courts: Sharia court of appeal of a state, and customary court of appeal of a state. Part three stipulates the provisions on Election Tribunals. Part four has Supplemental on other aspects of the Judiciary.

The last chapter (eight) is divided into four parts and twenty-four sections. Provisions made in this chapter concern in particular the Federal Capital Territory, Abuja and general Supplementary Provisions. Part one made provisions on the Federal Capital Territory, Abuja. Part two dwells on miscellaneous provisions such as procedure for proclamation of state of emergency, resignations, restriction on certain citizens, and restrictions on legal proceedings. Part three dwells on transitional provisions and savings in regard to citizenship, staff of legislative houses, standing orders, special provisions in respect of first election, system of revenue allocation, debts, existing law, existing offices, courts and authorities, and succession to property, rights, liabilities and obligations. Part four interprets and explains some code words, mentioned necessary citations, and the last section (320) officially declares the commencement of the said Constitution on 29th May, 1999.

The seven Schedules of the Nigerian Constitution form the last part of the constitution. The first Schedule is divided into two parts. The second and third Schedules have three parts respectively. The fourth Schedule is not further divided. The fifth Schedule has one part, while the sixth and seventh Schedules are not further divided.

Before we go further in this section with other constitutionally-related issues, permit us, for the sake of clarity on those issues, to highlight on the Institutions that in various ways influenced the 1999 Nigerian Constitution. There is no doubt that the establishment of Institutions like the 'African Commission on Human and Peoples' Rights' and the 'National Human Rights Commission of Nigeria' contributed immensely to the amendment of the present constitution, which allowed the incorporation of more rights and Nigeria involvement in international human rights Treaties and Conventions. Hence a brief history of these Institutions is necessary for the historical purpose of this survey.

1.2.2 African Commission on Human and Peoples' Rights[26]

As a result of the human rights network in Nigeria, which owes its link to the external aid and influence, it is pertinent to bring into this context the historical contribution of the African Commission on Human and Peoples' Rights, and its influence over the National Human Rights Commission of Nigeria, and of course the said amendments of the Nigerian Constitution. I do not in any way intend to neglect the foremost influence of the 1948 Universal Declaration of Human Rights over the former. I wish to presume the wide knowledge of the UDHR. I will nevertheless, where necessary, make references to the Universal Declaration of Human Rights in different areas.

The African Commission on Human and Peoples' Rights was formed as a result of the pressures, which the African Union (formerly Organization of African Unity OAU) was confronted with as regards its supposed duty failure. In the early days of its existence, the Organization had to be confronted with very strong and founded criticisms against its administration. Different groups, which included the Media, churches, inter-governmental and non-governmental organizations mounted pressure on the OAU by exposing some of the most gruesome human rights abuses on the continent. They accused the Organization of abandoning its primary goal of restoring the dignity of the humiliated African peoples. It was accused of double standards for condemning apartheid in South Africa while failing to condemn the rampant human rights violations perpetrated by some of its own members. At the same time, the said pressure groups were encouraging the establishment of a human rights protection mechanism on the continent. Thus, starting from the 1961 Lagos conference organized by the International Commission of Jurists (ICJ) to the 1979 UN sponsored Monrovia Seminar on the Establishment of Regional Commissions on Human Rights with special Reference to Africa. Pressure and assistance were simultaneous to ensure that OAU and its leaders uphold the spirit that motivated the struggle for political independence to restore to the African peoples their dignity lost during slave trade and colonial eras – a cause for which they won international sympathy and support.

26 The historical description of this Commission is culled mainly from the following sites: www.achpr.org/english_info/history_en.html; http://en.wikipedia.org/wiki/African_commission; and www.dfa.gov.za/foreign/multilateral/african/afrhr.htm.

In July 1979, the OAU Assembly of Heads of State and Government met in Monrovia, Liberia and decided to place its members under international obligations through a positivist approach. Accordingly at this summit, a resolution was adopted calling on the OAU Secretary General to form a committee of experts which would draft an African Charter on Human and Peoples' Rights, providing among other things, for mechanisms to promote and protect the rights embodied in the Charter. This group of experts began work on a draft Charter in 1979 and produced a draft, which was unanimously adopted at a 1981 meeting of the OAU Heads of State and Government in Nairobi Kenya. The Charter propagated 26 rights and 3 duties, which are unevenly distributed among the two chapters of part one. The rights and some of the duties cut across equality of all persons before the law and equal protection of the law (Ch. 1, arts. 3 and 7); respect for every individual life and integrity (art. 4); recognition of man's legal status (art. 5); right to liberty and security of persons (art. 6); freedom of conscience and religion (art. 8); freedom of expression, association and assembly (within the law) (arts. 9, 10 and 11); freedom of movement (both within and without) (art. 12); right to equal enjoyment of public services and property, and right to own property (arts. 13 and 14); right to work and equitable pay (art. 15); right to attainable state of physical health (art. 16); educational and cultural rights (art. 17); rights of women and children (with special reference to the International Declarations and Conventions) (art. 18); equality and equal respect for all (art. 19); right to life, economic and political rights (art. 20); right to free disposition of wealth and natural resources (art. 21); right to economic and cultural development (art. 22); right to national and international peace and security (art. 23); environmental rights (art. 24); the independent right of the Courts (art. 26); and freedom from discrimination (both as a right and a duty) (ch. 2, art. 28). This Charter provides for a Human Rights Commission to ensure implementation of the rights enshrined therein. This acceptance of a limitation on sovereign national authority (at least on human rights related issues), albeit minimal, was hailed as a significant step by African States. The move was generally viewed as ushering in a new era of recognition of individual rights as enshrined in the Universal Declaration of Human Rights.

On 21 October 1986, the Charter on Human and Peoples' Rights came into force, and the Commission was officially inaugurated on 2nd November 1987 in Addis Ababa, Ethiopia (in terms of Article 30 of the Charter), after the election of its members in July of the same year by the OAU

23rd Assembly of Heads of State and Government, and the creation of its headquarters in Banjul, the Gambia in 1989. The Commission is a quasi-judicial body charged with ensuring the promotion and protection of Human and Peoples' Rights throughout the African Continent, as well as interpreting the African Charter on Human and Peoples' Rights and considering individual complaints of violations of the Charter. In pursuit of these goals, the Commission is mandated to "collect documents, undertake studies and researches on African Problems in the field of human and peoples' rights, organize seminars, symposia and conferences, disseminate information, encourage national and local institutions concerned with human and peoples' rights and, should the case arise, give its views or make recommendations to governments" (Charter, Art. 45).

With the creation of the African Court on Human and Peoples' Rights (under a protocol to the Charter which was adopted in 1988 and entered into force in January 2004), the Commission has the additional task of preparing cases for submission to the Court's jurisdiction. In July 2004 decision, the AU Assembly resolved that the future Court on Human and Peoples' Rights would be integrated with the African Court of Justice. The Commission has six special Mechanisms that address thematic issues of a continental nature. The Mechanisms are: Extra-judicial, Summary or Arbitrary Executions; Freedom of Expression; Human Rights Defenders; Prisons and Conditions of Detention; Refugees and Internally Displaced Persons; and Rights of Women. Members of the Commission are appointed as Experts who monitor, investigate and report on allegations of violations in member states of the African Union.

With the above described extensive roles of the Commission, one cannot but imagine the silent influence it has wielded and still wields (as a 'Continental Police') over the National Human Rights Commission of Nigeria and the amendments done to the Nigerian constitution so far. But before I dwell into the link between the two commissions a brief presentation of the African Charter on Human and Peoples' Rights and its similarities and differences with the Universal Declaration on Human Rights is necessary. This presentation gives more meaning to the link between the African and Nigerian Commissions on Human Rights.

1.2.3 The African Charter on Human and Peoples' Rights and the Universal Declaration on Human Rights: Similarities and Differences.

The African Charter on Human and Peoples' Rights is a document that is considered as the text that paved the way to the current discussion on human rights in Africa – an African version of the Human Rights Declarations drafted in 1981. Although it has much in common with the Universal Declaration on Human Rights (UDHR) as a result of its heavy dependent on the declaration, the document theoretically differed from the UDHR on the grounds of its advocacy for a human rights' view point that is consistent with the African way of life.[27] This document is said to have evoked some questions as to whether "human rights are to be defined as claims ascribed to moral persons as such, or should it be based on the recognition of some major variants like cultural, ideological, political, economic and religious differences?."[28] This understanding has over the years now opened up a debate that seems to create a tension between the UDHR and the African Charter on Human and Peoples' Rights. Following the concept of ethical universalism that characterises the UDHR, some African scholars argue that it is a Western imperialism and hence advocate for cultural contextualism. It becomes very pertinent at this point to note that there is no substantial difference between the UDHR and the African Charter on Human and Peoples' Rights. In the mean time, one can accept the theoretical discussion on the character of universalism versus contextualism, not with regard to the texts of the documents, but with regard to the legal and judicial applications of some rights concerned. For instance, there is a legal and judicial right covering the legality of abortion and euthanasia in The Netherlands and Belgium, while in Nigeria abortion and euthanasia are not legalised. Another example is the legalization of gay-marriage in The Netherlands, Belgium, Spain, Canada and some States in the U.S.A., but not legalized in Nigeria.

So the principle in this matter is that human rights are universal and at the same time contextual. In other words, contextualization has to occur in each and every country. What this implies in the whole debate is that the concepts of universalism and contextualism have to be bridged for better

---

27 Tarimo, A., Human Rights, Cultural Differences and the Church in Africa, Salvatorianum Publications, Tanzania, 2004, p. 1.
28 Ibid.

collaboration. This bridge means the *localization* of rights discourse in order to encourage "involvement and interplay between local and international standards of human rights."[29] This localization process should not be regarded as too absolute. The theology of Inculturation is considered as a typical example of the mediation process between universalism and contextualism.[30]

These two concepts are meant to take care of the transcendental and cultural characters of human beings as elements acquired through participation, communal bonds, and solidarity.[31]

1.2.4 National Human Rights Commission of Nigeria[32]

The National Human Rights Commission of Nigeria was established in 1995, in response to the Vienna Declaration and Program of Action adopted by the World Conference on Human Rights in Geneva. At the Conference, all United Nations member States, including Nigeria, were enjoined to establish National Institutions for the promotion, protection and advancement of human rights, for the sole Purpose of advancing Universal Human Rights Standards and values within the confines and peculiar national and regional environments.

The establishment of National Institutions is to demonstrate the extent of importance human rights matters have assumed worldwide and within local settings. Nations that consistently and willfully violate the rights of their citizens risk being isolated by the international community. In order to demonstrate its commitment to observance of Human Rights, The Federal Republic of Nigeria through the NHRC is said to be developing a National Action Plan (NAP) for the promotion and protection of human rights in Nigeria. This is to serve as measurement tool for measuring Nigerian human rights process.

29 Ibid. p. ix.
30 Ibid. p. 24.
31 Ibid. p. 39.
32 Information on the National Human Rights Commission of Nigeria was obtained from: www.nigeriarights.gov.ng/mission-vision.htm

The National Human Rights Commission of Nigeria was established by the Human Rights Commission Act of 1995. This Act took into consideration the United Nations Charter, the Constitution of the Federal Republic of Nigeria and the principle of the dignity and equality of all human beings. The National Human Rights Commission of Nigeria is not a substitute or rival to law courts. Its complaint treatment mechanism is to complement the work of the courts, whose constitutional duty it is to enforce fundamental human rights. The target of the Commission ought to be the poor and vulnerable as well as the rich, by offering services, which are inexpensive, non-technical, less time consuming and more accessible to the public.

The objectives of the National Human Rights Commission are said to include, facilitating Nigeria's implementation of its various treaty obligation, including but not limited to, the Universal Declaration of Human Rights, the International Convention on the Elimination of all Forms of Racial Discrimination and the African Charter on Human and Peoples' Rights; to create an enabling environment for extra-judicial recognition, promotion and enforcement of all rights recognized and enshrined in the 1999 Constitution of the Federal Republic of Nigeria and under the laws of the land; to provide a forum for public enlightenment and dialogue on Human Rights matters and to limit controversy and confrontation over allegations of human rights violations by public officers and agencies and to reaffirm the sacred and inviolable nature of human rights and other fundamental rights.

Most importantly the Vision of the Commission ought to be committed to institutionalizing the observance, promotion and protection of human rights for everyone by encouraging national values built on the principles of democracy, good governance and respect for the rule of law. There is no doubt that the Commission is formed on very laudable standards and principles irrespective of the military junta that formed it. But one wonders to what extent its standards and principles are translated into the realities of the present day Nigeria human rights situation and demands?

1.3 THE NIGERIAN CONSTITUTION AND THE ISLAMIC SHARIA LAW

Following the above highlight on the Institutions that influenced the Nigerian Constitution so far, permit me to come back to the Constitution and its relation to Sharia Law in Nigeria. Sharia law is said to be as old as Nigeria itself. Historically the 19th century muslim invasion of the northern part of Nigeria by Shehu Usman Dan Fodio[33] played a very significant role towards the establishment and consolidation of Islamic practices and culture in this part of the country. It is in this era that the Sharia law received its vital position as a major aspect of the Islamic religious practice in northern Nigeria.

The word Sharia means "the path to a watering hole". It denotes an Islamic way of life that is more than a system of criminal justice. Sharia is a religious code of living for Muslims, in the same way that the Bible offers a moral system for Christians. Sharia offers a code for living governing all elements of life, from prayers to fasting and donations to the poor. It decrees that men and women should dress modestly, which in some countries is interpreted as women wearing the veil and the sexes being segregated.

There is a specific set of offences in Sharia Law known as the Hadd offences. These are crimes punished by specific penalties, such as stoning, lashes or the severing of a hand.[34] The penalties for Hadd offences are not universally adopted as law in Islamic countries.

According to Wael Hallaq, Hadd offences carry specific penalties, set by the Koran and by the prophet Mohammed. These include unlawful sexual intercourse (outside marriage); false accusation of unlawful intercourse; the drinking of alcohol; theft; and highway robbery. Sexual offences carry a penalty of stoning to death or flogging, while theft is punished with cutting off a hand.

"Sharia governs the lives of people in ways which are not governed by the law," says Lynn Welchman, director of the Centre for Islamic and Middle

33 Shehu Usman Dan Fodio was a Fulani and a pious Muslim who lived between 1754 – 1817. He began a holy war in 1804 to reform the practice of Islam in northern Nigeria. His son Muhammad Bello continued in his stead after his death in 1817 to consolidate the establishment of Islamic practice in northern Nigeria. Uunder Usman and his son, Muslim culture flourished in the Fulani empire.

34 More on ‚Hadd' or as Quranic punishment *Hudud* could be read from:Hallaq, W.B., Sharia: Theory, Practice and Transformations, Cambridge University Press 2009, pp. 36,124, 269,270, 271, 307, 310, 311, 322, 334, 342-345, 348-352, 383, 439, 480, 484, 490, 524, 526, 551-552.

Eastern Law. It is adopted by most Muslims to a greater or lesser degree as a matter of personal conscience, but it can also be formally instituted as law by certain states and enforced by the courts.

The Nigerian Constitution provides the legal foundation for the introduction of the Sharia Court of Appeal on the federal and state levels. Chapter VII, sections 260 – 264 and 275 – 279 respectively, carefully outlined the provisions of this practice. The constitution officially declares that the Sharia Court of Appeal (on federal and state levels) shall be competent to decide on: (a) any question of Islamic personal law regarding a marriage concluded in accordance with that law, including a question relating to the validity or dissolution of such a marriage or a question that depends on such a marriage and relating to family relationship or the guardianship of an infant; (b) where all the parties to the proceeding are Muslims, any question of Islamic personal law regarding a marriage, including the validity or dissolution of that marriage, or regarding family relationship, a foundling or guardianship of an infant; (c) any question of Islamic personal law regarding a wakf[35], gift, Will or succession where the endower, donor, testator or deceased person is a Muslim; (d) any question of Islamic personal law regarding an infant, prodigal or person of unsound mind who is a Muslim or the maintenance or the guardianship of a Muslim who is physically or mentally infirm; or (e) where all the parties to the proceedings, being Muslims, have requested the court that hears the case in the first instance to determine that case in accordance with Islamic personal law, any other question.

The form of Sharia law implementation, especially in northern Nigeria has resulted in to various kinds of unrest between Christians and Muslims, thereby raising the question as to the constitutionality of Sharia inclusion in the Nigerian Constitution. Proponents of the Sharia lay claim on the

35 „wakf' means the permanent dedication by a person professing Islam, of any movable or immovable property for any purpose recognised by the Muslim law as pious, religious or charitable and includes - (i) a wakf by user but such wakf shall not cease to be a wakf by reason only of the user having ceased irrespective of the period of such cesser; (ii) „grants", including mashrut-ul-khidmat for any purpose recognised by the Muslim law as pious, religious or charitable; and (iii) a wakf-alal-aulad to the extent to which the property is dedicated for any purpose recognised by Muslim law as pious, religious or charitable, and „wakf" means any person making such dedication.

constitutional recognition of the Sharia in the 1999 Constitution of the Federal Republic of Nigeria. They argue that such inference is in compliance with the wordings of Section 38 (1) and Section 275 (1) regarding the right and freedom to "manifest and propagate one's religious beliefs, teachings, practices, and observances." Of course as I earlier pointed out, they also claim that these sections of the constitution authorize any State of the federation to establish a Sharia Court of Appeal. There is no doubt about the constitutional clarity of their claims, but the manner of its implementation in most of the States that have introduced Sharia leaves one to wonder the rationality of its inclusion since it is purely a religious legal code guiding the lives and religious practices of Muslims. Its official recognition in the constitution therefore is opposed to the provision of this same Constitution (chapter 1, section 10) prohibiting any form of State religion in Nigeria. This brings to mind the critique of Prof. Madunagu, that the Nigerian Constitution was "a product of the (then) ruling bloc to accommodate all their major factions". This indicates the strong influence of Islam in the Nigerian politics.

Nevertheless, events since 1999 regarding the introduction and implementation of the Sharia Criminal Penal Code have led to the controversy among rights activists and millions of Nigerians (both Muslims and Christians) of whether Sharia law, as a fully-fledged legal system, should be reflected in the Nigerian Constitution – or not, given its contentious religious content, taken into cognizance the status quo, and the multi-ethnic and multi-religious nature of the Nigeria society. This Sharia Criminal Penal Code allows the introduction of flagellation (whipping), lapidating (stoning) and amputation. Between 1999 and today, twelve northern states have ratified the implementation of the Sharia Penal Code, of course supporting their argument with the provisions of the constitution in this regard. But a close study of the Section 277 (2) (a) – (e) shows that Sharia courts shall be competent to decide only issues of Islamic personal law which (as I mentioned earlier) include, among other things, marriage, guardianship of infants and persons of unsound mind, foundling, wakf, gift, will and succession (inheritance). The introduction of Criminal Penal Code in the Sharia court of Appeal is then an inclusion of civil matters into the religious domain, and as such opposes the prescriptions of the Constitution in this regard. This could then be viewed as an overstepping of boundaries.

Of a similar nature is imposition of the Sharia law by some of the States also on non-Muslims, which is opposed to the wordings of Section 277 (2), where it is clearly stated that for that provision to be used, the persons involved must be Muslims, who must have (voluntarily) requested the court to handle their case in accordance with the Islamic personal law. Non-Muslims could be bound by the Sharia law only when they voluntarily opt to be tried under Sharia law. A Muslim is also not obliged if he or she decides the contrary. Against this background some Islamic scholars[36] believe and affirm that under the Sharia law every person irrespective of country of origin, religion, race, sex, status, age or color has basic human rights that should be respected. Such rights include: the rights to life, right to justice, right to equality, right to be free from discrimination, right to freedom from slavery, respect for the chastity of women, right to freedom from want, right to security of life and property, right to personal liberty, right to freedom of expression, and equality before the law. Where is then the justification and constitutionality of the imposition?

The Nigerian Constitution is supreme by virtue of the provision of section 1 (1). Section three categorically states that any other law, which is inconsistent with the provisions of the constitution, shall be null and void. Chapter four of the constitution dwells on fundamental human rights, which include rights to freedom of thought, conscience and religion (Section 38). The stipulations of the Sharia law as affirmed by some Islamic scholars tend to be consistent with the Nigerian constitution, but as a matter of practice (especially with regard to the Sharia Criminal Code), the Sharia law in Nigeria is in many cases not consistent with the constitution, and as such could be considered to be unconstitutional. Women and in some cases, Christians, are the immediate and vulnerable victims of the practice of Sharia law in northern Nigeria. Such inconsistencies and ambiguities between the Nigerian constitution and the Sharia law create the space for the neglect and in most cases, violation of women's rights and rights to freedom of religion and expression. Unfortunately, federal legislation does not specifically uphold the rights of women in areas where the custom or religion violate their constitutional rights.[37] The 'patriarchal' nature of the

36 The claim to this regard is affirmed by Abiola Akiyode-Afolabi in her article: *Democracy, Women's right and Sharia law in Nigeria,* in www.peacewomen.org/news/Nigeria/newsarchive03/Shariawomen.html

37 There is no specific mention of such protection for women in the whole of the Nigerian constitution.

Nigerian constitution in this case backs up such provisions against women in the Sharia law and leaves them very vulnerable to their men counterparts, who in most cases handle them as personal property that ought to stay available to their whims and caprices.

In the light of the above description of the Sharia law and the Nigerian constitution, one doubts the supremacy of the constitution and wonders what is left of it for the common man. In principle the Sharia law ought to bind only Muslims. Unfortunately the events of the recent past in the northern Nigeria show something contrary to its practice. I shall later return to this. However, permit me to remark here that Nigerians are human beings of equal status and as such ought to be given equal opportunities. It is worrisome that Nigerian leaders have not been able to tactfully resolve this problem, which has led to lost of thousands of lives and destruction of property worth millions of Naira. The Nigerian constitution ought to be an instrument of mediation for the common man and in essence ought to provide appropriate means of ensuring this equality and peaceful co-existence of all Nigerians.

1.4 THE NIGERIAN CONSTITUTION AND HUMAN RIGHTS

It is believed that the heart of every national Constitution is, and should be, the body of rights which the citizens should enjoy. Many constitutions refer to this as the *Bill of Rights.* The Nigerian Constitution calls it *fundamental rights.* Nigeria's relation to the Universal Declaration on Human Rights dates back to the nationalist's period which drew attention to provisions of the declaration in making their case for determination and independence. Article 21 of the Universal Declaration was often quoted in correspondence to the British overlords. "Everyone", says the article "has the right to take part in the government of his/her country, directly or through freely chosen representatives". Paragraph three of the article further posits: "The Will of the people shall be the basis of the authority of government; this Will being expressed in periodic and genuine elections shall be by universal and equal suffrage and shall be held by secret vote or by equivalent free voting procedures". The moral authority of the General Assembly of the United Nations, which proclaimed the Universal Declaration, forced the British government to set in motion the machinery for independence in her colonial territories including Nigeria. This external influence that led to the decolonization of Nigeria brought about a more indigenous representation in the government administration and granted Nigerians the opportunity of being directly involved in drawing up a Constitution during one the major constitutional reforms in 1951[38].

It is therefore no surprise that at independence, the Nigeria Constitution borrowed extensively from the Universal Declaration of Human Rights. Such rights as freedom of movement, expression, speech and protection from arbitrary arrest and detention were expressly enshrined in the Independence Constitution. The basic rights stated in the Independence Constitution included the right to life, freedom from inhuman treatment, freedom from slavery and forced labor, the right to personal liberty, the right to fair hearing, freedom of conscience and religion, freedom of expression, freedom of peaceful assembly and association, freedom of movement and residence; freedom from discrimination, and the right to family life[39], which took a pride of place in the African Charter on Human and Peoples' Rights. The bill of rights in the constitution was accepted by most Nigerians and at the same time criticized because of its theoretical and practical limitations, hence necessitated future Drafts and amendments.

The introductory part of the Nigerian Constitution as the 1999 amendment has it (above), gives further explanation regarding commitments in the Constitution. Both the 1979 Constitution and the Draft Constitution of 1995, and the amended Constitution of 1999 of the Federal Republic of Nigeria not only recognize human rights but also made specifications in Chapter IV, sections 33 to 44 on "Fundamental Rights"[40]. These are: the right to life (33), the right to dignity of the human person (34), the right to personal liberty (35), the right to fair hearing (36), the right to private and family life (37), the right to freedom of thought, conscience and religion (38), the right to freedom of expression and the press (39), the right to peaceful assembly and association (40), the right to freedom of movement (41), the right to freedom from discrimination (42), and the right to acquire and own immovable and moveable property (43 and 44). Section 45 authorizes derogation's and restrictions from sections 37, 38, 39, 40 and 41 of the Constitution, provided the derogating legislation is justifiable in a

38 Bonny Ibhawoh, Ibid., 162.

39 Ibid., 166.

40 The full text of the Nigerian Constitution could be found from: www.nigeria.law.org/ConstitutionofTheFederalRepublicOfNigria.htm#Chapter_4.

democratic society in the interest of defense, public order, public morality or public health or for the purpose of protecting the rights and freedoms of other persons. The section further permits derogation from sections 33 or 35 during periods of emergency, to the extent that those measures are reasonably justifiable for the purpose of dealing with the situation that exists during the period of emergency. The "period of emergency" here means any period during which there is in force a Proclamation of a state of emergency declared by the President in exercise of the powers conferred on him under section 305 of the Nigerian Constitution.

Section 46 (1) offers the citizens of Nigeria the opportunity to freely apply to the High Court in any State for redress in cases of alleged contravention of the provisions of this chapter.

One wonders to what extent this supposed security and yardstick goes as regards to the promotion and protection of human rights in Nigeria. The following section of this chapter is meant to give some highlight to this uncertainty.

1.5 CURRENT TRENDS IN HUMAN RIGHTS QUESTION IN NIGERIA

According to the 2003 *Country Reports on Human Rights Practices – 2002*, released by the Bureau of Democracy, Human Rights, and Labor[41], the situation of human rights in Nigeria is all but nothing to be proud of. The report says that the Government's human rights record remained poor; although there were improvements in several areas, serious problems remained. This report is collaborated by the Amnesty International separate reports of November 2003 and November 2004. The latter only added the cases of political violence that results into increased political assassinations and promotion of impunity;[42] and environmental pollutions caused by oil exploration in Nigeria.[43] There are not yet convincing positive changes on this situation report till date. The increasing level of corruption, mismanagement and inefficiency rob Nigerians of their fundamental rights.

41 Bureau of Democracy, Human Rights, and Labor at: www.nationbynation.com/nigeria/Hum.

42 www.amnesty.org.nz/web/chogm.nsf/opendocument.

43 www.globalpolicy.org/socecon/tncs/2004/1109amnestynigeria.pdf.

The January 31 2007 Report of the Human Rights Watch reported, that the squandering of public revenues deprive the poor of Nigeria the basic necessities such as health and educational services.[44] Government actors including the police, military, and elected officials continued to commit serious and persistent abuses against Nigerian citizens. The lack of political Will to improve the country's poor human rights situation and ensure accountability for abuses not only threatens to undermine the fragile gains made since the end of military rule but also poses daunting challenges to holding credible and violence-free elections in 2007.[45]

With this preview on the current trends in human rights question in Nigeria, I wish to survey these trends within the domain of the ***three generations of human rights.*** The division of human rights into three generations was initially proposed in 1979 by the Czech jurist Karel Vasak at the *International Institute of Human Rights* in Strasbourg. He used the term at least as at November 1977.[46] His divisions are in consonance to the three watchwords of the *French Revolution: Liberty, Equality, and Fraternity.* First-generation human rights deal essentially with liberty and participation in political life. They are fundamentally civil and political in nature and are meant to protect the individual from excesses of the state. First generation rights include: *freedom of speech, the right to fair trial, freedom of religion and voting rights.* They were the first enshrined at the global level by the *1948 Universal Declaration of Human Rights.*[47] The Second-generation human rights are related to equality, and began to be recognized by governments after *World War I.* They are fundamentally *social, economic, and cultural* in nature. They ensure equal conditions and treatment for different members of the society. Second generation rights would include a *right to be employed, rights to housing and health care*, as well as *social security and unemployment benefits.* Like first-generation rights, they were also covered by the Universal Declaration of Human

---

44 January 31, 2007 Report of Human Rights Watch in: www.hrw.org/doc/?t=africa&c=nigeria

45 Ibid.

46 www.en.wikipedia.org/wiki(Three_generations_of_human_rights

47 Articles 3 to 21 of the Universal Declaration of Human Rights, and the *International Convention on Civil and Political Rights* have special emphasis on the First Generation Human Rights.

Rights.[48] Third-generation human rights are those rights that go beyond the mere civil and social, as expressed in many progressive documents of *international law,* including the 1972 *Stockholm Declaration* of the United Nations Conference on the Human Environment, the *1992 Rio Declaration* on Environment and Development, and other pieces of generally aspirational *"soft law"*. Because of the principle of *sovereignty* and the preponderance of would-be offender nations, these rights have been hard to enact in legally binding documents. It is pertinent to point out that the term "third-generation human rights" remains largely unofficial, and thus houses an extremely broad spectrum of rights,[49] including: *Group and collective rights, right to self-determination, right to economic and social development, right to healthy environment, right to natural resources, right to communicate, right to participation in cultural heritage and rights to intergenerational equity and sustainability.*

Due to co-relational purposes between the theoretical and the empirical aspects of this project, I wish to limit myself to the following aspects of the three generations of human rights: civil and political rights, judicial rights, socio-economic rights and environmental rights. These three generations of human rights are interdependent on each other since they are equally based on the concept of human dignity and ought to contribute equally to enjoyment of freedom from fear and want.[50] By virtue of their concepts, the violation of any one of them invariably implies violation of the others.

The description of the situation of human rights in Nigeria here is not meant to be exhaustive. The major positive aspect of human rights trends in Nigeria I can make mention of here is using the analogy of a Nigerian adage: "all Lizard are lying low on their stomachs". It is a positive development that the number of human rights activist and NGOs is on a constant increase. These persons and groups constantly oppose and challenge the rising perpetration of all kinds of human rights violations in Nigeria. The impacts of their oppositions are constantly being suppressed by the governmental structures and personnel. That is why the picture of human

---

48 See: Articles 22 to 27 of the Univesal Declaration, and the *International Convention on Economic, Social, and Cultural Rights.*

49 www.en.wikipedia.org/wiki(Three_generations_of_human_rights

50 Van der Ven, J.A., Dreyer, J.S., and Pieterse, H.J.C., Is There a God of Human Rights?, Brill, Leiden, 2004, p. 111.

rights trends in Nigeria is mostly colored by violations. The cases that would be cited here are just samples of broader patterns of the current human rights trends in the country since the beginning of the year 2000. It is unavoidable to make extensive references to the Sharia law in this aspect because of its influence in the Nigerian political arena. Some other related aspects would be discussed in the following chapter.

1.5.1 Civil and Political Rights

1.5.1.1 Right to Life

The right to life, which forms the basis of the entire range of human rights, is the subject of section 33 of the Nigerian Constitution. Section 33 (1) provides that "every person has right to life and no one shall be deprived intentionally of his life except in execution of the sentence of a court in respect of a criminal offense of which he has been found guilty in Nigeria." The second sub-section of this section however provided another dimension to this right by stating that: "A person shall not be regarded as having been deprived of his life in contravention of this section, if he dies as a result of the use, to such extent and in such circumstances as permitted by law, of such force as is reasonably necessary – (a) for the defense of any person from unlawful violence or for the defense of property; (b) in order to effect a lawful arrest or to prevent the escape of a person lawfully detained; or (c) for the purpose of suppressing a riot, insurrection or mutiny".

With regard to the above stipulation one sees a "give and take" attitude in the constitution: It provides for everyone's right to live and at the same time gives conditions for doing so. The concepts "intentionally" and "except" makes it clear that capital punishment is a tolerable and lawful process in Nigeria. Permit me to avoid delving into the intricacies of death penalty in Nigeria since that would warrant a complete full topical discussion. Nevertheless, the matter of right to life warrants addressing briefly the right against torture. Although torture belongs to a different right, but permit me to draw a link of right to Life and rights against torture in the Nigerian context, whereby a person who dies of 'officially permitted torture', as stipulated by the sub-section (2) of the constitution is not regarded as having been deprived of his right to life. This dimension serves as a license to authorities in this area to inflict inhumane torture to victims, which is most likely to lead to the loss of life. This is a consequential basis that warrants the stark connection of the two Rights.

The right to torture is an age long practice of forcing culprits to admit to accusations and in some other cases naming accomplices. This age long practice is nevertheless propagated against since the eighteenth century.[51] The popular argument of this campaign heavily depended on the immanent dignity of the human person as an entity of body and soul. Torture is then proffered as an unacceptable method for seeking truth and justice since it exposes the victim to untold inhumane conditions and could lead to an eventual death of the victim. And when it brings about the death of the victim the right to life is abused. Although the section 34(a) of the Nigerian Constitution is against torture and inhuman or degrading treatment[52], the dimensional definition it gave to section 33 allows a room for ignoring the common practice and justifies this aspect of removing life with beautiful clauses.

On a related issue the 2003 *Country Reports on Human Rights Practices – 2002* reported among others, that the Nigerian national police, military, and security forces committed extra judicial killings and used excessive force to apprehend criminal suspects and to quell several incidents of ethno-religious violence. Police, military, and security forces sometimes beat protesters, criminal suspects, detainees, and convicted prisoners. The effects of the Government's continued efforts to curb torture and beatings of detainees and prisoners are not being felt. In most cases, neither the state anticrime taskforces, nor the police, nor the military were held accountable for excessive force or the death of persons in custody, the *Report* concluded.

51 The calous torture of a sixty-four-year-old French Protestant named Jean Calas in the 1760s and of other culprits contributed to the debate of abolishing torture as a lawful process in France. From France the campaign spread to other parts of European regions: Lynn Hunt, *Inventing Human Rights.* W.W. Norton & Company, New York, 2008. p. 70 ff.

52 This section of the Constitution reads: "No person shall be subject to torture or degrading treatment".

The Nigerian Law approved wide discretionary powers to the police in matters of arrest. An extensive report of Udo Jude Ilo of the *Human Rights Law Service HURILAWS* in Nigeria elaborates further on this matter:

> From facts on the ground and testimonies of victims some trigger happy Policemen kill suspects for no just cause and hide under the excuse that such a person is trying to escape arrest. In some cases it has been argued that the police shoot innocent people in order to protect the actual culprits. Arthur Onyejekwe reports that during his detention he witnessed death of suspect who was trying to escape from detention. Lawrence Onyo in his testimonies recounts how on several occasions he was taken out of the police cell and asked to leave the police station. On each occasion he refused to leave. The police latter informed him that he was lucky and that he would have been a dead man if had accepted to walk out of the police station.[53]
>
> This report also highlighted other extra judicial killings by militia groups that were sponsored and legitimized by the governmental institutions. The *Bakassi* vigilante group and the *Odua People's Congress* call to mind.[54] Although the two groups mentioned above were eventually officially disbanded by the government there are more of such similar groups existing in the rural areas, whose activities are purportedly ignored by the government.

Several aspects of death penalty in Nigeria are still of special concern. The widespread procedural irregularities leave the whole practice with a question mark. The condition on death row is very dehumanizing and the operation of Sharia law, especially with regard to adultery and sodomy calls for revision. During the visit of the Special Rapporteur to several prisons in Nigeria in 2004,[55] it was discovered that the Nigerian Police are said to be applying torture to extract confessions from convicts and that these confessions have often been critical to the conviction of persons charged with capital offences. Moreover many defendants in capital trials have effectively had no legal representation, and legal aid is not available for appeals. In addition, many of the prisoners with whom he met on death row were tried when Nigeria was governed by a military regime, when various constitutional rights were suspended and capital trials were sometimes conducted by military tribunals. The procedural probity of such tri-

---

53 Udo Jude Ilo: *The Rope: Country Report on death penalty application in Nigeria.* HURILAWS Lagos Nigeria, 2004. pp. 39-40.

54 Ibid. pp. 40-41.

55 Details of the Special Rappoteur's visit is given in: www.extrajudicialexecutions.org/law

als was almost flawed. Another problem with the death penalty in Nigeria is its imposition for the crimes committed as a minor. Due to uncertainties linked to condemning convicts to death many State governors are said to be reluctant in signing the death warrant of condemned convicts in their States. This trend has led to the psychological damage to human dignity of such convicts. Majority of them wait endlessly for the hang man's noose, and in most cases suffer from mental disabilities prior to their proposed death. Such illnesses owe to their long stay behind bars, and by so doing are inflicted with double jeopardy.

Sharia courts have continued to sentence persons to harsh punishments including amputations and death by stoning. The 111-page report, entitled *"Political Sharia?: Human Rights and Islamic Law in Northern Nigeria"*, published by the Human Rights Watch, on September 21, 2004, extensively reports human rights violations since the Sharia was introduced to cover criminal law in 12 northern states.[56] Among other issues, it reported that in northern Nigeria, many Muslims who had initially supported Sharia have become disillusioned with the manner in which it has been implemented. They told Human Rights Watch that this was not "real Sharia but political Sharia", but are fearful of being labeled "anti-Islamic" if they say so publicly. In this vein, the report said that state governors have championed Sharia simply to boost their popularity and enhance their political standing.

Due to the increasing rate of corruption in the country, matters of security are of a no class discussion. Instead of providing basic security for her citizens those at the helm of affairs in the governance of the nation are more concerned about their own safety. The statement of the former Inspector General of Police (Rtd), Mr. Musiliu Smith corroborated this situation: "Nigerians should not expect adequate protection of their lives and properties as long as the police force is not properly funded".[57] As a result of this lack rampart killings are being recorded almost on daily basis, ranging from political killings, ethno-religious killings to armed robbery killings. In most cases those who are involved in these killings are not brought to book, especially when the poor citizens are affected. It is now a question

56 This extensive report on violations of human rights from the perspective of Shari'a by the Human Rights Watch could be viewed from: Hrw.org/english/docs/2004/09/21/nigeria9364_txt.htm.

57 Daily Trust (Abuja), February 8, 2007, at www.allafrica.com/stories/

of security-purchase power. Those who can afford it make private arrangement for security outfit, and in most cases involving the official security outfit of the nation –the Nigerian Police Force (NPF). The lives of the poor citizens, who cannot afford this purchase power, are left at the mercy of providence and the powerful. The rich cultural and religious values of right to life in Nigeria have been relegated to the relativism of her existential era.

1.5.1.2 Right to Freedom of Religion

Due to the plurality nature of religion in Nigeria, Nigeria adopted the right to freedom of religion in her Constitutions. Section 38 of the 1999 Constitution, for instance, guarantees that "every person is entitled to freedom of thought, conscience and religion, including freedom to change his religion or belief, and freedom (either alone or in community with others, and in public or in private) to manifest and propagate his religion or belief in worship, teaching, practice and observance." On the right to freedom of religion in Nigeria, the 2004 International Religious freedom Report[58] commented that though the Federal Government generally respects religious freedom, there were some instances where limits were placed on religious activity to address security and public safety concerns. This report lamented the allegation by some Christians that Islamic religion has been adopted as a de facto state religion in several northern states, citing the reintroduction of criminal code into the Sharia Law and the continued use of state resources to fund the construction of mosques, the teaching of the Q'uran, and Muslim doctrines, and pilgrimages to Mecca (hajj). This report is an indication that freedom of religion in Nigeria remains problematic, hence necessitated Nigeria's 7th position among the 13 countries worldwide named currently as "countries of particular concern" by the U.S. Commission on International Religious Freedom, as it pertains to violation of the right to religious freedom[59].

Human Right to freedom of religion went through various difficult hurdles before assuming its present position in human rights history. The Medieval period in European history played a major role in the struggle for freedom of religion as a human right. Prior to the struggle that brought about the

58 Details of this report are also found on: www.ecoi.net/doc/en/NG/content/4/941-961.
59 *Religious Freedom under Threat,* John Flynn. LC, Zenit.org, Rome May 10, 2009.

institution of this right, minority religious groups such as Muslims and Jews suffered untold hardships in the hands of the dominant Roman Catholic Church of the era. Micheline Ishay elaborated extensively on this fact:

> The pervasive Christian fear of the Turks, a result of the Crusades…, contributed to sharpening Catholic intolerance toward other religious groups. In addition to Muslims, European Jews were considered foreigners and often personae non gratae in Western Christendom, and as such were subjected to various levels of discrimination. The fourth Lateran Council (1215), for instance, banned Jews from government employment. In 1920, Jews were expelled from England, in 1306, from France. In Spain, initial tolerance gave way to persecution during the Inquisition (1492), and Jews were forced to choose between conversion and eviction. In addition, Jews were often accused of performing acts of sacrilege and murdering children, charges that intensified during the Crusades and the Black Plague (1347-1351), and as a result were often targeted as scapegoats and massacred.[60]

Against this background the rise of Protestantism posed a significant challenge to this existing Catholic dominance and paved the way for great reformations, which took place at the 1555 Augsburg Peace and the October 1648 Treaty of Westphalia. In its first official style, the Levellers' spokesman, John Lilburne (1614-1657) citing the equality of all human beings, proclaimed during the English civil war, according to *The Clarke Papers,* that: "all men by nature are the children of Adam, and regardless of religious differences, they are equal and alike in power, dignity, authority and majesty."[61] Among the reformators of this era, the English philosopher John Locke, with his famous *Letter concerning Toleration* (1690) opened a significant chapter in the struggle for freedom of religion as a human right. His emphasis was based on the individual's right, rather than the state's, to choose religion. He argued that such a right emanates from a personal conviction.[62] John Locke went further to consolidate his struggle by strongly calling for a clearer separation between the church and the state.[63]

The Nigerian case is not far from that of the European medieval era. Freedom of religion is a Right problem in Nigeria, which is explicitly and greatly owed to the introduction and practice of Sharia law in the public

60 Micheline R. Ishay, The History of Human Rights: *From Ancient Times to the Globalization era.* University of California Press, London, 2004. p.75.

61 Ibid. p. 77

62 Ibid. P. 78

63 Ibid. P. 79

sphere. As indicated above, Sharia law came with the advent of Islam in Nigeria. Until its recent public introduction it has always been practiced in the private religious sectors and family boundaries. The matter is made more complicated due to the reluctance, and if I may say, weakness of the government to implement to the latter the dictates of the Constitution in this regard. This lukewarm attitude has led to the illegal adoption of Islam as State religion and the Sharia law in most northern States.

The International Religious Freedom Reporter[64] reported that more than ten northern States have adopted and introduced the Sharia Law. Theoretically, non-Muslims are not bound by these laws, but in practice non-Muslim residents in these States are meant to choose less severe options when they are found guilty. This is more or less an imposition of the said laws on non-Muslims. Christian nurses in some of the States, for example, are dismissed because they refused to wear Sharia compliant uniforms. Many tend to live false patterns of lives in order to escape undue punishment. This same agency also reported that several northern State governments continued to ban public proselytizing under the guise of avoiding ethno-religious clashes and tensions. This is an indirect way of hindering other religious bodies to be popular in such Muslim-dominated zones. In most of these areas, localized discrimination and violence against religious minorities persisted. Subsequently, Christian groups complained that they are being denied land for building churches.[65] The forceful introduction and implementation of Sharia Law in most of the northern States have led to bloody clashes between the Christians and Muslims resulting to the deaths of many innocent citizens of those States.

This religious intolerance in Nigeria, especially in most of the northern-Islamic States has led to all kinds of religious clashes and killings between Muslims and Christians. One even begins to wonder the rational behind these clashes unleashed, in other cases by Muslims. Two cases reported by *Human Rights Watch* illustrate my claim in this regard: in October 2001, violence erupted in the northern State of Kano following protests against the United States military attacks on Afghanistan. The said violence was directed against Christians who live in this State[66]. Another example is the

64 Ibid., www.ecoi.net/doc/en/NG/content/4/941-961.

65 Dickson Adeyanju, *Governments Inability to End Sharia Worries Bishops*, in THE GUARDIAN (September, 19 2000) at www.ngrguardiannews.com

66 Human Rights Watch Nigeria 2001 available at: www.hrw.org/reports/2001/nigeria

recent Danish cartoon of Mohammed in 2006. This event that took place in the Scandinavian country Denmark sparked up another bloody violence against Christians in the northern State of Maidugri, which resulted in the death of a catholic priest and many other peoples' lives.

Some people argue that the adoption of Sharia is indeed a political issue. It is regarded as a game plan by the northern leaders to hold on to power since Sharia strongly recommends that non-Muslim should not rule over Muslims.[67] As a result of the adoption of Sharia in some northern States there has been an increased rate of human rights abuses. A good number of death sentences by the Sharia courts have been passed and inhuman penalties (such as amputation) have been carried out based on offences such as marital infidelity, pre-marital sex and theft. In most cases the convicts are not allowed access to legal representation and appeal.

As a matter of fact the provisions of the Nigerian Constitution on this Right are not reflected in the practical application and implementation of the said Right, especially as it pertains to Islamic religion (in the northern part of Nigeria).

1.5.1.3 Right to freedom from discrimination

The Nigerian Constitution of 1999 under section 42 gives every Nigerian citizen the right to freedom from discrimination: "A citizen of Nigeria… shall not… (a)be subjected either expressly by, or in the practical application of, any law in force in Nigeria or any executive or administrative action of the government, to disabilities or restrictions to which citizens of Nigeria of other communities, ethnic groups, places of origin, sex, religion or political opinions are not made subject; or (b)be accorded either expressly by, or in the practical application of, any law in force in Nigeria or any such executive or administrative action, any privilege or advantage that is not accorded to citizens of Nigeria of other communities, ethnic groups, places of origin, sex, religious or political opinions". Under this section, grounds of discrimination pertaining to particular community, ethnic group, place of origin, sex, religion or political opinion is mentioned. It is however unfortunate to indicate that the provisions of this section are

67 Ben Omoni, *Sharia and Religious Intolerance in Nigeria,* in NIGERIA WORLD FEATURE (June 20 2000), at www.nigeriaworld.com

too general. The section, for instance, did not include discrimination on basis of health. This provision did not also include marital status, family status. There is also no legislation in Nigeria that seeks to provide punishments or sanctions from people who engage in discriminatory acts, for instance where a person is denied or dismissed from his/her employment on health basis such as HIV/AIDS infected persons.

The human rights trend in Nigeria with regard to discrimination has assumed all kinds of cultural and religious interpretations without due consideration or regard to the dictates of the Nigerian Constitution.

I mentioned above that Nigeria is signatory to numerous International Conventions and Covenants on human dignity. One of such is the International Convention on the Elimination of all Forms of Discrimination against Women. The Constitution did not in any way discriminate between men and women, but certain laws and practices relating to personal status and family relations carry clear discriminatory biases against women. In some areas where women's rights are not abrogated by law, socio-cultural constraints rooted in customs and tradition continue to pose serious problems to the full realization of their rights in practice.[68] This aspect of neglect of women's rights is basically recorded in the form of violence women experience almost on daily basis. Generally, violence against women include: violence at home, sexual harassment at school or place of work, rape and defilement, harsh punitive widowhood rites, female genital mutilation, forced childhood marriages, sexual violence in conflict situations and during execution of armed robbery, enforcement of gender biased laws, discrimination against the girl child, denial of inheritance to wives and daughters, and harmful traditional practices. These have physical, psychological and socio-economic consequences on women. It violates their rights to physical integrity.

From the religious perspective the situation is not better. Religions in Nigeria are considered to be bodies which promote liberation and emancipation. It may seem an overstatement to refer to religions as being propagators of human rights abuses, but in a way, the structures and ideologies of the major religions in Nigeria (African Traditional religion, Christianity

---

68 John Oziegbe, Open Society: JUSTICE INITIATIVE, Anti.Discriminatory Law in Nigeria, at www.justiceinitiative.org

and Islam), are made in such a way that they indirectly recognize their perpetuation. The patriarchal structures of these religions have continued to provide possibilities of discrimination against women (in particular) in the society and, even within their circles. Some details on this aspect would be discussed in the following chapter.

Outside the ambient of religion, other domestic violence against women remained widespread, and some forms were sanctioned by traditional, customary, or Sharia laws. Quoting Amnesty International on this matter, a reporter at *Nationbynation.com* reported that "Discrimination against women remained a problem. Female genital mutilation (FGM) remained widely practiced in some parts of the country, and child abuse and child prostitution is still common. Trafficking in persons for purposes of prostitution and forced labor remains a problem, and the collusion of government officials in trafficking was alleged".[69]

I cannot avoid an analysis of the role Sharia Law plays in this aspect. Unlike in some Muslim countries where Sharia Laws are implemented, in northern Nigeria, Sharia Laws are not meant to apply to other citizens who are not Muslims (as I mentioned earlier). Nonetheless, non-Muslims have been directly or indirectly affected by certain aspects of Sharia Law, as reported by *Human Rights Watch* Report, and representatives of some churches and Christian organizations have reported instances of discrimination and marginalization. It is further reported that while Christians have always been a minority in northern Nigeria and complained about social and cultural marginalization and discrimination before the advent of Sharia Law, these complaints have increased since the scope of Sharia Law was extended in 2000.[70] The *Civil Liberties Organization* also reported that a radio station in Zamfara State, for instance, discriminated against Christians in the State by rejecting commercials and paid Adverts containing Christian literature.[71] The *Human Rights Watch* also noted that even on internal basis, the Sharia Law warranted a form of discrimination among Muslims themselves. The case of Zamfara State is yet another example.

69 See: www.nationbynation.com/nigeria/Hum

70 See Human Rights Watch Report IX. *Freedom of Conscience and religion, and the impact of Sharia on non-Muslims*, September 2004, at: www.hrw.org/reports/2004/nigeria0904/9.htm

71 CLO's Report, Supra note 185.

A number of Muslims were arrested in December 2001 for not complying with the government's orders for prescribed period of prayers in preparation for the beginning of Ramadan.[72]

Another deplorable report on the right to freedom from discrimination has to do with HIV/AIDS patients. The UNAIDS 2001 Report reported that "an estimated 3.2. Million Nigerians between the ages of 15 and 49 are currently living with HIV/AIDS".[73] The humiliating aspect of their situation is the "denial of treatment in some health care institutions, breaches of privacy and confidentiality, termination of employment, ejection from housing, and other forms of social exclusion".[74] Ignorance of the populace about the contagious nature and process of this sickness has also contributed a lot to the victims being discriminated against. An appellant once made an appeal to the Lagos State Court of Appeal seeking to challenge her unjust dismissal from work on the grounds of being infected with HIV/AIDS. Out of ignorance, the presiding Justice had to call an expert witness to testify if the Plaintiff would not infect the court audience with HIV virus, if she were to be invited as a witness.[75]

With the House of Representative Committee on Human Rights' consultation around a bill known as *Discrimination Prohibition and Enforcement of Equality Act*, Nigeria is said to have taken a giant step to curb the wide spread of discriminatory practices rampart in Nigeria. This Act is meant to extend the laws covering discrimination in Nigeria particularly discrimination on grounds of ethnic origin, sex, age, religion, marital status, family status and conviction that has been pardoned etc.[76] As has always been the case in Nigeria, initiation of ideas are always wonderful, but their lack of implemention has rendered those ideas ineffective.

---

72 See: www.hrw.org/reports/2004/nigeria0904/9.htm

73 Culled from a paper prepared by the Centre for the Right to Health for the POLICY Project titled: *HIV/AIDS and Human Rights in Nigeria* sited from: www.dec.org/pdf_docs/PNACX553.pdf

74 Ibid.

75 John Oziegbe, Ibid.

76 Ibid.

1.5.1.4 Right to Freedom of Expression

Section 39(1) of the Nigerian Constitution states that: "every person shall be entitled to freedom of expression, including freedom to hold opinions and to receive and impart ideas and information without interference." Freedom of expression and opinion is regarded as one of the fundamental human rights since it offers the human person the grounds for making his feelings and thoughts known. The contributions of the English political pamphleteer John Milton (1608-1674) towards this struggle cannot be ignored. In a protest against the practices of his time, John Milton turned the tide in the following words in *Areopagetica*[77]: "He who kills a good book kills reason itself, kills the image of God… in the eye. (G)ive me the liberty to know, to utter, and to argue freely, above all liberties…. If truth is let free, it will overcome and win over all possible errors."[78] These statements formed to a large extent good basis for the universal recognition of the right to freedom of expression.

Unfortunately, Nigeria is still lacking in her respect of the freedom of expression. The atmosphere of tyranny and dictatorship still becloud the democratic regimes, even of the present day. The Government generally respected freedom of speech and of the press; however, there were problems in some areas, reported the *Bureau of Democracy, Human Rights and Labor*.[79] Further Reports from *San Frontieres* and *Reporters Without Borders*[80] show that there is a continued arbitrary arrest and detention of journalist and social activists in the country. Such numerous attacks on press freedom lead to growing climate of lawlessness. In some cases, foreign journalists are barred from entering the country for coverage, with the accusation of being biased. On May 14 2006, agents from the State Security Service (SSS), raided the Abuja office of Daar Communications

---

77 *Areopagetica* is a book that remains a classic plea from John Milton for the freedom of the press addressed to the parliament of England in the days of the persecution of the press.

78 John Milton, *Areopagetica: A Speech for the Liberty of Unlicesensed Printing, to the Parliament of England,* in *Selected Essays of John Milton,* p. 42 & p. 128, quoted by Michelin Ishay, Ibid. p. 79 (Original text is unfortunately beyond reach at the time of writing).

79 Centre for the Right to Health for the POLICY Project titled: *HIV/AIDS and Human Rights in Nigeria* sited from: www.dec.org/pdf_docs/PNACX553.pdf Ibid.

80 From Reporters Sans Frontieres/ Reporters Without Borders, 2003, at: www.ecoi.net/doc/en/NG/content/4/941-953.

Limited, owners of Ray Power FM radio and the Africa Independent Television (AIT), and seized the master tape of a documentary film.[81] It was further reported that "upon arrival at the premises, the security agents halted further transmission of the documentary, which partly dealt with the extension of President Olusegun Obasanjo's term in power, and seized the master tape for the documentary".[82] The Chairman of the Communications outfit said that the agents who raided the office claimed to have come from the Presidency.

Critics of the government, especially the media and human rights and political activist are still almost on daily basis exposed to all kinds of humiliations and arbitrary arrests from the said SSS. The Human Rights Watch reported that brutal measures have been used to repress peaceful expression. In extreme cases, the government's reaction to dissent or protest has resulted in extrajudicial killings.

Democracy and Minority Rights in Nigeria[83] also reported that one of the effects of the introduction of Shari'a law in some northern states is an assault on culture since it bans also cinema houses and video production, singing and dancing. Though the government is making effort to stop such assaults, the enforcement agents of Shari'a law believed that all traditional music, singing and dancing in Hausa land must stop. This attitude hinders Muslim artistes to develop their talent in consonance with their culture and invariably rob most Hausa communities access to their cultural values found in music and dances. These restrictions point to the violation of the 1999 Nigerian Constitution, section 39. On another note, some critics of Shari'a law claim that the introduction of Shari'a law has led to a further clampdown on freedom of expression in the northern part of Nigeria. Those most affected in this regard are Muslims rather than Christians. Human Rights Watch reported that "there were instances, soon after Shari'a law was introduced, when government critics, including some Islamic leaders and scholars, were publicly discredited or ridiculed.[84] Open discussion on the Shari'a law was strongly prohibited by the government. The reluctance

---

81 Media Rights Agenda (Lagos), Press Release, May 15, 2006 at: www.lists.mayfirst.org/pipermail/friends/2006-May

82 Ibid.

83 www.ecoi.net/doc/en/NG/content/4/941-953 Ibid.

84 Human Rights Watch Report, *The Impact of Sharia on Freedom of Expression,* September 2004, at: www.hrw.org/reports/2004/nigeria0904/9.htm

of critics to express their views about the Sharia law appears to be primarily based on a fear of being labeled anti-Islamic. Human Rights Watch further reported that "the politicization of religion has meant that criticism of northern State governments is also automatically labeled as criticism of Islam, even when it is not connected to issues of religion or religious law, and even when it focuses on specific legal or technical points".[85] It is however reported that this situation in the northern part is sober now than it was some two or three years ago. Nonetheless, the atmosphere of freedom is still lacking in this regard. As a result, most of the public critics of Sharia law are either from the Christian folk or from other parts of the country, or foreign or international organizations. The sad news of the external criticisms is an increased polarization of opinion, and propaganda that Christian or Western organizations are leading the "attack" against Sharia law, and possibly against Islam.

Freedom of expression within the church does not generally receive public applause, especially from her critics. Some members of the church do not feel very free to express themselves on controversial religious matters, mostly under the fear of being denied membership or one sacrament or the other. Further elaboration on this will come up in a later chapter.

With the above mentioned deplorable situation of right to freedom of expression, Nigeria is in breach of several international and regional conventions which guarantee freedom of expression.

1.5.1.5 Right to Freedom of Association

On the right to freedom of association the 1999 Constitution of Nigeria, Section 40, states: "Every person shall be entitled to assemble freely and associate with other persons, and in particular he may form or belong to any political party, trade union or any association for the protection of his interests". The right to freedom of association is closely linked to the rights to freedom of religion, freedom from discrimination and freedom of expression. Violation of the said rights denies the human person of his fundamental right to existence, albeit the freedom to live freely and enjoy the common goods of the earth.

85 Ibid.

The right to freedom of association and effective recognition of the right to collective bargaining are the first of the four core labour standards, according to the International Labour Organisation (ILO) standard. Freedom of association is regarded as safeguarding individual civil liberties and acknowledged as a fundamental right in international law. Generally speaking and in comparison to the military and para-military regimes, there is progress in the government's enforcement of respect for workers' right to organize and assemble in Nigeria. This notwithstanding the Bureau of Democracy, Human Rights and Labor, further reported that the Government placed some limits on freedom of assembly and association, citing security concerns. With regard to this right, the 2004 UN Integrated Regional Information Network *(IRIN)* report[86] indicated that associations that protest against some ideologies of the government are still being suppressed, attacked, and in some cases, people are killed in the process. Several public meetings and demonstrations are often banned by the police forces, and of course on the Federal or State Government's orders. The International Center for Not-for-Profit Law (ICNL) in its Journal of August 2006 reported that trade unions in Nigeria have continued to suffer crude treatment and abuse from the government despite the dispensations of the democratic governance.[87] The Nigerian trade unions are well known for their nationalist movement, which eventually led to the Nigerian independence and freedom of its citizens. But most of these trade unions have remained under a continued attack and suppression from the governmental bodies in Nigeria. The ICNL Journal gave an extensive report of such violations of the right of the trade unions to assemble:

> "Violence against trade unionists is endemic, including murder, disappearance, intimidation, torture, and detention. In 2002, shortly after the Nigerian Labor Congress (NLC) declared a nationwide strike over the increase of petroleum prices, security agents rounded up Adams Oshiomhole, the NLC president, and several other labor leaders, including Dr. Dippo Fashina, president of the Academic Staff Union (ASUU). Sixteen other union leaders were arrested in Port Harcourt, Rivers State, while twenty-five persons, including the state secretary of NLC, Wale Olaniyan, were locked up in Ogun State by the police. In the course of the Abuja arrests, the police

86 IRIN 2004 Report at: www.ecoi.net/doc/en/NG/content/4/941-951.

87 Ovunda V.C. Okene, *Curbing State Interference in Workers'freedom of Association in Nigeria,* in The International Journal of Not-for-Profit Law, Volume 8, Issue 4, August 2006; published at: www.icnl.org/knowledge/ijnl/vol8iss4/art_2.htm

> exhibited excessive brutality. … ASUU president Fashina had his shirt turn and one of his fingers broken. Throughout a twenty-four hour stint in detention, they were not allowed to receive any medical attention".[88]

From the tone of the recent warning to the NLC from a government spokesman to curb the extent of their confrontation on governmental policies, it gives a clear indication that these attacks and suppression are backed by the government.[89] In collaboration to the above report, the NLC reported that the Nigeria's New Trade Union Amendment Act, which was adopted recently, "fails to address adequately problems identified in the report with regard to the freedom of association and the right to collective bargaining, the right to strike and anti-union policies".[90] This recently adopted Act and the Nigerian Public Order Act prevent unions from gathering without official permission from the authorities and empower the authorities to prohibit gatherings or mass meetings generally.[91] Human Rights Watch reported that in July 2006, the Police, under the guise of the said Public Order Act, broke up a meeting of civil society groups convened in Abuja to discuss the human rights records of Obasanjo administration.[92] This indicates that not much has changed.

All these suppressions and attacks mentioned above also point to (a greater extent) breech of the stipulations of UDHR and African Charter on Peoples and Human Rights.

1.5.2 Judicial Rights

Equal judicial rights for all

The general situation-report on the question of judicial rights in Nigeria goes about the deplorable prison conditions and the consequences of inefficiency, underfunding, understaffing, manipulations and corruption in the judiciary system. Country Reports on Human Rights Practices – 2005,

---

88 Ibid.

89 Ibid.

90 *Labour Standards remain poor in Nigeria.* afrol News, 29 April 2007, published at: www.afrol.com/articles

91 Ovunda V.C. Okene, Ibid.

92 Nigeria: *Events of 2006,* at http://hrw.org/englishwr2k7/2007/01/11/nigeria

released by the Bureau of Democracy, Human Rights, and Labor, March 2006 reported a very deplorable and shameful situation of the Nigerian judiciary system, ranging from beatings of prisoners, detainees, and suspected criminals; harsh punishments by Shari'a courts; harsh and life-threatening prison conditions; arbitrary arrest and prolonged pre-trial detention, to executive interference in the judiciary and judicial corruption.[93]

Akin to the violation of the right to life is the state of Nigerian prisons. Prison conditions are still harsh and life threatening and the lack of sufficient food and adequate medical treatment contribute to the death of numerous inmates. Police and security forces continued to implement arbitrary arrest and detention. Prolonged pre-trial detention remains a serious problem. The judicial system is often incapable of providing criminal suspects with speedy and fair trials. This is also an infringement on people's rights to liberty and security, rights to dignity and humane treatment while in detention, and rights to fair hearing, as explicated in the Sections 35 and 36 of the Nigerian Constitution, respectively. Section 35 clearly states in some of its subsections thus: (1)"Every person shall be entitled to his personal liberty and no person shall be deprived of such liberty save in (some) case (as extensively mentioned by the constitution) and in accordance with a procedure permitted by law"; (3) "Any person who is arrested or detained shall be informed in writing within twenty-four hours … of the facts and grounds for his arrest or detention"; (4)"Any person who is arrested or detained in accordance with subsection (1)(c) of this section shall be brought before a court of law within a reasonable time[94], and if he is not tried within a period of (a) two months from the date of his arrest or detention in the case of a person who is in custody or is not entitled to bail; or (b) three months from the date of his arrest or detention in the case of a person who has been released on bail, he shall … be released either unconditionally or upon such conditions as are reasonably necessary to ensure that he appears for a trial at a later date". Section 36(1) complements the former thus: "In the determination of his civil rights and obligations, including any ques-

93 Country Reports on Human Rights Practices – 2005, March 8, 2006, at www.state.gov/g/drl/rls/hrrpt/2005

94 "a reasonable time" here means (a) in the case of an arrest or detention in any place where there is a court of competent jurisdiction within a radius of forty kilometres, a period of one day; and (b) in any other case, a period of two days or such longer period as in the circumstances may be considered by the court to be reasonable.

tion or determination by or against any government or authority, a person shall be entitled to a fair hearing within a reasonable time by a court or other tribunal established by law and constituted in such a manner as to secure its independence and impartiality".

The provisions of the Nigerian Constitution not withstanding, the nation's judicial procedures are plagued with an obnoxious practice, commonly known as "holding charges", whereby the police obtains the endorsement of a court which lacks jurisdiction to remand a criminal suspect in prison custody indefinitely. There is the possibility that suspects held under the holding charge regime may remain in detention as Awaiting Trial Prisoners for upwards of five years without their cases ever being heard in a court of competent jurisdiction either due to the ineptitude of the police that cannot conclude investigations, or simply that the case file of the individual is lost. Buttressing this point, statistics, as mentioned by the former Secretary General of The Catholic Secretariat of Nigeria, George Ehusani, show "for example that over 60% of the prison population in Nigeria are Awaiting Trial Prisoners, and of the 1771 inmates of the Ikoyi Prisons, 1631 are Awaiting Trial Prisoners".[95] Ehusani goes further to decry that these "citizens who are presumed innocent until proven guilty of a crime after due process of a court or a tribunal, are (while in detention) subjected to the most degrading and dehumanizing conditions that can be imagined. They are often held for periods much longer than they would have served on conviction, yet a number of them could well be innocent of the crimes for which they are being held".[96]

It is also a common phenomenon that a normal Nigerian prison generally lacks the basic conditions of prison welfare in the modern civilized society. Many prisons, as at 2004, held 200 to 300 percent more persons than they were designed to accommodate.[97] The scenario paints a picture of total neglect of the stipulations of the Constitution as regards the rights of suspects or prisoners.

It is worrisome that in most cases institutions and laws fail to contain the abuses. The government simply threw the rule of law aside while the ju-

---

95 Ehusani, G., *Forward,* in: Oilisa A., and Ibe, S, Travesty of justice: An Advocacy Manual Against the Holding Charge, Hurilaws publication, Lagos, 2004, p.vii.

96 Ibid.

97 Details of this claim are found on: www.ecoi.net/doc/en/NG/content/4/941-963.

diciary, its first custodian, looks on. I mentioned earlier that section 46 (1) of the 1999 Constitution on Fundamental Rights, offers the citizens the opportunity to freely apply to the High Court in any State for redress in cases of alleged violations of their rights. But regrettably, most of these law courts have failed to live up to the expectations. They are mostly now pictured as places where bribery and corruption walk on their four legs in flamboyant-style domination. The law courts are no more abodes of justice. They have become places where the highest bidder gets the 'commodity' (justice). The poor invariably become defenseless and voiceless in such a situation. Law and human rights instruments are most often inadequate to cope with the exigencies of everyday human degradation. And this development is directly opposed to the 1999 Constitution, chapter two, Section 17, which states: "The independence, impartiality and integrity of courts of law, and easy accessibility thereto shall be secured and maintained".

Section 6 of the Nigerian Constitution succinctly upholds the sovereignty of the courts. Some Nigerian Lawyers have over the years, continued to protect the integrity of the law courts as the most robust of the Nigerian constitutional institutions. This effort on the part of lawyers is being marred by the continuous interference of the executive institutions into the judiciary system, coupled by political, psychological and physical attacks and intimidations our honorable judges and lawyers go through in the course of their constitutional duties. Few quick recent examples (among others) by Reuben Abati substantiate this report:

> "One, in February *(2007),* the detained leader of the Niger Delta Peoples Volunteer Force (NDPVF), Mujahiddin Asari Dokubo who is standing trial for treason at the Federal High Court Abuja, decided to vent his spleen on the presiding judge in his case, Justice Peter Olayiwola whom he tongue-lashed, abused, and openly intimidated. He told the judge: "This is an evil court; this is a judge from the bottom of hell fire. I will come after you, and I will bring you to your knees. I will destroy you. You think Obasanjo can save you when he could not save the expatriates in the Niger Delta. You will see, I know where you live. I know where your family lives." Asari Dokubo further told the judge: "You are an idiot, a very stupid old man. We must not continue this trial before this judge.""[98]

This is a case of open intimidation and assault. A case of direct and physical attack and assault on Judges took place on 20 March 2007 in Gombe State

98 Reuben Abati, *Attacks on Judges;* March 2007, at www.nigeria.com

Magistrate Court, where the Chief Magistrate, Mr. Joseph Garba Shinga was brutally beaten and wounded while hearing a case involving a former Governor of Gombe State who was accused of inciting his supporters to engage in civil disturbance that resulted in the destruction of public property.[99] An example of a direct interference of an executive institution into the judicial matters involved a Minister of the Federal Republic of Nigeria, Mallam Nasir El-Rufai, Minister of the Federal Capital Territory (FCT), and the Executive Secretary of the Federal Capital Development Authority (FCDA), Mallam Mohammed Al Hassan. The Federal High Court charged the two for contempt of the court.

> "Both El-Rufai and Al Hassan had ignored the court; but an angry Justice Mudashiru Oniyangi tried to protect the sovereignty of the judiciary, insisting that the Inspector-General of Police must produce El-Rufai and Al Hassan by all means. But what did he get in response? This week, officials of the FCDA pasted a demolition notice on the court building, making it an illegal structure: "You are hereby ordered to vacate this site you are illegally occupying/ developing and report to Development Control Department at No. 1 Asamara Street, Zone 6, Wuse District, Abuja. Failure to comply will lead to demolition of your structure and legal action will be taken against you. To avoid embarrassment please comply." The court was in session while FCDA officials were busy pasting this Quit Notice. Nothing could be more farcical or mischievous."[100]

This is not only farcical and mischievous but a disgraceful exhibition of ignorance and unpatriotism since the High Court belongs to the Federal Government of Nigeria. It is an indication of the extent of the combined work of the executive to dictate for the judiciary.

The above described images and scenario of the law courts in Nigeria have resulted into the emergence of passive judges and lawyers, who prefer to dance to the tune of the executive, and worst, has led to a disregard of the law Courts by most Nigerians as places where lawyers waste time over arguments, and a criminal with a good lawyer can escape unpunished. Jungle justice hence appears to be a more effective and quicker means of conflict resolution.[101]

---

99 Ibid.
100 Ibid.
101 Ibid.

It is now very clear that the people must possess their institutions and make them work, but how would they do this in an atmosphere were the threat to life is real and where fear rules supreme? The fear of loosing one's life looms every time there is a confrontation with the authority. The overriding motive then becomes survival. But how do the people survive in such a pitiable situation?

1.5.3 Socio-economic Rights

1.5.3.1 Rights to decent standard of living and equal employment opportunities

The socio-economic rights, according to the article 22 of UDHR, are directly linked to the dignity of the human person and the development of his personality. The modern struggle over economic right is said to have emanated from the industrial revolution and the subsequent working class movement. But calls for economic justice originated in ancient times. Special reference could be made here to the traditions of Hammurabi's code and the Islamic and Christian thoughts.[102] (This special aspect shall be revisited in the next chapter).

There is no doubt that Nigeria's constitution, consciously or unconsciously, borrowed her stipulations on socio-economic rights from the said struggles and calls for economic rights and justice. The Section 16 of the Nigerian Constitution states: (1) "The State shall, within the context of the ideals and objectives for which provisions are made in this constitution, (a) harness the resources of the nation and promote national prosperity and an efficient, a dynamic and self-reliant economy; (b) controls the national economy in such a manner as to secure the maximum welfare, freedom and happiness of every citizen on the basis of social justice and equality of status and opportunity; (2) The State shall direct its policy towards ensuring: (a) the promotion of a planned and balanced economic development; (b) that the material resources of the nation are harnessed and distributed as best as possible to serve the common good; (c) that the economic system is not operated in such a manner as to permit the concentration of wealth or the means of production and exchange in the hands of few indi-

102 Micheline, Ishay, Ibid. p.35.

viduals or of a group; and (d) that suitable and adequate shelter, suitable and adequate food, reasonable national minimum living wage, old age care and pensions, and unemployment, sick benefits and welfare of the disabled are provided for all citizens". Complementing this section, section 17(3) states that: "The State shall direct its policy towards ensuring that – (a) all citizens, without discrimination on any group whatsoever, have the opportunity for securing adequate means of livelihood as well as adequate opportunity to secure suitable employment".

Nigeria is globally known as the largest oil producer in Africa and the sixth-largest oil producer in the world. Going by this record, one naturally expects that the citizens of such a naturally rich nation ought to live at least averagely above poverty level. But due to incompetence and corruption in the governmental system, the reverse is the case. According to the United Nations Development Program report, 70% of the citizens of Nigeria live in abject poverty (on less than one dollar a day), the United Nations specified poverty line and Nigeria ranks 151st out of 175 countries in the UN Human Development Index.[103] Other sources disclose that the 90% of the nation's wealth rest within the reach of 10% of the citizens. This is widely considered as the measure of abject poverty by the World Bank. The unfair distribution of the nation's wealth has left such social rights[104] such as right to an adequate standard of living unfulfilled for many Nigerians.

Reporting on the general situation of socio-economic rights in Nigeria, Amnesty International commented: "The Nigerian State, despite the availability of resources, has failed to take the necessary steps to ensure the core content of these rights, in violation of international law. It has not provided enough essential services, nor built the social and physical infrastructure in large parts of the country, necessary to ensure a minimum acceptable level of the rights to health, education, and access to drinking water, and an adequate standard of living."[105] Amnesty International believes that Nigeria

---

103 United Nations Development Program, *Human Development Report,* New York: United Nations Publications, 2004 (online) http://hdr.undp.org/statistics/data/cty/cty_f_NGA.html

104 Cf. The Constitution of the Federal Republic of Nigeria, Chapter 11, Section 16, 2 *(Fundamental Objectives and Directive Principles of the State Policy).*

105 Amnesty International; Nigeria: *Are Human Rights in the Pipeline?,* 9 November 2004, at: http://web.amnesty.org/library/index/engafr

has a duty to set measures that can be applied in the entire (West African) region, in her capacity as a leading producer of oil in the world and the biggest in Africa.

The Federal Government is the sole beneficiary of the huge revenue earned from the crude oil export, but she has invested very little of this resource to the socio-economic detriment of the poor of the nation. In many parts of the country, continues the Amnesty report, many roads are in a constant state of despair; power outages are frequent; the water available is of poor quality and is often contaminated; schools are almost non-existent in many remote places; and most state-controlled hospitals and clinics are under-equipped and short-staffed, or both.[106] Because of this unfair distribution of the national wealth, oil companies' personnel and assets such as pipelines are continuously targeted for attack and sabotage, resulting in jungle justice as quick means of settling conflicts and partaking in the national wealth.

The Nigerian law sets a minimum wage, which should be constantly under review. The minimum wage for private sector workers as at 2005 was \$56.70 (7,500 naira) per month, and \$41.70 (5,500 naira) for workers at the public sector.[107] This national minimum wage, however, did not provide a decent standard of living for a worker and family.[108] The increment of the national minimum wage (at the national or state level) is most often achieved through civil strike actions or demonstrations. In such a situation most people and families cannot provide for themselves nor have access to adequate food, adequate housing, adequate education, adequate health-care, etc.

The above mentioned Sections of the Nigerian Constitution upholds the provision of employment opportunities as a way of uplifting the living standards of the citizens, by ensuring a promotion of a planned and balanced economic development and a reasonable national minimum wage. This notwithstanding, unequal employment opportunities remains a problem in Nigeria.

106 Ibid.

107 Country Reports on Human Rights Practices – 2005, March 8 2006, Ibid.

108 Ibid.

One of the major evils of unequal employment opportunities in Nigeria is the policy of indigeneity. This policy, which has been enacted by many state and local governments, denies many Nigerians the access to one of their economic rights of being gainfully employed in any part of the country they choose to live. The federal government policy on this indigeneity is not helping matters. Human Rights Watch Report of April 2006 buttresses this fact: "State and local governments throughout Nigeria have enacted policies that discriminate against non-indigenes and deny them access to some of the most important avenues of socio-economic mobility open to ordinary Nigerians. In many states, non-indigenes are openly denied the right to compete for government jobs and academic scholarships.... Instead of working to combat this discrimination, federal government policies have often served to legitimize and reinforce it."[109] This report paints for us a picture of racial discrimination and political immorality. Nigerian politicians, who are to wage war against this trend, are utilizing the trend to "curry favor with their indigene constituents by excluding non-indigene from scarce opportunities that should be available to all."[110] Mediocrity in the civil service and labor sectors undoubtedly becomes one of the consequences of this trend. The trend does not promote hard work and excellence.

This form of discrimination that denies many Nigerians access to scarce employment opportunities is also seen on a religious sphere, especially in the northern region, where the practice of Shari'a Laws is in vogue. A case was reported in 2002 of Christian nurses being dismissed from their work because they refused to wear Shari'a compliant uniforms.[111] Recently in Kaduna State (in northern Nigeria), local officials improperly denied certificates of indigeneity to people who do not share their religion, which eventually led to Christian-Muslim tensions in the state.[112] In most cases issuance of such certificates is fraught with all forms of bribery and corruption, and goes to promote the evil of racial discrimination on this basis, whereby the minority religious persons are either forced to flee their state, convert to the major religion in the state or live in poverty. The Christian

109 *Nigeria: Indigeneity Policies Marginalize Millions.* Human Rights Watch News, April 25, 2006, at http://hrw.org/english/docs/2006/04/nigeri13260.htm

110 Ibid.

111 Nogi Imoukhuede, Women Rights Watch- Nigeria: *2003 Report on the State of Women's Rights in Nigeria..* *www.rufarm.kabissa.org/pressrelease/report03.htm*

112 Human Rights Watch News, April 25, 2006. Ibid.

religion is not left out in this practice. It has been also observed that some churches do not employ persons who are not members of their religion or denominations. It is part of discrimination based on religion.

The consequences of the evils of unequal employment opportunities and unemployment in Nigeria are not different from one's expectations of the state of a nation that is plagued with corruption, unaccountability, fraud, tribalism, culture of impunity, brain drain and civil disturbances. One continues to wonder: "Quo Vadis Nigeria?"

1.5.3.2 Rights of women and children

Globally speaking, women and children constitute the majority of the world's poor, weak and, in most cases, uneducated population. They are said to be the most vulnerable to the highest percentage of global human rights violations. The cause of women and children in the developed countries has greatly improved. In most of the so called "underdeveloped nations" and "developing nations", the story is still different. Fortunately there is a constant call to elevate and improve the global cause of women and children. Western nations have continued to exert unflinching effort in this regard both within and without. NGOs in most of the "underdeveloped" and "developing" nations are tirelessly pressurizing their governments to create and enforce policies designed for the protection of the rights of women and children. Nigeria is not left out of this effort.

Unfortunately, as argued by some activists, the Nigerian Constitution basically lacks gender sensitivity in its interpretation of human rights provisions. Because of the 'woman question', one would expect explicit gender stipulations regarding the special role of women and their rights in the constitution. Gender sensibility was only shown in the Section 42(1) with regard to the right to freedom from discrimination, where the 'sex' question was made mention of but in a general sense. Nonetheless, one may not expect something else from the constitution of such a patriarchal society like Nigeria's. The above mentioned argument is however of a secondary level of the consideration of the rights of women in Nigeria. My interest in this part is of a basic nature. On a similar note, no mention of the specific child's rights is made in the Nigerian constitution.

Generally speaking, one can say that the state of the rights of women in Nigeria has relatively improved in comparison to about 10 to 15 years ago. In January 2003, for example, Dr. Dora Akunyili, the former Director General of the National Agency for Food and Drug Administration and Control (NAFDAC), was declared the person of the year.[113] Dr. Akunyili is the first woman to ever direct such a delicate Ministry since the history of the government of the Federal Republic of Nigeria. Hers (among other laudable examples) is a portrait of hope for the future of women emancipation and empowerment in Nigeria. Nevertheless, the protection of the rights of women in Nigeria is yet to meet the international standard. Protecting the rights of women in Nigeria is a complicated matter because of the principles of cultures and, in some cases, religions in Nigeria. These principles do not guarantee the rights of women in the strict sense of human rights.

The current state of the rights of women in Nigeria is that of continued cases of violence and discrimination, which are being promoted by the discriminatory laws regarding divorce and employment, hence making it difficult for women to evade such situations. In its 2006 Report on Nigeria, Amnesty International USA extensively reported that "women were raped and subjected to other forms of sexual violence by government agents as well as partners, employers and others. In some communities, female genital mutilation and forced marriages were still practiced. The numbers of women killed, injured, raped and beaten by their partners remained high. Despite the lack of official statistics, nearly two-thirds of women in certain groups in Lagos State, for example, were estimated to be victims of violence in the home. Discriminatory laws and practices, dismissive attitudes within the police, an inaccessible justice and lack of shelters for victims contributed to violence against women being widely tolerated and underreported.... By the end of 2005, national law had not been amended in line with the protocol to the African Charter on Human and peoples' Rights on the rights of women in Africa, which had been ratified by Nigeria in December 2004".[114]

The untold plight of widows in Nigeria following the death of their husbands is still deplorable. Cultural beliefs in this case have contributed im-

113 Nogi Imoukhuede, Women Rights Watch- Nigeria: Ibid.

114 Amnesty International USA, *Annual Report. Federal Republic of Nigeria.* www.amnestyusa.org/annualreport.php?id=ar&yr=2006&c=N

mensely to their plight. The women custodians of the cultural beliefs make the matter worse against their fellow women. A part of the 2003 Report of the Women's Rights Watch- Nigeria commented that "women are generally regarded as capable of doing immense evil and so, for instance when she marries in Edo land, she is traditionally made to swear allegiance to her husband and his family. Part of the rites are oaths administered that she will not poison her husband, she will not flirt and such other averments. It is so bad that it is believed that if a child is sick, it must be as a result of the woman's flirtations."[115] One would tend to immediately ask about the part of their male partners in this whole process of oath-taking. The patriarchal structure of the Nigerian society militates against equal treatment in this regard. It goes also to say a lot about the number of women who have been sentenced to death penalties since the introduction of Shari'a laws in most northern states. In most cases, their male counterparts are set free due to lack of evidence.[116] Women are forced to bear alone the brunt of an extra-marital relationship that involve them and their male counterparts on cultural, and in some cases, religious grounds. The case of a woman in Delta state, who was allegedly accused of committing adultery calls to mind. Her allegedly accusation of adultery was said to have led to her husband's illness. As a result she was compelled to walk the streets of Ubulu-Uku naked, as a way of saving her husband from premature death.[117] Her husband was eventually reported to have died from the illness. Most women are so intimidated that they shy away from reporting their plight to the authorities. In most cases, the authorities have done so little or nothing to assist the women claim their rights, thereby discouraging them from coming up further. The right to inheritance of the girl child or a widow is still a hot debate in most parts of the nation. As at 2003, only three states (Enugu, Edo and Oyo) have passed laws against punitive widowhood rites, but the cultural practices and influence still play a dominate role, thereby sabotaging the efforts to promote and protect the rights of women, especially in rural areas.

Akin to the deplorable plight of Nigerian women, or worst still, one may say, is the plight of Nigerian children. The state of the rights of Nigerian children is even more complex. It is so because a nation that does not

---

115 Nogi Imoukhuede, Women's Right Watch- Nigeria: Ibid.

116 Ibid.

117 Ibid.

recognize the dignity of children as persons with specific human rights, cannot guarantee herself of patriotic leaders. Generally speaking, Nigerian public is yet to know the difference between the rights of the child and privileges or charity. The rights of the child in Nigeria are far more from being respected, irrespective of the Nigerian signatory to the *Convention on the Rights of the Child* (CRC) since 1991, and the African Charter on the Rights and Welfare of the child since 2001. The abuse of the rights of the child in Nigeria has different faces.

Human Rights Watch reported that "child labor, such as exploitation of children as domestics and as laborers in quarries, as well as child trafficking within Nigeria and across borders, remained serious problems during 2006.[118] On a good note, she also reported that hundreds of trafficked children from Nigeria as well as from Benin, Cameroon, Togo and other African countries have been rescued by Nigerian authorities.[119] This report on the long run, indicates that Nigeria has been a safe haven for the abuse of children, even involving other neighboring nations. As a result of economic hardship a high number of children engage in all kinds of work to enhance meager family sustenance. Most of these children are employed as beggars, street peddlers, bus conductors, and domestic servants in urban areas. A survey conducted by the National Modular Child Labour Survey Nigeria between 2000 and 2001, indicated that approximately 15 million children are working in the country. Of these, more than six million were not attending school and more than two million were working 15 or more hours a day.[120]

The Report also said that private and government initiatives to curb child labor problems continued but ineffective. It is no surprise that the efforts are ineffective following the recent history of the child rights promotion question in Nigeria. The Child Right Act was first drafted in 1993, but was only adopted as law ten years later, in 2003. Only three years later has it been enacted into law in three states, Ogun, Lagos and Edo states, out of the 36 states of the federation. This explains the wide gap between the principles of the Act and the actual practice.

---

118 Human Rights Watch World Report 2007 – Nigeria, www.unhcr.org/home/RSDCOI/45aca2a316.html

119 Ibid.

120 Country Reports on Human Rights Practices – 2005: Ibid.

In 2005, the Minister of Women Affairs, Hajia Inna Ciroma went on a tour of the northern states, trying to educate local leaders on the importance of the CRC.[121] The former president of the federation, Olusegun Obasanjo, is also said to have appealed to states on May 27 (National Children's Day), to ratify the CRC.[122] These two examples are indicators that the rights of the Nigerian child are still at the mercy of the legislators; hence no court can prosecute violators of the CRC in states that have not enacted it. Most of the arguments by states that have not enacted it are based on the diversity of cultures and religion. This is the root of the complexity of this problem in Nigeria.

1.5.4 Environmental Rights

Right to healthy environment, and nature preservation

The only words on the Environment found in the Section 20 of the Nigerian Constitution reads: "The State shall protect and improve the environment and safeguard the water, air and Land, forest and wild life of Nigeria". Due to the verbous nature of the Nigerian Constitution, one would naturally expect more words on this aspect as was done in most others, especially with regard to procedures of safeguarding the environment and penalties that accrue by violations. Nonetheless, let us presume the great strength and power of those few words on the environment. When one talk about environmental rights in Nigeria what comes to mind is the corporate efforts of local and international bodies and organizations to curb the extent of environmental pollutions caused by the oil explorations companies in the oil-producing regions of the nation. The Nigerian economy is largely dependent on the production of crude oil. Oil exports is said to account for 98.5% of Nigeria's total exports.[123] It is however unfortunate that the government's efforts to control the environmental pollution from oil spillage are marred by bribery, corruption and greed. A general description of environmental current issues is "soil degradation; rapid deforestation; oil pollution – *(water, air and soil have suffered serious damage from oil spills)*;

121 Chukwunwike Okumephuna, 2005, "A Case for Children", in *The Guardian Newspapers, Nigeria,* Wednesday, 7 September, 2005, p15

122 All Africa.com, 2006, Nigeria: President Obasanjo seeks nationwide Adoption of CRC, 30 May, 2006, http//allafrica.com/stories/200605300495.html

123 Amnesty International; Nigeria: *Are Human Rights in the Pipeline?* Ibid.

loss of arable land; rapid urbanization."[124] The local and international bodies urge the federal government of Nigeria to ensure enforcement and proper implementation of the environmental protection legislation in order to enable a fully inclusive consultation process and clean up of oil spills.

The federal government of Nigeria is largely blamed for the abuse of the environment through the operation of oil companies because of her attitude to these (mainly foreign) companies. Nigeria is not the only country that produces oil. Many other countries, especially in the Middle East, Europe and America also produce oil in large quantities. So one discover that the attitude of companies differ in these countries because of the attitude of the governments. In Europe and America, and in most Arab nations, news about environmental pollution by means of oil spillage and harness are seldom heard. When that is the case, it is in most cases, out of mistake. But the case of Nigeria is different since it has become a daily occurrence and has to led to all kinds of conflicts in the oil-producing regions of the nation, which has resulted in the violations of human rights of the inhabitants of such regions.

The inability of the federal government to handle the crisis properly, according to Amnesty International, has led to local communities taking laws into their hands as a short-cut to claiming their rights. In most cases, personnel and assets of the oil companies have come under continued target and attack because of their failure to clean up polluted land after oil spills.[125] In other cases, the oil companies end up entering into private agreement with the individual communities for various kinds of compensation and oil spill clean-up policies. But Amnesty International reported that the effect of such theoretically sound policies is often far from being realizable and compensating: "Companies typically provide benefits and facilities to the communities closest to their area of operations. But by so doing, the companies often end up antagonizing other parts of the region, which do not benefit from the companies' community development programs. Even within communities, divisions emerge, between those benefiting from particular projects, and those who do not. This divides communities and in many instances, creates conditions for conflict, re-

---

124 Environment current issues, at: www.cia.gov/cia/publications/factbook/geos/ni.html

125 Amnesty International; Nigeria: *Are Human Rights in the Pipeline?* Ibid.

sulting in human rights abuses of the people living in the communities around their area of operations."[126] The conflicts arising from oil spillage in oil-producing areas of Nigeria have often made news around the world. The federal government has done most of its part to calming the situation by sending troops to the regions, to provide security for the companies' personnel and their assets, which has often involved horrible gun-shot exchanges between the government troops and the local armed groups, often referred to as 'rebel groups'. Such resolution strategies do not address the root of the problem. They have rather led to the death of many innocent lives of the local population in the regions and the destruction of property worth millions of Naira.

Such conflicts are also partly blamed on the unrealistic expectations of the local populations from the oil companies. Some of the local communities expect the oil companies to provide amenities, which are in the domain of the government to provide. It is worth mentioning at this point, that the oil companies are not legally obliged to provide basic amenities for communities, where they are operating. It is the duty of the federal and state governments to provide them, and of course, through the revenue being generated from the oil explorations.

The government's failure to provide her citizens with basic amenities has also resulted into other abuse of environmental rights such as soil degradation, air pollution, rapid deforestation and loss of arable land. The government's failure, for example, to provide for a basic standard of living for all accruing from provision of employment opportunities, has left many people in abject poverty. In this case, a poor man (according to Nigerian standard) cannot be able to have access, for example, to cooking gas, or even one of the most scarce common man commodity, Kerosene. In such a situation he has as an option the use of firewood for cooking needs and other household energy. By so doing, he not only causes deforestation and soil degradation, but also causes serious air pollution by the emission of a large amount of carbon dioxide into the atmosphere. The unrestricted logging for timber in Nigeria is another cause of deforestation.[127] There is no standard control over the manner of logging. The same crave to survive has en-

126 Ibid.

127 Nathaniel, Imeh T. and Nathaniel Adebobola, *The Effects of poverty in conservation of biodiversity: The Nigerian Experience,* in "Science in Africa", (online) at http//www.scienceinafrica.co.za/2001/nov/Nigeria.html

riched a good number of Nigerians through logging, but has left the most parts of the country with very poor environment. Deforestation in Nigeria is also reported as a result of industrialization, commerce, agriculture and the activities of rural dwellers.[128] The primitive agricultural practices of rural farmers do not help matters in this regard. The 'shifting cultivation' and 'slash-and-burn' methods of these farmers has led to the exploitation of forests by means of over demand for farming land, causing more forests to be cleared for farming ends.[129] These sorts of environmental attitudes also end up in desertification and extinction of the beauty of nature.

The success of the preservation of the beauty of nature in such a deplorable state of environment such as Nigeria's, is in a serious doubt. A friendly environment is all that it takes for the beauty of nature to be preserved. The government's failure to control and set a standard for hunting in Nigeria, and of course, the crave of the poor for survival, has led to the extinction of many rare species of animals in the forests. If these species are not endangered by the rapid deforestation and desertification, they are endangered by the human crave to hunt them for food or for commercial purposes. An example of endangered specie is the Nile crocodile, which was once found in Nigerian coastal waters right up to Lake Chad. This specie is fast disappearing because of indiscriminate hunting attitude and loss of habitat.[130] It has been reported by forestry experts that about 65 of Nigeria's 560 species of trees are in the danger of extinction, while others are at different stages of risk.[131] "Most of the people hunting wildlife in Nigeria has little or no economic alternatives." These are threatened to extinction because of little or no replacement. Poaching has remained a serious threat to the preservation of the beauty of nature and wildlife in Nigeria.

Nathaniel Imeh T. et al, give us hope and comfort from the efforts of the governmental agencies and Non-Governmental Organisations to protect and preserve the environment, such as the Nigerian Conservation Foundation (NCF), the Federal Environmental Protection Agency (FEPA), the National Resources Council (NARECO), in collaboration with the United Nations Environmental Programme (UNEP) and the World Wild Fund (WWF). Nevertheless, they reported that their beautiful policies are hin-

128 Ibid.
129 Ibid.
130 Ibid.
131 Ibid.

dered by the government's preoccupation with economic problems to the extent of not been able to "allocate enough resources for conservation, for research and monitoring of conservation programmes, for the creation of gene banks and education of the public concerning the importance of preserving the biosphere."[132] All the same, Nigeria is said to be committed in her environmental protection efforts through tree planting, "but tree planting only preserves a part of the original biodiversity in an environment, it does not result in a return of the vast and varied flora and fauna hitherto destroyed."[133] As long as seven of each ten persons in Nigeria continue to live below one dollar a day, environmental rights would remain only unrealizable heart's desire.

Summary

This first chapter painted the image of "progress" of human rights development in the Nigerian context (past and present). It is an effort to answer how human rights question got into Nigeria; the understandings of human rights in the Nigerian context; and to what extent human rights are being respected, promoted and neglected or abused in Nigeria. By means of the description of the structural problems of human rights in Nigeria, a picture of the human rights situation in Nigeria has been painted in this chapter. One gets a strong indication that the extensive inclusion of human rights in the Nigerian Constitution has little or no impact in the application of human rights in its practical sense. The influence of the African Commission on Human Rights and the National Commission on Human Rights were not overlooked as far as the Nigerian Constitution is concerned. It is also made very clear in this chapter that the violations of human rights in Nigeria are attributable to almost all institutions – civil, religious, economic and cultural institutions. It is also an amazing fact to discover the extent of latency religions are said to provide towards the perpetration of human rights violations in Nigeria. This is observed in the aspects of freedom of religion, freedom to non-discrimination, freedom of expression and socio-economic rights, especially as it regards to right to equal employment opportunities. I regard this observation as an indication of one of the aspects the church's urgent attention is being called to. This implies

132 Ibid.
133 Ibid.

that since all are involved in one way or another towards the perpetration of the human rights violations in Nigeria, all also ought to be involved in the struggle towards a positive change.

CHAPTER TWO

CULTURAL AND RELIGIOUS TRADITIONS IN NIGERIA AND HUMAN RIGHTS

Introduction

There are still controversies and debates regarding the origin of human rights. Some trace it's origin to Judaism and Christianity, others trace it to the great Asian religions, others trace it to Islamic principles, still others trace it to the ancient cultural traditions. But some others claim the influence of the contemporary era as being the spark-point. In one of the arguments for instance, René Cassin (1887-1976), one of the members of the International Human Rights Commission, strongly opined that religious and natural laws have their foundations in the modern understanding of human rights. He traced the origin of human rights to the Bible citing some examples: "the first article of the declaration corresponded to the biblical injunction "love thy neighbor as thyself" and "love the stranger as you love yourself" (Leviticus 19:18-33 Jerusalem Bible). Thou shall not murder is the right to life. Thou shall not steal is the right to own property…"[134]

The controversies notwithstanding, cultural and religious traditions are said to have influenced to a greater extent the understanding of human rights today. Our interest here is not to dwell into the arguments made in favor of or against the origin of human rights; nevertheless, it is necessary to note that human rights view points across cultures and religions add to the beauty and complications of the global response to the human rights question. The divergences in their ideological differences and practices pose obstacles to a universal understanding of human rights. It has not been an easy task from the global point of view to find a common language of human rights from a host of cultural and religious traditions. In order to construct a common understanding of human rights, a common understanding of the *common good* has to be created in consultation with cultural and religious traditions.

134 Micheline Ishay quoted, in: The History of Human Rights, op.cit. p.19

Nigeria as a multi-cultural and mutli-religious society has a similar difficulty in creating a common national understanding of human rights. Nevertheless, the diversities of her cultures and religions could be utilized in forming a common ground for the promotion and protection of human rights.

Nigeria is considered the most populous country of Africa with over 130 million people distributed unevenly among about 250 ethnic groups. Hausa, Yoruba and Igbo ethnic groups are the most prominent among the others. The Hausas are in the northern part of Nigeria. The Yorubas are in the western part, while the Igbos are in the south-eastern part. These biggest ethnic groups of Nigeria have very different cultural settings and languages. Their languages are also the most prominent languages of Nigeria. In a similar way three different religions have prominence in Nigeria: the Islam, Christianity and the African Traditional religion (ATR). Christians and Muslims are said to be about 45% respectively, while the ATR adherents are about 5%. These three religions are to be found in all parts of Nigeria. However, the majority of adherents of Islam live in the northern part, while majority of adherents of Christianity live unevenly in the eastern and western parts. The ATR is basically found in all parts of the country as a result of its originality to the Nigerian peoples. For most Nigerians religion and culture are considered important aspects of everyday life. The two aspects control the laws, thinking and behavior, as well as beliefs and values of the people.

This chapter aims at answering the question of religious and cultural aspects of human rights hence the investigation into the influences cultural and religious traditions have on human rights understanding in the Nigerian context. Of particular interest here is finding out the positive and negative influences of culture and religion on human rights as a later tool for utilizing their divergences in creating a common understanding of human rights. This chapter is therefore divided into two sub-parts: the first part is an endeavor to address cultures and some cultural values in Nigeria and their relationship to human rights. In a similar fashion the second part dwells on the religious traditions in Nigeria as they relate to human rights. As a multicultural and multi-religious country, a comprehensive study into the cultures and religions of Nigerians in relation to human rights would be cumbersome. But for the purpose of this work, cultures of the three prominent ethnic groups in Nigeria and the three major religions have been chosen for study.

2.1 NIGERIAN CULTURAL TRADITIONS AND HUMAN RIGHTS

Culture in this context is understood as unscripted values that determine the behavioral pattern of a people. A certain pattern of behavior can be seen differently in different cultures. The Nigerian cultures (**Hausa, Yoruba and Igbo**) are expressed in daily living, religion and arts. Over the time these cultures have been identified with and traced to certain culture centers.[135]

2.1.1 The Hausa cultural tradition

According to the historical traditions of these culture centers, the **Hausa** culture is identified with the NOK culture. Hence

> "...the NOK culture is identified with the "Hahm" or "Jaba" people of Northern Nigeria. The largest town of the area is Kwoi, which is 144 kilometer west of Jos and 198.4 kilometer south of Kaduna. The famous archeological findings of NOK culture were made in this area. NOK, which possibly means "to start" in Jaba language, is the village where NOK terra-cotta excavations were started in 1936. Since then a great deal of ancient pottery has been uncovered. An investigation carried out by Kato among the old men in Kwoi area as to the place of their origin proved that they have no myths of migration from any far away place. Their common sayings, whether in singing of direct narrative is that they came from Bitaro, which is only four miles away. They claim that their religion has origin from Njeng, which is twelve miles away".[136]

---

135 *Culture Centers* refer to Centers, as described by, Onwubiko Oliver in: African Thought, Religion and Culture, (Snaap Press Ltd. Enugu, 1991), p.5; as those places that have been accepted by either popular ovation or popular belief as sources of identifiable cultures; those places that are associated with mythological, ritual and historical/archeological evidences to support that they are an ancient home of a people who occupy a culture area. A culture centre then is the fount of the ideological matrix responsible for the cultural life's formation of a people in a given area.

136 Onwubiko, Oliver; Ibid. pp. 6-7.

There is yet no counter evidence to this historical tradition, hence it is assumed that Jaba must have lived at the archeological NOK area for at least two thousand years, and based on this assumption NOK is considered a cultural origin of the Hausa culture.

2.1.2 The Yoruba cultural tradition

The **Yoruba** culture is said to have its home in Ile-Ife. The claim to this origin has two oral traditions, which are told in a more mythological form. One of the traditions claims that "in the beginning, there was Olódumare, God – the archetypal Spirit. When he decided to create the world, Olódumare engendered Orishanla and sent him down to do the actual work. This he rapidly completed with the aid of other divinities. Orishanla then brought mankind out of the sky and settled them at Ile-Ife. From there they spread across the earth and cultivated it".[137] The second tradition has it that "it is not Orinshala who created the world at the bidding of Olódumare, but Oduduwa. Coming from somewhere far away in the East, Oduduwa then brought the Yoruba into their homeland, ruled them from Ile-Ife. He begot men and women who were to rule or provide rulers for other Yoruba communities".[138] It is still a problem till today reconciling the roles of Oduduwa and Orishanla in the historical traditions of the Yoruba cultural origins, but the common association of both with Ile-Ife settles the conflict that Ile-Ife is the cultural home of the Yoruba people.

2.1.3 The Igbo cultural tradition

The **Igbo** cultural origin is a bit more complicated than the former. Nevertheless, some Igbo scholars hold to two traditions for the identification of Igbo cultural origin based on traditions of *non-migration* and *migration.* The tradition of non-migration is here represented by the observations of V.C. Uchendu as cited by Oliver Onwubiko:

> "the belt formed by Owerri, Awka, Orlu and Okigwe divisions constitute this nuclear area. Its people have no traditions of coming from any other place. We assume an early migration from this area into Nsukka – Udi

137 Ibid. p.7
138 Ibid.

> highlands in the North and into Ikwerri, Etche, Asa, and Ndoki in the South. The eastern Isuama claim to have come from this centre. Ngwa traditions point to their secondary migrations from Mbaise".[139]

A proponent of the migration tradition is Professor A.E. Afigbo, who holds that the Igbo people "originated from the Niger-Benue confluence six thousand years ago. Migration led to the settlement in the areas they now occupy. They originally settled in the Northern Igbo Plateau – Amigbo Orlu, Nri, Awka, before dispersing to areas they now occupy, or which are in contest and across the Niger".[140] There is another tradition based on the *Umueri* mythology[141], but let us base our brief analysis on the above two traditions. The names of places mentioned in the two traditions are current existing places in Igboland. Some names such as Awka and Orlu were mentioned in the two traditions. Nevertheless, the former gives us information based on the originality of the origin of Igbo culture; and the latter gives us impression of a quasi borrowed culture. The two traditions, however, give us some elements of certainty about the origin of Igbo culture.

The above historical traditions regarding the origin of the three major cultural traditions in Nigeria strike a consensus that the cultures did not originate from outside of what is known today as Nigeria. The cited migrations were done within very short distances. But the resiliency of these cultural traditions was tested by foreign cultural contacts, which influenced their current standard to a great extent. The contacts meant here are foreign religious traditions that came into contact with them over the time. Islamic religion was the very first that initiated this contact beginning in the northern Nigeria. It came with the Arabic culture, which wielded and still wields a great influence over the Hausa traditional cultural values. Christianity was introduced through the western coast down to the eastern Nigeria, and of course fought its way into the behavior patterns of the people of Yorubaland and Igboland. Despite these external contacts and influences, these cultures maintain some elements of resiliency as could be witnessed in the daily lives of the people.

---

139 Onwubiko, Oliver, Ibid. p.8

140 Quoted from a lecture given on the occasion of the annual meeting of the Nigerian Library Association; Onwubiko, Oliver, Ibid. p. 9.

141 *Umueri* mythology is the story of heavently beings that played significant roles in the creation of Igbo people.

2.1.4 Common values of the Nigerian cultural traditions and the Human Rights Question

Despite the different ideological roots and practices of these cultural traditions, they share some common values, which Oliver Onwubiko represented as values of African culture[142]. I disagree with Onwubiko's presentation of African culture as an entity, because patterns of behavior are differently seen in various countries and as such tantamount to differences in cultures. To talk of a Nigerian culture, for example, would be an absurd, because the various ethnic groups have their various patterns of behavior different from each other. Nevertheless, it could be acceptable to talk of some common cultural values that run across these cultural traditions. It is on this basis that we group them together in our context borrowing from Onwubiko's presentation. Due to the difficulty in finding a written documentation of these cultures in their particularities, we have chosen to present the following values they share in common as aspects of their positive influence on the lives of the people and on the understanding of human rights.

2.1.4.1 The value of Communalism:

It is strongly believed that these cultural values exhibit a great *sense of community.* In this understanding the individual member of the community feels psychological and ultimate security due to the physical and ideological identity the culture gives its members. The aim of this is to prepare and present the individual as a *community-culture-bearer*. It is believed that culture is a property of the community and must therefore be *community-protected.* The community cannot exist without persons, and that explains why this type of care centers on the individual as a protector of the community and its culture.

Another important aspect of this cultural value is the solidarity it fosters over and above all. Explaining this further, Onwubiko differentiated between being poor and being a beggar. Because of the security offered by solidarity, it is not possible to have a beggar in this type of community since all care for the other. One can be poor, but no one lacks the basic

142 Onwubiko, Oliver; Ibid. pp. 13-31.

needs of life. It is necessary to point out here that promoting solidarity is not to the expense of individual private interest or loyalties, which ultimately do not endanger the community life.

We see in this context the promotion of the rights to freedom from discrimination, freedom of association, and to a decent standard of living.

2.1.4.2 The value of human relations:

This value is closely connected to the value of communalism based on the philosophical principle of *live and let live.* It is a further elaboration of communal solidarity. Each relates to the other in view of mutual assistance to one another. It is the principle of Eagle and Kite, which expresses itself in the Igbo Saying: *Egbe bere Ugo bere.* (let the Eagle perch and let also the Kite perch). The original version of this Igbo Saying actually reads thus: *Egbe bere Ugo bere, nke siri ibe ya ebela nku kwaa ya* (meaning: let the Eagle perch and let the Kite perch; any that refuse the other from perching ought to have its wings broken). However over the time the modern Igbos have changed this version to read: *Egbe bere Ugo bere, nke siri ibe ya ebela gosi ya ebe o ga ebe.* (let the Eagle perch and let the Kite perch; any who refuses the other from perching should show him where to perch). In other words this principle defines rights and duties, responsibilities and obligations towards the less fortunate. Hence there is no room for misgivings of any kind. Each thinks of the good and progress of the other. This value also offers the forum for dialogue and conversation in the sense that people are free to discuss their problem and look for suggestions and solutions together. The unwillingness to discuss one's problems with others is considered as bad manners or sign of enmity. It is practically believed that he who discusses his problems with others hardly run into difficulties or makes mistakes. Nevertheless, the discussions must respect individual sentiments; hence conversations that may cause misgivings are avoided. Malicious killing of a kinsman is not only abhorred but also regarded as an abomination. Its punishment is immediate death of the doer. But if an outsider is killed the punishment takes a different shape. This however does not imply that killing of an outsider is allowed. The cultures encourage the extension of the cherished values of one's community to other communities. These values ought to enable the individual community member to appreciate what others have and to cherish the other man as his brother and a fellow human being.

Another offshoot of this cultural value is the sense of hospitality it offers, which is still alive. Strangers are easily incorporated and made to feel belonged. There are different symbolic ways of expressing welcome. The Igbos, for example, express it in the form of Kola nut presentation. This shows that the visitor is accepted and safe. Other ethnic groups offer traditional gin, coconuts or cohise cholk. Among the Igbos, the basis of hospitality is the generally accepted principle that a guest must not harm his host and neither should the host be hostile to the guest.

The above analysis gives us some basic sense of the modern understanding of the right to freedom of expression (partly), and right to life (to an extent).

2.1.4.3 The value of the sacredness of life

The traditional Nigerian cultural setting prohibits violence per se because shedding of blood is abhorred. Capital punishment was allowed only when the existence of the killed is threatening to the peace of the entire community. Killing at war or in self defense is allowed, but the killer thereafter ought to cleanse himself in a traditional form obtainable in the community, of the blood of the slain person since it is absurd for someone to exterminate life of the other and go on living as if nothing happened. This cleansing ritual reflects the high regard for blood irrespective of who is involved. In a similar dimension suicide is never permitted. The body of anyone who takes his/her own life is not buried, as a way punishment. It is thrown into the forest to be eaten up by wild beasts. In this way others are deterred from committing similar acts.

In a similar connection unborn children are protected thereby making abortion an abominable act. Sources of life are regarded as very sacred and as such sexual intercourse and sex organs are handled with respect. In the traditional cultural setting sex before marriage is not encouraged. This practice stems from the fact that Nigerians believe that "the blood of virginity is the symbol that life has been preserved, that the spring of life has not already been flowing wastefully, and that both the girl and her relatives have preserved the sanctity of human reproduction".[143] But through the culture contacts the practice of this aspect of the Nigerian culture has been seriously altered, but remains however a highly regarded cultural practice.

This cultural practice of the sacredness of life reflects the current understanding of the human right to life.

2.1.4.4 The value of religion

This cultural value has no direct link to our topic, but its presentation is necessary for the purpose of a later analysis. It is generally believed that in traditional African societies there were no atheists because religion is not an independent institution and thus not separable from the culture of the people. Exactly the same could be said of the Nigerian society. The people's entire action is reflective of their religious concepts and practices as is seen in the ordering of society. This is because social morality is directly linked to religion. The analysis of Bola Idowu about the Yoruba people also gives articulation for other ethnic groups in Nigeria: "With the Yoruba, morality is certainly the fruit of religion. They do not make any attempt to separate the two; and it is impossible for them to do so without disastrous consequences".[144] It could be said with some certainty that Nigerians do not know how to live without religion due to their religious inclinations and attachment. The importance of religion in the traditional Nigerian cultural context points to the great role religion could play in the promotion and protection of human rights in Nigeria.

There are other aspects of the Nigerian cultural values, which Onwubiko presented, such as value of time, value of authority and respect for the elders, and value of speech and proverb as cohesive of community. But these values are of no immediate value to our topic. Hence we go into the next part of this work to reflect the aspects of human rights violations, which are caused in the practice of some of the traditional Nigerian cultures.

143 Mbiti, J.S.; African Religions and Philosophy, Lond. Heinemann, 1975, p.262.
144 Idowu, E.B.; Oludumare – God in Yoruba Belief. London Longman, 1962, p.11.

2.1.5 Human rights violations in Nigerian cultural contexts

In its strict understanding, a culture is a pattern of life of people. The culture of a people influences their behavioral pattern and their pattern of thoughts. Culture begins at a certain point in time, changes in the course of time, but nevertheless retains some of its basic elements due to its resilience nature (as already mentioned above). The elements of cultural values that change in the course of time are either influenced by other cultural contacts or they have not benefited the society, hence the need for change. Today we talk of globalization. A concept that brings people nearer to each other thereby producing globalised culture. Through the so-called cultural contacts, peoples have the opportunity of experiencing other values other than what they have been used to. In this way, people begin to compare their values to those of others thereby asking themselves questions about the practicability or benefit of their own values. Today people also talk about different cultures from the point of view of relativism. When we talk of human rights culture, for example, we talk of a culture that comes into existence as a result of man's inhumanity to man, which does not benefit the human race. Hence it is a culture that came into existence in the course of time in view of improving the relational attitudes between persons. This explains the heuristic character of human rights. Through the promotion of this culture over the years, we are able to distinguish between violation and protection of the human rights. It is in this connection that we talk of the negative influences the Nigerian cultures have on the promotion of human rights in the Nigerian context.

Some of the above mentioned traditional Nigerian cultural values are in themselves very pro-human rights. Nevertheless, the nature of some of them warrants the danger of 'give and take' approach, which gives them anti-human rights picture. Most written books so far on African cultural values focus on promotion of the said values. Very little has been put in the orthodox written form by way of explicit exposition of the negative sides of the values as seen in the eyes of today's world. Authors may not be totally blamed for this approach since African cultural values are still on the promotional stage. Therefore some of the following criticisms of the Nigerian cultures against human rights culture are based on personal experiences as a first-class witness. However, the elaborate empirical research carried out by the Project Alert on Violence against Women in Nigeria ("Beyond Boundaries" by Josephine Effah-Chukwuma and Ngozi Osarenren) would be extensively utilized, especially as it regards women rights.

2.1.5.1 Right to life

The Nigerian cultural value of the sacredness of life promotes in itself the right to life. Life is seen as sacred, and shedding of blood is abhorred. However an aspect of its practice gives us a picture of two-sided coin. One side promotes, while the other abuses. At some points it looks like a contradiction. We have already seen above the side that promotes. The other side of the coin that abuses is seen from the point of view of capital punishment, which eventually leads to the spilling of blood as against the cultural abhorrence of shedding of blood.

In a similar manner, blood of the innocent is spilled in cases of some cultures, particularly among some parts of Igboland, where a human head is a prerequisite for the funeral of the King of the community. This practice was in vogue in almost the whole of Igboland until the advent of Christianity. Fortunately most Igbo communities no longer practice this culture today, but there are some very remote areas that are vehement on its practice but in an utmost secretive way. This practice contradicts the Igbo cultural value of the sacredness of life and the human right to life.

There is a negative cultural offshoot that is common today in Nigeria, especially in the western and eastern part. It is the killing of human beings for ritual purposes. This is commonly called *ritual killing*. Almost on weekly basis the media relate cases of ritual killings. Some have happened without traces, while some others were exposed to the public. In most cases people took laws into their hands to expose and exterminate propagators of this abominable culture. The Nigerian cultures do not support this practice per se, but as a result of culture contacts, it came into existence as a cultural offshoot. In its July 23, 2009 Report the Zenit Catholic News Agency in Rome reported that the albino children are kidnapped and murdered by witch doctors due to the belief that their body parts are regarded to be very potent for magical potions.[145] This practice is said to be very common in Tanzania, but many cases of missing albino children have been reported also in Nigeria.

2.1.5.2 Right to freedom from discrimination

The traditional Nigerian cultural values of communalism, human relations and hospitality evoke a culture of sharing and community spirit on the basis of *live and let live* philosophy. These cultural values do not smack of discrimination. But there exists in this aspect also attitude of *give and take*. According to the Zenit News Agency, a couple of children were discriminated against and rejected because they are albinos with white skin and hair.[146] This discrimination is based on the belief that such children bring ill-luck to their families, and as such they are either thrown away at birth, killed or at later ages rejected. In this sense right of the child to grow normally and be accorded healthy upbringing is violated.

As against this cultural background women are, at a second degree discriminated against. They are often victims of all kinds of abuses in homes and communities, without cultural security guarantee for their cause. But before the colonial era, women occupied leadership positions in some traditional Nigerian cultural communities. Eugene Elochukwu Uzukwu gave an account of the exercise of power shared among the sexes. According to him, Igbo women, for example, exercised enormous economic and political power before the colonial era. There were women chiefs, who were responsible for women concerns in the communities.[147] Colonial and religious policies altered this balance of power between men and women thereby relegating women as second-class citizens. It was this development that led to the Aba women riot, which we already made mention of in the earlier chapter. This calls our attention once again to the so-called cultural contacts, which influence cultures. Prior to this, however, some traditional communities, ab initio, generally regarded women as second class citizens. They are said to be weaker sex and as such are meant to be dependent on their male counterparts. They are not free to express themselves freely

145 Zenit.org, ZE090723; July 23, 2009: "Nigerian Nuns: Children are Jewels".

146 Ibid.

147 Uzoukwu, Eugene; „Die Kirche in Afrika im Dienst an Versöhnung, Gerechtigkeit und Frieden – eine Antwort aus nigerianischer Perspective", in Forum Weltkirche; No. 4 (July/August 2009), p. 20.

and assume desired positions and opinions on public matters, except on matters within women's gathering. Unfortunately such practices are still in vogue in some cultural settings in Nigeria, especially in the villages and some private homes. From this analysis, we see not only discrimination against women, but also a repression of their right of expression.

2.1.5.3 Rights of women

The violation of women's freedom in the traditional cultural setting is closely linked to robbing women of their rights. Women are said to be victims of violence at home, polygamy, prostitution, disinheritance and various repressive rites and rituals.[148]

2.1.5.3.1 Women as victims of violence

There have been several cases, when women reported of violence at home to security officers (like the police), and were told to go home and be obedient to their husbands. Josephine Effah-Chukwuma and Ngozi Osarenren gave a first-class account of such anomaly from their empirical research:

> "In most cases of domestic violence for instance the police right from the counter, where the case is reported, determine provocation. They start asking the victim ridiculous and embarrassing questions such as: Did you deny your husband sex? Did you serve him food on time? Were you rude to your husband or in-laws? Did you keep the house tidy? By so doing already the victim is being blamed for acts of violence perpetrated against her. She becomes the villain and as such is doubly abused and violated".[149]

Christianity as a culture contact fanned this cultural attitude with her teaching of St. Paul's address to women to be under the obedience and control of their husbands. Islam has a similar standard on this matter. The cultural settings force them to be at the disposal of the whims and caprices of their husbands. There are other cases of negligence of matters concerning women in relation to violence in the society, which leaves them vulnerable and helpless, thereby making them constant victims of persecution and intim-

148 Ibid. p. 19.

149 Effah-Chukwuma, Josephine and Osarenren, Ngozi; Beyond Boundaries: Violence against women in Nigeria, Project Alert on Violence against Women, Lagos, 2001, p. 123.

idation. This practice is only a cultural offshoot as a result of the culture contacts. But there are typical traditional cultural practices that directly harm women.

2.1.5.3.2 The Traditional bride price

The traditional bride price is another factor that encourages the intimidation of women. Men brag of their "women purchasing power", and that means the women's rights are also been bought at a price. This gives men the impetus, in a traditional setting, to marry as many wives as they wish irrespective of the wish of the existing wife. This attitude has a direct link to the arbitrary use of women as sex objects in prostitution. Women are put to the loss of their dignity as a result of the repression they suffer in the hands of their men counterparts. As a way of escape some of them take recourse to prostitution so as to free themselves from such men, who lord their whims and caprices over them. Nevertheless, they do not escape the slavery of being seen and used as sex objects. The traditional Nigerian cultures abhor prostitution, but indirectly constrain women into the practice by means of robbing them of their rights.

2.1.5.3.3 Right of inheritance

There is a common desire among couples in Nigeria to beget at least a male child. This owes to the cultural concept of inheritance. A typical Nigerian father wishes the continuation of his lineage. That means the continued existence of his *Name* in his children and children's children. The implication of this is that only male children can make this happen since the female child is expected to marry and answer the *Name* of her husband and establish her own family. But the male child stays within the environs of his father and is expected to carry the lineage of his father further. Therefore only the male child has right to inheritance of the parents' property. So the female child has no right to the said inheritance. This implies the preference of a male child. This practice makes women to feel insecure because they fear loosing their place in the family and as such are forced to doing everything possible to beget male children, and in most cases, even to the detriment of their health and life.[150] This practice is still tenable till date and is common in most parts of Nigeria, especially among the Igbos

150 Ibid. pp. 113-114.

of south-east Nigeria where inheritances go to sons. However, by means of western education some couples nowadays are beginning to see child bearing positively irrespective of the sex.

Another dimension of the denying women of the right to inheritance is with regard to widowhood. Among the Igbos, for example, it is presumed that all landed properties of a deceased father belong to the boys. Neither a daughter nor a wife has right to inheritance. Quoting a traditional ruler, Effah-Chukwuma and Osarenren reported:

> "Where a widow has no son, she can use the property until her death. The properties of the deceased will however be inherited by his brothers or other male relations. But if she is inherited by her late husband's brother, then both of them shall inherit the man's property if on the other hand the widow has son/sons, the senior son and the mother will inherit the property".[151]

The total exclusion of female children in this case is really obnoxious. Among the Yorubas of South-west Nigeria, inheritance by a wife is said to be out of the discussion if the deceased dies intestate (that is, without leaving a Will behind) or was married under customary law.[152] The woman is considered to be a property that ought to be inherited by any of the late husband's relatives. Among many Hausa communities in the North Central Nigeria inheriting widows is a common practice. After the traditional mourning period of a decease husband, the wife is summoned to select a husband from the brothers of her husband.[153] It is said that she has no other choice than to make this selection if she doesn't want to loose the right to her late husband's property and custody of her children. This means the woman is forced against her wish to remarry and remarry to another man, who may not be her choice.

2.1.5.3.4 The traditional widowhood rites

The cultural traditions being discussed here also subject women to repressive rites of widowhood. According to most Nigerian customs, a woman and her children are considered to be the property of a man – the head of the family whose duty theoretically is to provide for them. Then the

151 Ibid. p.109.
152 Ibid. p. 110.
153 Ibid.

sudden death of the husband begins a time of sorrows for the woman. It is already a misfortune to loose a husband, but in most Nigerian cultural settings, it is a double misfortune, which leads most women into wishing to die before their husbands. This is because they are subjected to all kinds of inhuman conditions, all in the name of tradition.

In an Igbo traditional cultural setting, for example, a woman is subjected to a rite of purification at the death of her husband. In most cases this rite has dangerous consequences for the woman and her children. In the case of *Isa ahu* purification rite, the woman is taken to a local river to bathe herself. In the process she is examined to determine her periodic circle. If she is found to be menstruating at the time, she is declared a persona non grata, and is sent back to her father's home with a strict prohibition of setting her feet in her husband's home.[154] It is commonly believed that her periodic circle at the time of the husband's death determines if she is innocent of her husband's death. It is therefore an abomination for her to be menstruating at the time. What has the woman's biological system got to do with the death of her husband?

According to the focus group discussions with one hundred and twenty-five women in six geo-political zones of Nigeria organized by Effah-Chukwuma and Osarenren, other widowhood rites prevalent in most Nigerian cultures include: shaving of hair (including pubic hairs), sitting and sleeping on the floor, drinking of water used to bath corpse, jumping over corpse, sitting/ sleeping with corpse, eating from a broken plate, crying out loud early in the morning.[155] An account of one of the women in the south-east Nigeria is worth narrating:

> "When a man dies, the woman is expected to shave her hair completely. She wears black clothes, stays indoors for one month, sits and sleeps on a mat, and take her bath in the bush. If she is suspected of having a hand in her husband's death, she has to prove her innocence. She is expected to do this by either sleeping with the corpse or jumping over it or performing any other rites as may be demanded by the custom and tradition of the area her husband is from. In fact in Ohafia and Abriba areas of Abia State, the man's

154 Odoeme, Paul; Isa Ahu rite of purification in Uturu; unpublished paper at Bigard Memorial Seminary, Enugu, 1995, p. 21.
155 Effah-Chukwuma, Josephine and Osarenren, Ngozi; Ibid. p. 105.

> family will go as far as asking the widow to leave her husband's house, and collecting all his belongings and not caring if the children eat, go to school or even have a roof over their heads. It is really terrible".[156]

Within this focus group discussion forum other practices were narrated such as wearing unkempt hairs, being forced to remain with the corpse until the funeral is done, being barred from taking normal bathe, from taking a normal route to the toilet, observing personal hygiene, moving about, seeing the inside of the grave, eating pounded yam and chicken meat and goat meat and some other food items, from cooking for anyone during the mourning duration, wearing sackcloth and placing grass on her head. Widows are meant to mourn their deceased husbands for a specified period of time depending on the stipulations of the various customs. In most cases, the women folk (for example the *Umuadas* in Igboland) are direct executors of these widowhood customary rites.[157] The widowhood rites is a gross abuse of women's right, which not only maltreats and denies them of their human dignity, but also denies them of their right to movement and freedom of speech.

2.1.5.3.5 Female Genital Mutilation (FGM)

A similar rite being culturally imposed on women in Nigeria is the female genital mutilation (FGM). Mention has been made of this in the earlier chapter, but it deserves detailed approach at this point. "Female Genital Mutilation is defined as comprising all procedures that involve partial or total removal of the female external genital and/ or injury to the female genital organs for cultural or any other non-therapeutic reason".[158] Some refer to it as circumcision as in the case of males, thereby placing the two practices on the same par. But because of the harmful physical and psychological effects the practice has on women, it cannot be equated with male circumcision, hence befitting of the name FGM.

Effah-Chukwuma et al[159] recorded four types of Female Genital Mutilation in Nigeria: (i) *Sunna or Clitoridectomy* - This process involves the excision of the prepuce, with or without excision of part or the entire clitoris. (ii) *Excision* – This means the excision of the clitoris together with partial

156 Ibid. p. 105 ff.
157 Ibid. p. 106 ff.
158 Gachiri, E.W.; Female Circumcision, Paulines Publication Africa, 2000. p. 30.
159 Effah-Chukwuma, J., and Osarenren, N.; Ibid. p. 97ff.

or total excision of the *Labia minora* (small lips at the opening of the genitalia). This involves also the removal of some parts of the *Labia majora* (large lips). (iii) *Infibulation* – This is said to be the most severe form of FGM. The word means to fasten with a clasp or buckle. It involves the excision of the clitoris, labia minora and some parts or entire part of the labia majora. It also involves the stitching together of the two sides of the vulva, leaving only a small opening for urine and menstruation. (iv) *Unclassified* – A number of methods are involved in this fourth classification. They include: pricking, piercing, or incising of the clitoris and/ or labia; stretching of the clitoris and/ or labia; cauterization by burning of the clitoris and surrounding tissue; introduction of corrosive substances or herbs into the vagina to cause bleeding for the purpose of tightening or narrowing it; any other procedure involving partial or total removal of the external female genitalia or other injury to the female genital organs whether for cultural, religious or other non-therapeutic reason.

A research conducted by the National Baseline Survey revealed that "the most prevalent type of the four classifications of FGM practiced in Nigeria is Type I (Clitoridectomy) found mainly in the South-East, South-South and South-West. Type iii (Infibulation), which is the most severe form, is practiced in some parts of Northern Nigeria… Infibulation has also been found to exist in parts of … South Eastern Nigeria and … South-Western Nigeria".[160]

Several reasons have been given for the practice of FGM based on the empirical research of Effah-Chukwuma, et al.[161]

- *Maintenance of cleanliness:* The proponents of the FGM often argue that the removal of the genital organs promotes cleanliness in the private part. According to them, the secretions produced by the glands in the clitoris, labia minora and majora are foul-smelling and unhygienic.

160 Akumadu, T.U., Repudiating Repugnant Customs; Supra, 2000, p. 10.
161 Effah-Chukwuma, J., and Osarenren, N, Ibid. p. 100 ff.

- *Prevention of Still-Births in pregnant women:* In some communities FGM is performed on pregnant women in the belief that if the clitoris is not cut off at the first child delivery, the baby will die, and subsequent babies could be affected if this mutilation is not done.

- *Preventing promiscuity:* FGM is defended in Nigeria as a way of preventing women from being promiscuous. It is believed that if the clitoris is left intact, it causes women to be too sexy and always in high demand for sex. So it is said to be beneficial to the married couples so that wives, who do not get enough of sexual satisfaction from their husbands are not driven into extra-marital relationships. And also to help single girls to avoid having multiple sex partners.

- *Enhancement of Male sexual performance:* it is a common belief that the presence of the clitoris during sexual intercourse generates additional excitement, which results in early ejaculation by the male partners. On the belief that a man should be in total control of all aspects of sexual relations, it is argued that this role of the clitoris denies him this right. Therefore the whole idea of the Infibulation type of FGM is to bring about increased pleasure to the man during sexual intercourse.

- *Preservation of virginity:* Akin to the promiscuity argument, FGM is performed in young girls in order to help them abstain from sex until marriage.

- *Fertility enhancement:* It is believed that a young woman who does not perform this rite stands the danger of being infertile in marriage because the secretions produced by the clitoris kills the spermatozoa deposited in the vagina during sexual activity.

- *Good health:* it is believed that the performance of this ritual on women make them healthier. The ritual is said to have supernatural powers.

- *Promotion of socio-political unity:* This last reason argues that in order to be recognized and accepted in a particular community, members have the obligation of identifying themselves with the customs and traditions of such communities. In this regard, cir-

> cumcision in some communities is a ritual which confers full social acceptability and integration upon females. Without it they face the danger of being ostracized in their communities and denied of their rights as members of such communities.

None of the above mentioned reasons for performing FGM on women in some traditional Nigerian cultural settings, irrespective of how morally plausible they may seem, can be compared to the physical and psychological trauma the women go through in the process of this ritual and the rest of their lifetime. Majority of them are forced to believe that the life of a woman without this rite is worthless, and could ultimately lead to the untimely death of the woman. There are numerous consequences of this cultural practice on the quality of the life of women, ranging from health related problems, which occur at different stages with various complications, to other psychological damages such as frustration and depression,[162] and the loss of their dignity and right to their bodies, and freedom of expression.

2.1.5.3.6 Child marriages

Child marriage is another form of harmful custom in some parts of Nigeria. The victims of this tradition are young girls between the ages of 10 to 15. The little girls are forced into marriage at such tender ages. It is a practice more prevalent among the Hausas of Northern Nigeria. According to the empirical research of Effah-Chukwuma, et al, these little victims are forced to abruptly end their childhood once puberty sets in. "These little girls often do not decide whom or when to marry. This decision is taken on their behalf by their parents or guardians. Only in very "unusual conditions" would a little girl about to be married have a say on her needs. In most cases, the men in question are more than twenty years older than the girls and already married with two or three wives.[163]

It is revealed that this custom is practiced for the following reasons: (a) desire to avoid dishonor to the family as virginity can only be guaranteed between ages eight (8) to ten (10) years; (b) for economic gains accruing

162 Effah-Chukwuma, J., and Osarenren, N.; Ibid. p. 103 ff.

163 Ibid. p. 111.

from the pride price; (c) desire by parents to reduce the burden of a large number of children to take care of. Hence they give off their girls and shift the responsibility of caring for them to someone else.[164]

This practice of child marriage is said to have some social and health consequences on the female child. Most of the girls, who are fortunate to find a means of escape, run away to major cities and towns, where they are forced into becoming commercial sex workers, or escaping from the practice by means of committing suicide.[165] The major health consequence of forced child marriage is the medical condition known as Vesico-Vaginal Fistulae (VVF). They are exposed to difficulties at child delivery because of their underdeveloped delivery organs, which leads to health complications for mother and child.[166] As a consequence of early marriage, the girls are exposed to *gishiri cut.* Gishiri (an Hausa word) is a traditional operation carried out in Northern Nigeria meaning Salt, particularly believed to be helpful in relieving obstructed labour and enabling easy penetration during sexual intercourse with girls of under 13 years of age.[167] It involved cutting of the anterior and rarely posterior parts of the vagina using a razor blade or knife. Sometimes the bladder is mistakenly cut, thus resulting in VVF. Sadly enough, victims of VVF, according to Effah-Chukwuma, et al,

> "...are socially discriminated against. They are forced to leave the home by the very husbands who are the direct cause of their predicament. They are also rejected by their parents who made them to marry so young in the first instance. Rejected by husband, parents and the entire community, VVF patients either resort to begging or become commercial sex workers. They also become permanent visitors to health institutions because after the reconstruction through an operation if she engages in active sexual intercourse, it breaks down again".[168]

The above mentioned negative influences the traditional Nigerian cultures have on human rights, question the authenticity and sincerity of the cultural values in general, and stand against the common African high regard of the role of women in the societies as mother and protector of life.

---

164 Ibid. p. 113.
165 Ibid. p. 112.
166 Ibid.
167 Ibid. p. 1113.
168 Ibid.

2.2 RELIGIOUS TRADITIONS IN NIGERIA AND HUMAN RIGHTS

The old and popular view of the Kenyan Religion Philosopher John S. Mbiti that Africans are notoriously religious could also be said of Nigerians in particular. For most Nigerians religion and belief determine their everyday life activity. According to the survey on religion made by Bertelmann Foundation,[169] Nigeria is identified as the most religious country in the world and 92 percent of Nigerians identify themselves as deeply religious. The advent of the foreign religions did not make the people of Nigeria religious. From the beginning they naturally had their religious values, ideologies and practices. In their natural religious practices they express belief in the one and supreme God, who created the heavens and the earth, which the foreign religions (such as Islam and Christianity) share in common. The Igbo traditional religious institution, for example, is hierarchically structured: the supreme God is at the peak of this hierarchical ladder; at the second rank are the gods, who are considered the representatives of the supreme God on the various aspects of human life on earth. Next in the rank are the ancestors, who could be compared to the Christian saints and Islamic holy men and women. And then the priests who are considered the bridge between divine beings and human beings. The natural religions of other parts of Nigeria such as among the Yorubas of western Nigeria and the Hausas of the northern Nigeria share similar practices and ideologies. The religiosity of the peoples explains why the foreign religions could rapidly and quickly spread all over the country. It was like a change of old clothes into new ones.

The traditional cultural values of these cultural areas are synonymous with the values of the natural religions. The traditional cultural ideologies determine the religious ideologies. The two are inseparable. What the culture permits is also permitted in the religious circle. The culture is the religion! Since we have discussed extensively the cultural values of the three major ethnic groups in Nigeria we have invariably discussed the religious values of the natural religion (ATR) and their positive and negative influences on

169 The Bertelman Foundation Survey as presented by MISSIO in her power point presentation in preparation of World Mission Sunday 2009 under the Motto: “Peace and Reconciliation“; MISSIO, Aachen, Germany, 2009.

the understanding of human rights. With the advent of Islam and Christianity they were forced to operate almost underground, but their presence and influence are still being felt all over the country.

We now shift our attention to an account of the two major foreign religions in Nigeria – Islam and Christianity. Some aspects of the attitudes of these religions to human rights have been partly mentioned in the previous chapter, but in this part a more detailed account will be presented as it regards their ideologies and practices, and how these positively or negatively affect human rights understanding in the Nigerian context.

2.2.1 Islam and human rights in Nigeria

Since almost one thousand (1000) years, the Islamic religion formulates all aspects of life in Northern Nigeria. For example, the educational upbringing begins with memorizing the Koran. A systematic Islamization of the Hausa folk began officially in 1804. Although there is no official State religion in Nigeria, Islam works as a non-official State religion since it is being claimed to be greatest religious body in the country. All the Islamic free days are celebrated with big pomp all over the country. The yearly pilgrimage to Mecca, the Hajj, is a national event. The Friday prayers are strongly observed even in Christian-dominated areas. Like in Christianity the Islam has also different sects. The most popular in Northern Nigeria is the Islamic sect of the Cameroonian "Prophet", Maitatsine. This sect present themselves as fundamentalists, who through their activities caused a number of bloody religious crisis in Northern Nigeria in the years of1980, 1982, 1984 and 1985, against their fellow Muslims who do not believe in the teaching of Maitatsine, whom they notably identified as "unbelievers". There have been more cases of such sects instigating conflicts in the name of spreading the real teachings of Islam and propagating the adoption of Islam as a State religion in Nigeria. The Boko Haram sect is still a similar sect that instigated religious violence that left hundreds dead in four northern states in August 2009, in an attempt to install the Sharia as a law system in the northern states, if not in the whole of Nigeria. Nevertheless, the practice of Islam in Nigeria sometimes contradicts the real teaching and ideologies of Islam as a religion of peace.

When we talk about Islam and human rights there are some pertinent questions that come to mind: does Islam support human rights? Do human rights principles threaten Islamic institutions? These questions come up every now and then because human rights question remains contested in the Muslim world. Divided opinion among Muslims on human rights makes it difficult to know the stance of Islam on human rights. Nonetheless, the formulation of the Universal Islamic Declaration of Human Rights (UIDHR) and the Cairo Declaration on Human Rights lead to associating human rights with Islam and thereby the enhancement of its legitimacy among some Muslims. Whether it measures up with the international standard is a different question (which may come into play alongside further analysis). Ann Elizabeth Mayer, who made an extensive investigation into Islam and Human rights in some core Muslim countries, indicated that "Muslims have energetically condemned the human rights abuses perpetrated in the name of Islam in *(some)* countries. Even Muslims who do not use the terminology of modern human rights often display attitudes revealing their beliefs that justice and respect for human life and dignity are such central principles of Islam that a legal system that fails to honor these cannot be in conformity with Islamic requirements".[170] It is also said that Muslims who are disturbed by the human rights violations in the name of Islam count among prominent Islamic clerics. These are said to have denounced oppressive measures undertaken by governments to infringe on rights in the name of Islam.

The mission of Islam as a decentralized religion is said to be Liberation. The late Ayatollah Taleghani[171], one of the Iran's most distinguished clerics and a religious leader, emphasized the liberation aspect of Islam's mission by maintaining that Islam does not retard people's freedom. He accused and opposed leaders who use a "self-definition of Islam" to execute their personal and selfish interests. Although he did not use the language of human rights, he is said to have "effectively called for respect for human rights and treating Islam and human rights as natural allies".[172]

170 Mayer, Ann Elizabeth, Islam and Human RIghts: Tradition and Politics (Third Ed.); Westview Press, U.S.A., 1999, p. 24ff.

171 Ayatollah Taleghani's ideas are said to be mostly acceptable among younger, left-leaning Iranians He opposed the Khomeini regime which constantly invoked Islam as it sought to cut down on freedoms, whereas in his view the protection of freedom is a central concern in Islam. Ibid.

172 Ibid.; p. 26

Based on this liberative mission of Islam, Dr. Ali Abdel-Wahid Wafi introduces us into the human rights issues in Islam beginning with the Islamic understanding of equality.[173] He first of all laid a claim that Islam acknowledged human rights before any other institution or culture. He argued that although the language of human rights was not employed, but the principles and ideologies of Islam ab initio protected the human dignity and equality of all persons. Corroborating this claim Mayer wrote: "The Islamic heritage offers many philosophical concepts, humanistic values, and moral principles that are well adapted for use in constructing human rights principles".[174] These principles are deeply rooted in the Islamic traditions, and are strictly guided by the same. From this point we go into the analysis of human rights in Islam and particularly as it affects its practice in Nigeria.

2.2.1.1 Right to Equality in Islam

It is said that Islam advocates and promotes equality between persons irrespective of tribe, color or race. The only differences among persons are with regard to righteousness and good deeds, qualities and religion. The righteous fellow is believed to be more honored by God than an unrighteous fellow. The same goes to persons with better qualities, and adherents of Islam (as a superior religion).[175] Otherwise there is no difference between male and female in the essence of nature. This teaching is said to be backed by the Quran (Sura 13: Surat Al-Hujurat) and the Prophet Mohammed.[176] Islam regards persons as children of the same father and mother. Since God does not differentiate between his creatures humans ought also not to essentially differentiate among themselves.

This same principle of equality is also said to be extended to civil rights, for example "contractual right and possession without any difference between a prince or a pauper, a nobleman or a layman, rich or poor, popular or unpopular, near or far".[177] Islam is also said to apply the same principle of equality to people in the pursuit of learning and culture. But the empha-

173 Ali Abdel-Wahi explicates the principle of Equality in Islam in: Wafi, Ali Abdel-Wahid; Humn Rights in Islam (Translated by Derar Saleh Derar), Riyadh, 1998.

174 Mayer, Ann Elizabeth; Ibid., p. 43

175 Wafi, Ali Abdel-Wahid; Ibid., p. 13

176 Ibid. p. 14ff.

177 Ibid. p.23

sis on the pursuit of knowledge is deeply rooted on matters of religion and nature, especially as it regards to women.[178] In economic matters Islam advocates that "there should be laws that will give equal opportunities to people…, pave the way for each individual to obtain money, give each enterprising person his reward, work at the same time for achieving economic equilibrium, reduce the differences between classes, bring them closer together, stand in the way of accumulation of wealth, nib capitalism in the bud and strip it from means of influence and domination".[179] In order to achieve such an economic equality, Islam opts for moderate socialism.[180]

Islam advocates the equality in all these rights among Muslims and non-Muslims, but with a major difference. It stipulates that the *Thimmis* (that is non-Muslims who live under Islamic rule) have the same rights as Muslims and as such enjoy the same protection and care by the state as Muslims.[181] This special treatment on the basis of living under the Islamic law gives an impression that non-Muslim who do not live under the Islamic law are out of this packet.

A similar side of the coin is that Islam allows some discrimination, especially among men and women on the basis of nature and duty of each sex, taking into cognizance the welfare of society and family. This discrimination in Islam is applied to aspects of economic duties, inheritance, family supervision, giving witness, and obedience and divorce.[182]

In the economic field women are said to be placed under the total financial care of the men in order to protect them from social evils emanating from struggle to earn a living. Unmarried women are to obtain this care from their immediate family members, while married women are placed under the protection of their husbands. Similarly women are relieved of the duty of catering for family needs and supervising family matters. These are sole responsibilities of men. One of the reasons for relegating these roles to men is that men are said to be emotionally balanced than women, and as such are stronger personalities for such roles. The emotional qualities of

178 Ibid. p. 33.

179 Ibid. p.66

180 Moderate Socialism is described by Waffi Ali-Wahid as the system that takes the good in Communism and Capitalism, and ignores their evils.

181 Ibid. p.29.

182 These aspects are to be presented as treated by Wafi Ali Abdel-Wahid; Ibid. p. 121ff.

women are praised as God-given but they are meant for their task of being mothers. The role of leadership and supervision are said to require understanding, thinking and meditation. Therefore it is argued that these qualities are found more in men than in women. It strongly argued that women's status are not belittled or their civil rights lost by the headship of the family by men. She is said to be free to retain her family name and manage her wealth as she deems well. She still has a say in the family affairs.

In matters of inheritance, men are more favored than women. The men are said to be heads of the family and as such have greater and extensive responsibilities in the family. Based on this factor, men are bequeathed more in order to enable them meet their both financial and social responsibilities in the family as ordained by Islam. This is seen as just distribution of wealth on the basis of duty. It is also argued that Islam gives women a greater inheritance share by relieving them of financial responsibilities.

In Islam men and women are said to differ in acting as witness. This is applied mainly in matters like fornication, where only the witness of at least four reasonable men is required. Woman as a witness is not accepted. Women's witness is only accepted in feminine matters. The emotional nature of women is argued to be the reason for this practice because women are said to be carried off by their emotions thereby rendering their evidence or witness invalid.

The Islamic law obliges women to obey their husbands. Since the husband is solely incharge of the affairs of the family and caring for the wife, it is argued that she ought to be obedient to him, live with him wherever he wishes, and has to go with him to any place he thinks is good for their residence. This law suggests that men have the responsibilities and women have the duty of obedience, thereby suggesting an inequality between them.[183] Ali Abdel-Wahid concluded this section by positing that the Muslim law does not inflict any punishment on women for disobedience but it punishes men for failing in their obligations towards their wives. But the tone of the obligation by the law for the women to obedience is almost as stronger as the punishment inflicted on men by failing in their duty. The

183 Sura 228; Sura Al-Baqara of the Koran suggests this inequality: "And women shall have rights similar to the rights against them according to what is equitable, but men have a degree (of advantage) over them"; Ibid. p. 134.

compulsion involved in the case of women suggests disciplinary measures to make sure that this law is executed to the latter. The implications involved here may not be written but they are conspicuously implied.

Before we go on with further analysis of equality in Islam and its implications for human rights in the Nigerian context, let us present the nuance of Mayer on the other side of understanding equality in Islam. The mere mention of equality connotes the standard of international understanding according to the UDHR. But Mayer points our attention to the fact that equality could have a different meaning among many Muslims. Mayer beckons on the factors of social and cultural conditioning as influential factors in determining how people view equality. Based on these factors, "…it is easy for conservative Muslims to assume that the distinctions made between groups of persons in Islamic law are part of the natural order of things and to imagine that the retention of premodern Islamic rules does not in any way contravene the principle of equality. Thus, one finds Muslims who argue that Islam recognizes the principle of equality even while they uphold rules relegating women and non-Muslims to an inferior status".[184] What we see here is cultural and social conditionings, which make people to justify their religious practices on natural and religious rights basis even when such practices are incompatible with the universal standard.

This Mayer's nuance immediately gives us a picture of the negative effects Islamic traditions and practices have on equality principles in Nigeria, especially in the northern part. There is no need belaboring the obvious strong and enviable brotherhood and communalism that exist among Muslims in Nigeria. But it is worrisome that this communion exists only among Muslims. Non-Muslims are not part of it. The political situation in Nigeria worsens the matter by making non-Muslims enemies that should be exterminated. That explains the so many crises that occur in northern Nigeria under the guise of religion. Non-Muslims suffer untold hardships in the Islamic domains of Nigeria. The Sharia law has been adopted in eleven northern states as a law system, and in most cases, non-Muslims are forced to live according to the Sharia law system against their will and religious inclinations and against the stipulations of the Nigerian Constitution. Instances of this have already been mentioned in the previous chapter.

184 Mayer, Ann Elizabeth; Ibid., p. 84

The authorized discrimination against women in Islam gives their men counterpart in Nigeria an undue advantage of handling them as objects instead of fellow human beings according to stipulations of the Quran.[185] As indicated by our previous reports, the Islamic traditions, especially the Sharia law, are mostly utilized to justify personal interests and actions. Women are in most cases victims of such justifications. We have already made mention of inheritance rights in northern Nigeria and its implications for women. This shows that they have no will of their own to decide for themselves. Their emotional nature is even used against them in such matters (as we pointed above). Men are simply considered to be superior to women.

The case of Amina Lawal[186] immediately calls to mind here. She was accused and prosecuted of adultery for having a baby outside marriage. Her conviction was based on the evidence of her baby whereas the alleged father of her child was discharged on the grounds of insufficient evidence against him.[187] According to the Islamic tradition, there ought to be at least four men-witnesses to witness against the man, but it is very clear that it is difficult to have such witnesses to a single sexual act. Therefore the woman suffers on the basis of the evidential rules. Through the outcry of the International community and human rights activists, a higher Islamic court reversed the case of Amina based on genuine Islamic principles. Without the intervention of the international community and the higher Sharia court she could have been a dead person by now. Similar discrimination against women challenges the Islamic justice in a plural democracy such as Nigeria's, and questions the legality of the Nigerian constitution.

2.2.1.2 Rights of Women in Islam

Analogous to the analysis on equality in Islam is the understanding of women's rights. A lot have been already said in the previous chapter and partly here on the rights of women in Islam, but suffice it to make some

---

185 Verse 124 – Al Nisa-a (The Women) and Verse 32 – Al Nisa-a (The Women), in: Wafi, Ali Abdel-Wahid; Ibid., p. 31

186 Amina Lawal is a 30 years old mother of three children and divorced at the age of 14, who was prosecuted for adultery for having a baby outside wedlock in northern Nigeria in 2002.

187 Amnesty International, "Save Amina from Death" Urgent Appeal, posted at: http://www.mertonai.org/amina/amina.asp., November 2002.

brief mention of some other aspects of such interpretations in the Nigerian context. Historically it is said that Quranic innovations tend to enhance women's rights by conferring rights on women in the seventh century which women of the time in the West did not have. "The historical accounts regarding the status of women in the first decades of the Islamic community under the Prophet Muhammed suggest that women were originally accorded considerable freedom (which) enabled them to defend their interests, and that they participated in public and religious affairs on a footing of approximate equality with men".[188] The Muslim feminists deploy the current disabilities Muslim women suffer and blame the distortions of authentic Islam on male interpreters who had ulterior motives of preserving the patriarchal privilege. Hence it is argued that, "as a result of social conditions and the interpretation of many diverse cultural traditions, the inferior status of women was written into Islamic law".[189] In other words, the inferiority of women developed over the course of time and male biases and cultural traditions were disguised as religious precepts.

The UIDHR is one of the influential documents that came up in the course of time with a lot of ambiguities on the rights of women. It did not specifically admit that women are to be given second-class status. But on reading in between the lines, one discovers that a number of rights and freedom are denied women therein. Commenting on this Mayer said that "many of the provisions assigning women to a subordinate role do so only indirectly and are written in such a convoluted style that their significance may not be obvious to readers – and especially not to readers of the English version of the document".[190] An example of what we are saying here is found in the Article 19.a of the UIDHR, which states: "Every person is entitled to marry, to found a family, and to bring up children in conformity with his religion, tradition and culture." This provision stands against that of UDHR, which states: "Men and women of full age, without any limitation due to race, nationality or religion, have the right to marry and to found a family." The international standard took care of the limitations and dis-

188 Naila Minai, *Women in Islam: Tradition and Transition in the Middle East,*(New York: Seaview, 1981), 1-24; and Jane Smith, "Women, Religion, and Social Change in Early Islam", in *Women, Religion, and Social Change,* ed. Yvonne Hadad and Ellison FIndley (New York, 1985), 19-35, quoted in: Mayer, Ann Elizabeth; Ibid., p.98

189 Falzur Rahman, "The Status of Women in the Quran", in *Women and Revolution in Iran,* ed. Guity Nashat (Westview Pres, 1983), p. 38.

190 Mayer, Ann Elizabeth; Ibid. p. 106.

abilities posed by those elements, which the UIDHR ignores. That means persons are bound by this obligations irrespective of whether the traditional, cultural and religious principles offer uncomfortable, and sometimes, inhuman means of achieving them.

That is one of the ambiguities I mentioned above, and the Nigerian Muslim women find themselves in such situations. The Sharia law imposes restrictions such as barring them from marrying non-Muslims, and restricting them to monogamy. They are subjected to the male tutelage and control; subjected to subordinate role in the family and exclusively relegated only to domestic functions. Child marriage (which has been discussed above) is an offshoot of such subjugations. The girl child is married off at early age and against her will, and begins so early in life to experience religiously imposed restrictions: she must be obedient to her husband at all costs; her husband could terminate the marriage at will just by mere utter of a divorce formula, whereas she has to go through rigorous juridical procedures in order to obtain a divorce over her husband's refusal. To cap it all, she looses custody of her children to the husband after they passed the infancy stage.

From the tone of the Islamic principles in women matters, one gets the impression that only men have rights. What women enjoy in Islam could be better called *privileges* because they seem not to have the will of their own.

2.2.1.3 Right to Freedom of Religion in Islam

On freedom of religion, the Holy Quran (S. 2:256) says: "Let there be no compulsion in religion: Truth stands out clear from Error: whoever rejects Tagut[191] and believes in Allah has grasped the most trustworthy Hand-hold, which never breaks. And Allah heareth and knoweth all things". This pericope on tolerance suggests that religious adherence should be a matter of conscience. One wonders where the question of apostasy came into Islam. It is no where stipulated in the Holy Quran that a Muslim who converts to other religious bodies ought to be killed. Some liberal Muslim scholars repudiate apostasy in Islam and identify with religious tolerance that one of them even concluded that the Quranic principles of religious liberty have

191 Tagut means anything worshipped beside Allah

common backgrounds with the Western concept of religious liberty.[192] As against this background some extreme conservative Muslims do not yet accept this wind of change that is coming to the Muslim world. The Cairo Declaration on Human Rights fails to provide explicitly for freedom of religion. That such an important and influential document does not make such a provision is a deflating factor against this wind of change.

This deflating factor against the positive wind of change on religious freedom is very prominent among most Nigerian Muslims. They are still very much influenced by the version of Sharia law, which prohibits conversion from Islam to other religions, thereby vigorously pursuing their course to transform Islamic principles into state ideologies in the northern Nigeria. Apostasy do not only prohibit convert from Islam but limits Muslims from following their conscience in matters of faith.[193] Thus without doubt this prohibition limits their freedom of thought and expression; a freedom which Ali Abdel-Wahid argued as one of the acknowledged freedoms in Islam.[194] If Muslims are restricted in their freedom of thought and expression, one wonders about such tolerance with regard to millions of non-Muslims who live in the northern Nigeria.

The manner most Muslims, especially in northern Nigeria, go about the spread of Islam leaves one to doubt the motive behind such fanatical evangelization. The politicization of religion in Nigeria makes the matter worse since politics is played in a manner that suggests the appeasement of religion. Our previous examples (especially on matters of Sharia) buttress this fact. In most cases non-Muslims are forced to operate underground. In some core Muslim areas Christian proselytizing is completely forbidden. Ninety-nine percent of the religiously-termed crises in northern Nigeria have left non-Muslims, especially Christians as immediate victims, which led to the burning of their houses, Churches, business premises and worst of all, lost of somany of lives. The supposed causes of these crises suggest a climate of hate and unfounded aggression. We recall again the Danish Mohammed cartoon, which has nothing to do with Nigeria, but ended up

192 Abdulaziz Sachedina, "Freedom of Conscience and Religion in *the* Quran", in *Human Rights and the Conflict of Cultures: Western and Islamic Perspectives on Religious Liberty,* ed. David Little, John Kelsay, and Abdulaziz Sachedina (Columbia, 1988), pp. 53-90.
193 Mayer, Ann Elizabeth; Ibid., p.151
194 Wafi, Ali Abdel-Wahid; Ibid., p. 251

causing a crisis that led to loss of lives and destruction of properties in Nigeria. The frequency of these crises is an urgent invitation from the side of adherents of Islam to study deeper and possibly better the principles of Islam as a religion of peace and accommodation.

2.2.1.4 Right to protection of life in Islam

Islam is said to be keen in the protection of life. Ideologically murder is abhorred by Islam. Murderers are met with immediate death penalty. But a classical distinction is made in this regard between intentional murder and unintentional murder. Intentional murder gets immediate death penalty as a deterrent to others for committing such a crime. It is believed that a murderer is not only punished here on earth but also in the next world.[195] Unintentional murder attracts indemnity or 'Kaffara' (redemption) depending on the intensity of the crime. It could as well attract the two at the same time. Indemnity involves a financial compensation to the relatives of the victim. The 'Kaffara' is said to be usually borne by the murderer. It entails releasing a slave, or fasting for two successive months if no slave is available. Besides, the murderer is stripped of any bequest entitlements that include his name.[196] It is further said that an unintentional murder of a non-Muslim however attracts only the indemnity and no Kaffara.[197] This distinction here smacks of the aspect of inequality allowed by Islam, which at the same time contradicts Islamic principles that all human beings are equal as children of the same Father. Another give-and-take approach is seen in this regard.

In events of murder where the murderer is not known, fifty persons from the area are chosen to appear in the court. They would be required to oath-taking of no involvement in the crime. The punishment is dropped as a result of the oath-taking, but the community jointly pays the indemnity to the relatives of the deceased.[198] It is further said that some Jurists stipulate that corporal punishment be executed in events of murder, where the murderer is not known, based on strong grounds of suspicion by the relatives of the deceased. The suspicion here is authenticated by establishing an evidence of enmity that existed between the deceased and the suspect. If the

195 Ibid.; p.279
196 Ibid.; p.280
197 Ibid.; p. 281
198 Ibid.; p.283

relatives of the deceased attest to the accusation by oath the suspect would be thereby charged of murder and punished by killing. Charging and sentencing someone only on the basis of suspicion is a violation of the right to fair trial. This is however only opinion of some popular jurists, but presumed not to be representing Islamic principles. Moreover it goes against the stipulations of the Holy Quran S. 49:12, where it is recommended that suspicion should be avoided as much as possible.

Islam is also said to be opposed to removal of life irrespective of who is involved. A practical example was given by Ali Abdel-Wahid (quoting Mohammed Al-Hassan) that the Prophet Mohammed "condemned a Muslim to death because he killed an infidel and declared that of all people he must keep to his pledge".[199] Islamic Jurists argue that since difference in religion could lead to removal of lives such a rule is installed in order to deter people from committing such crimes. The seriousness of this law indicates that Islam respects life and advocates that it be preserved.

This said law is however contradicted by the popular belief (among fanatical Muslims) that killing a non-Muslim (infidel) attracts some heavenly rewards. At this point comes the Nigerian context in the fore. The rampart killing of non-Muslims (mostly Christians) in northern Nigeria at any least provocation suggests the wide acceptance and notoriety of this belief among many Muslims. Why would non-Muslims be targeted for crimes they are not connected with if Islam is lived and adhered to as a religion of peace and respect for human life? This remains an open question which ought to lead our Nigerian Muslims to rethink on their approach to Islamic religion.

Another factor is yet the Sharia. According to the international human rights standard, Sharia offences suggest claim of violation of the right to life and the dignity of the human person. The sentence of death by stoning passed against Amina Lawal was internationally condemned as a violation of her right to life and human dignity. The Nigerian constitution has a provision for death penalty (except passed in violation of regular law), but

199 Ibid.; p. 278

forbids any form of inhuman treatment.[200] But the manner of punishment according to the Sharia law suggests a violation of this constitutional stipulation. In a particular case, the Sharia Judge pronounced:

> "The convict should be stoned at his back and front but not at the face and private part. She should be stoned to death. Later to be bathed and prayed and taken to her last home of Muslim".[201]

This sounds like very brutal and humanly speaking horrific. But the argument here is not about the abolition of the Sharia law or capital punishment in Nigeria, but it goes about humane treatment of offenders still with the view of achieving the desired aim for the punishment. Although it has not yet been officially revealed that someone is stoned to death in Nigeria, but there abound cases of other Sharia law offences such as brutal floggings and amputations, which could lead to one's eventual death.

Sam Amadi is of the opinion that torture (inhuman treatment) may be universally precluded yet there is no commonly accepted standard about the fact of torture. Canning a child for wrong doing, for example, is no longer an acceptable standard in the western countries, but it remains a typical moral training for most Africans. Most religious and cultural traditions including Muslims base their argument on this religious relativism. But what makes the difference about this particular act of canning is the degrading effect it leaves on the child for his/her future development. The international standard of condemning canning of children is based on this moral effect and not as attack against cultures and religions. The dignity of the human person qua tale is at stake here.

Muslims, like adherents of other religions, have their religious and cultural rights to practice their religion according to its principles and ideologies. Nonetheless the universal standards on matters of human rights ought not

---

200 Section 34 of 1999 Constitution.

201 Judgment delivered by Mohammed Bello Sanyinnawal in Case No. USC/GW/CR/F1/10/2001, Commissioner of Police v. Yakubu Abubaka Tungar Tudu & Safiyyatu Husaini Tungar Tudu on October 9, 2001 quoted in Ayo Obe, "The Meshing of Legal Systems: The Challenge of the Sharia", a paper presented at a conference on "Unity, Governance, Law, and Conflict" at the Kennedy School of Government, Harvard University, 12-14 December, 2002, (not paged), cited by Amadi, Sam; "Religion and Secular Constitution: Human Rights and the Challenge of Sharia", posted at: http://www.ksg.harvard.edu/cchrp/pdf/Amadi.pdf

to be ignored since Muslims are living in the same world with other peoples who may be non-Muslims or non-religious. A pluralism of worldview and ideology is an inescapable feature of our world today, which ought to be accepted and harnessed in a harmonious manner. The appeal we try to convey here is calling for a more revision of the Islamic principles and ideologies as been practiced in Nigeria in comparison to the authentic principles and ideologies of Islam and their practices in other nations, but not in isolation of the international human rights standard. It has to be noted also that the international standard is not devoid of shortcomings. Hence warrants a collaborative approach. This aspect shall be addressed in a later chapter.

2.2.2 Christianity and human rights in Nigeria

The spread of Christianity to Nigeria cannot but be reported in the context of colonization and human slave trade. The inhuman trafficking in human lives went on for over three hundred years during which a large population of black Africans was transported into Europe, United States of America and Central and South America. At the end of the 18th century, Eastern Nigeria alone is said to have supplied 20,000 slaves in one year.[202] Many of the slaves died en route due to torture, starvation and exposure to the asperities of the weather. A large number of them however survived in the new world where many eventually became Christians.

Anti-slavery movements were formed in England many years before the official decree of abolition of slave trade in 1807. By 1841, slave trade abolitionists were advocating taking the campaign inside Africa itself as a means of regenerating the continent "by the Bible and Plough". This was seen as an effective way of ending the trans-Atlantic slave trade and seeking a form of reparation to Africa for the wrongs done to it by Europe and America. Emancipation did come at last. It is said that many of the slaves actually regained their freedom long before 1800. After the emancipation thousands of the ex-slaves wanted to return to their original homes in West Africa. They returned with their various Christian denominational beliefs and practices thus brought with them the new faith into

202 Roland, Oliver and Atmore, Anthony; Africa since 1800, London, 1978, p.38

that part of the world.[203] Hence Christianity was unofficially introduced and this unorganized introduction of the new faith paved the way for the first foreign missionaries to come to Nigeria for the evangelization of the numerous numbers of traditional religionists in the land. The Methodist and the Anglican Churches were the first to gain official entrance and establishment in 1841. In the consequent years came the Catholic Church, the United Native African Church (which is currently called the First African Church). The Christian faith in Nigeria was immediately confronted by the traditional African religious and cultural beliefs. This traditional institution was also immediately tagged 'paganish' by the early missionaries, and therefore warranted abolition. The Missionaries therefore set out to Christianize the native population with the Bible as their tool, targeting most especially the inhuman and harmful traditional practices of the time in view of promoting the human dignity.

The said promotion of human dignity forms the basis of the Christian approach to human rights question with a direct connection to the life and teaching of Jesus Christ, who promoted the universal notion of equal moral status for all human beings. We shall explore the Christ's connection of the Christian mission in details in the following chapter. But it suffices here to comment that Christ's teaching took its orientation from the Jewish Scripture, the Old Testament: "Do not think that I have come to remove the Law and the Prophets. I have not come to remove but to fulfill them". (Matthew 5:17, Christian Community Bible). With this statement Christ announced the basis of his teaching. Thus the New Testament as part of the Christian Bible (dwelling mainly on the life and teaching of Christ), was written on the basis of the Old Testament (the Jewish Scripture). The Christian combination of the two parts for her Bible is indeed a smart one since the New Testament complements the Old Testament in most sensitive aspects that would constitute violation of the modern understanding of human rights. Further analysis on this would be made in the course of this section.

Surely the word 'Human Rights' is not mentioned in the Christian Bible. But the basis of the Christian human rights engagement is to be found in it. Renè Cassin strongly supports this view by articulating that the human rights concept comes from the Bible, the Old Testament, citing first and

203 Ibid.

foremost the Ten Commandments.[204] He argues that these concepts were at the time given in form of 'duties', which eventually developed into the modern understanding of 'rights'. This is a similar argument with the traditional concept of 'rights' understood as 'duties' among the traditional local population in Nigeria prior to colonization. In a similar vein, the Polish historian Sergius Hessen (1887-1950) was of the opinion that the Christian roots form the basis for modern understanding of democracy, thus human rights. He explains that true charity means equality, liberty and brotherliness – as inseparable aspects of Christian love.[205] According to some Theologians and Bible Scholars the Old Testament is especially described as 'duties', while the New Testament is seen as the fundament of 'Freedom' positing Jesus Christ as the Liberator. In this sense the smart blend between the Old Testament and the New Testament is made through the mediation of Jesus Christ.

This blend made possible by Christ became the source of other Christian Traditions such as the Canon Law and Catechism of the Catholic Church. Such Traditions borrowed extensively from the Biblical Traditions and seeks to correct some of the past mistakes of the Church which led to the Church's violation of the said human rights she sought to promote and protect. The Inquisition and the Crusades are typical examples of such mistakes. It is not however our duty to dwell in this matter, but suffice it to say that the Church[206] has the tendency of repeating *similar* mistakes by means of some of her ideological structures and norms inherent in the *intrusive, ethnocentric,* and *triumphalist* tendencies in some of her methods. Because of such tendencies the Church is constantly exposed to allegations of human rights violations, and the Church in Nigeria is not left out of this. Such tendencies resulted into expression of the tension between the secular human rights ethos and the hierarchical constitution of the Church and her self-view. Nevertheless, the Mission of the Church remains the mandate of Christ, which is carefully analyzed in the Vatican II Council Document:

---

204 Cited in: Ishay, Micheline; Ibid. P.19

205 Sergius Hessen, "The Rights of Man in Liberalism, Socialism and Communism", in Maritain, *Human Rights,* 117; in: Ishay, Micheline; Ibid., p.25

206 The mention of the *Church* as from this point would be made mainly with regard to the Catholic Church since she is the major focus in this project. Other Christian denominations would be mentioned when necessary.

> "Having been divinely sent to the nations that she might be "the universal sacrament of salvation (Lumen Gentium, 48)," the Church, in obedience to the command of her founder (Mt. 16:15) and because it is demanded by her own essential universality, strives to preach the Gospel to all men. ... the Church, the salt of the earth and the light of the world (cf. Mt. 5:13-14) is even more urgently called upon to save and renew every creature...."[207]

The preaching of the Gospel to all peoples, and salvation and renewal of all creatures as fundament of the Church's mission has political, economic and social consequences. In this way she ought to be the solicitor for human rights, world peace and justice. It is therefore to be said that the mission of the Church is inseparably connected to the promotion and protection of human rights. It is then on this basis that we go to analyze Christianity and human rights in the Nigerian context. We shall give particular attention to areas where she is found wanting in human rights matters.

2.2.2.1 Right to Equality in Christianity

One of the major Christian basis of human rights is found in the creation account of humankind: "God said, "let us make man in our image, in our likeness, and let them rule over... (all the earth)..." So God created man in his own image, in the image of God he created him; male and female he created them". (Gen.1:26-27). The universality of equality is emphasized in this passage. As long as human beings are created in the image and likeness of God, they share the same nature and status with God and with each other. That means as long as God is to be respected human beings are also to be respected. Another strong emphasis stressed in this context is the dignity of human beings. This dignity then forms a strong basis for the respect of humankind and her rights. This calls for reciprocity, which the book of Genesis further emphasized: "And from each man, too, I will demand an accounting for the life of his fellow man. Whoever sheds the blood of man, by man shall his blood be shed; for in the image of God has he made man". (Gen. 9:5,6). God gives human beings responsibility over each other and thereby discourages all barriers of race, tribe and nations. In Paul's letter to the Colossians, a similar emphasis is made: "There is no distinction between Jew and Greek, between circumcised and uncircumcised. There are no strangers, barbarians, slaves or free men, but Christ binds all and is in all". (Col. 3:11). While giving his disciples the evan-

207 Vatican II Council Document, *Ad Gentes Divinitus,* 7 December, 1965, no. 1

gelizing mandate (Mt. 28:19), Christ indicated that they should go to all nations without boundaries. And this gospel's invitation led the Church to accepting "a universal application of the image of God for all humankind by …making all equal..."[208]

The Church in Nigeria makes serious efforts to live out this missionary mandate according to these principles of the sacred scripture. She makes her social structures (such as schools, hospitals etc) available and beneficial to all and sundry irrespective of religion, denomination or tribe. This is a very great credit for her evangelizing mission. However, hatred mingled with her triumphalist attitude towards pluralism of faith in Nigeria contradicts this universal concept of the *image of God* as a basis for equality of all human beings. Naturally the hatred and suspicion that exist between Christians and Muslims in Nigeria is as a result of frequent clashes often initiated by Muslims against Christians in the northern part of Nigeria. But among the numerous Christian denominations there exists also tendencies of concurrency and antagonism. Each strives to outshine the other. The Pentecostal groups are fonder of such tendencies, but in most cases the Church sees herself as being superior to others. Such attitudes contradict her missionary basis and mandate, and she is therefore called upon to intensify her contributions towards interreligious dialogue and ecumenism as a way of living above these contradictory tendencies in her missionary endeavors.

2.2.2.2 Right to Freedom from discrimination in Christianity

Freedom from discrimination is analogous to the right of equality of all human beings. Some of the biblical passages cited above make references to it. Another example from the Old Testament is God's mandate to Noah to allow every creature (clean and unclean) entrance into the Ark without any form of discrimination.(Gen. 7:1-10). St Paul calls to mind in the New Testament as a model of equality of all human beings. He wrote to the Galatians in a similar tone as he did to the Colossians: "Here there is no longer Greek or (difference) between slave and freedman, or between man and woman: but all of you are one in Christ Jesus". (Gal. 3:28). In a seem-

208 Bentley, David, "Created in the Image of God: a shared hope for understanding human rights among Jews, Christians, and Muslims", November 2004, posted at: www.sanford.edu/lilyhumanrights/papers.html

ingly contradictory manner St. Paul calls on wives to be totally submissive to their husbands (Eph. 5:21ff). Paul made a similar call in 1 Tim. 2:11-15, but using stronger words describing what role a woman ought to assume owing to her nature. Biblical scholars[209] defend Paul's address as reflecting the culture of his time. The society of his time warrants it; but Paul makes a difference by relating the obedience he talks about as obedience to Christ. His teaching is said not to be against feminism since the cultural model of his time suggest a particular mode of relationship between husband and wife. By linking all to Christ as a model indicates he opted for a more humane relationship between man and woman. Thus making the husband the head of the family just like Christ is the head of the Church indicates a servant-role the husband ought to play in the family, since Christ himself said that he did not come to be served, but to serve. Over and above all Paul calls on the husband to love his wife as Christ loved the Church and gave himself up for her. This indicates to the husband that he ought to be loyal to his wife even to the point of laying his life for her cause. This suggests a mandate to protect the rights of the woman.

As against this background, the Church's promotion of equality is contradicted by some of her attitudes towards the female sex. The Church in Nigeria has no explicit laws against women, but that is implied in the limitations placed against roles women could play in the Church. (This has been briefly commented on in the previous chapter). One can say that the patriarchal structure of the local cultures still have some significant influence on the Church in this matter. In some cases women regard themselves as inferior to men and as such legitimize the societal judgment on them. Unfortunately this latter part of Paul's teaching on the role of women in the Church is sometimes given a different interpretation in order to suite some patriarchal tendencies within the Church and in some Christian families. The Church's intrusive tendency is suggested in this context. The Church's silence in this regard does not help matters. That is why it is imperative on her to intensify her mission in this aspect through good education on matters of rights.

Another aspect of discrimination observed within the Church in Nigeria has to do with funerals. Although the Canon Law of the Church does not

---

209 The exegesis of this passage is taken from its commentary in Christian Community Bible, Claratian Publications, Philippines, 1994.

stipulate the denial of funerals to people in irregular marriages and suicides,[210] the Church in Nigeria is been constantly accused of and criticized for such discrimination. In most instances this aspect of discrimination has been counterproductive for the Church and questions her credibility and integrity, hence her intrusive tendency. By virtue of her salvific mission the Church ought to intercede for the soul and leave final judgment to God.

On Social and Economic rights the Church in Nigerian champions the cause by working against the unjust structures of the Nigerian society that suppress and oppress the poor. She does her best to create employment opportunities within the limits of her strength, by trying to secure economic security and rest for the laborer and the poor. But she has often been accused of some discrimination in matters of employment when members of other religions or Christian denominations are involved. In her ethnocentric tendency she even discriminates and denies her own members employment opportunities on ethnic or tribal grounds.

In some other cases, the Church's hierarchy in Nigeria is accused of keeping scandalous relationship with the civil government to the extent that she gives up her prophetic role in the Nigerian society as the voice of the voiceless. Acceptance of flamboyant gifts and favors from the civil government that do not care much about alleviating the poor conditions of her citizens makes her a toothless dog as a moral solicitor. In such a romance she expresses a tendency towards the rich to the discrimination of the poor. The result of such behavior is antagonism from the poor faithful, who may become lukewarm in faith or decide for a different denomination or religion.

With this last example permit us to conclude this section and chapter with the criticism and admonition of Oscar Wermter SJ:

210 The Legionary of Christ Father Edward McNamara, Professor of Liturgy at the Regina Apostolorum university, Rome, indicated this in his Question and Answer forum on "Funeral Masses"; posted at Zenit.org on August 18, 2009.

> "The criticism of the Church is definitely not enough. The burden of witnessing lies on the shoulder of each person. It is a Church in transition which must still learn to confront the Powerful (despots) without compromises".[211]

This criticism and admonition calls the Church to be more conscious of her prophetic role without loosing ties to the footprints and examples of her founder and Master. The Church's engagement for justice, peace and reconciliation cannot be deeply rooted until she steps out to address the root causes of injustice and crises without comprises since peace cannot be separated from justice.

Summary

This chapter with its various sections involves a long articulation of the beauty and richness of the cultural and religious traditions in Nigeria, with particular emphasis on the major three cultural and three religious traditions. Thus the multi-cultural and multi-religious nature of Nigeria is clearly articulated here. On a deep study of the ideologies and principles of these traditions, one gets an impression of ideologies and principles that support the promotion and protection of human rights. The practical aspects of these traditions mostly suggest contradictory signs that suggest anti-human rights tendencies inherent in them. In some aspects, the principles and ideologies directly contradicts the international standards on human rights matters. But in most cases, the problem is the actual blending of theory and practice according to the authentic principles and ideologies of these traditions. In other words the practice contradicts the theoretical aspect. In order to achieve a consensus, each is expected to look inwards and make some necessary revisions of her ideologies and principles and make some self-examination regarding her method. Thereafter they converge on a dialogue table to disagree in order to eventually agree.

211 This criticism and admonition of Oskar Wermter was reflected by Schalück Hermann, „Die Katholische Menschenrechtsdebatte"(The Catholic Human Rights Debate), in: Jahrbuch Mission, p.77 (Original copy in German; translation is mine).

CHAPTER THREE

THE MISSION OF THE CHURCH FROM THE PERSPECTIVE OF THE MISSION OF CHRIST.

Introduction

Human rights concerns are often regarded as issues that have to do with political, economic and social attitudes with the tendency to elbow religion out of the task. When it comes to the church's involvement in human rights issues, some people become very skeptical about her role. Such people opine that the church's mission is strictly speaking a spiritual one, which should not be mingled with political or economic matters. They argue that human rights issues are matters of law and as such belong more to the juridical area. While others are of the opinion that the church has taken a very reserved position in the past with regard to human rights question and even perpetrated and is still perpetrating some human rights abuses, hence they do not understand the role she can play towards human rights promotion and protection.

Without any doubt, the above mentioned contentions prove that the church is not an institution *of* human rights, but it does not preclude the chance that the church can be an institution *for* human rights, especially with regard to her concern for the respect of human dignity. This is where the church's mission of Liberation expresses itself. That means liberation that does not underplay the transcendental and eschatological dimensions. So the liberation in question here is geared towards realizing the ethical principles of the Kingdom of God in peoples' lives: justice, love, equality, freedom, peace, mercy, truth, holiness of life, tolerance, community, work and human dignity.[212] It becomes very pertinent to ask at this point: to what extent can the church's mission of liberation be really seen as an integral one that propagates these ethical principles as they relate to human rights question? That is the task of this chapter: to attempt an answer to *why* should Christianity or the church engage herself with human rights issues. In other

212 Kiss, I., *The Gospel and Human Rights*, In: Halama, J. (ed.), The Idea of Human Rights: Traditions and Presence, Prague, 2003, p.63.

words, it asks for the proof of legitimating the mission of the church towards human rights. This chapter navigates essentially into the mission of Christ as the foundation for the mission of the church, starting by tracing the biblical and historical sources of Christ's mission in conjunction with the mission of the church today, to an exposition of liberation as a perspective for the church's mission; and human rights as an instrument with which the church can do her mission of liberation. Christ as a missionary par excellence did not shy away, when necessary, from dialogue with peoples of other beliefs or opinions in his time. Hence this chapter concludes with some insight into the church's mission of Dialogue, especially with members of other religious beliefs.

3.1 BIBLICAL SOURCES OF CHRIST'S MISSION

The mission of Christ to the world was done within the religious, social, economic and political contexts of his Jewish era. The direct access to the story of Christ that is available to us is through the New Testament authors, especially the Evangelists that authored the four gospels. Christ's life history is told based on the Jewish background of his time. He did not live in a political vacuum. He is to be placed in the historical context of his time regarding the political and religious matters of the time. It is only in this way that the vitality of his message could be better appreciated today.[213]

The political and economic situation at the time was tied to the Roman domination of the Jewish territory, politically and economically. This Roman domination was clearly expressed by the organization of a census and the collection of taxes from the Jews around AD 6.[214] The Israelites endured their long tradition of external domination in the prophetic hope of a "Messiah", who will liberate them from the shackles of their political and economic lords. They expected a political fighter who will wage wars to bring down the reign of the Romans and other dominators over them. It is within this context that Christ introduced himself as that Messiah (liberator). This political aura contributed immensely to his being viewed as a political revolutionary. Nevertheless, the messianic expectations of the an-

213 Wilson, B., How Jesus became Christian.Orion Books, United Kingdom, 2009, p. 55.

214 Bosch, D., Transforming Mission: Paradigm Shifts in Theology of Mission, Orbis Books, Maryknoll, New York, 1991, p. 26.

cient Israel were somehow different from the conceptions of Christ, which were purely for spiritual benefits (of body and soul). According to the Israelites of old, a Messiah

> … must help overthrow foreign authority, establish an independent Jewish state, be the Davidic king and, with God's help, usher in an era of universal peace, establishing the universal rule of God, the Kingdom of God. During his time, the wicked will be eradicated and the righteous will be rewarded. The righteous dead will suddenly reappear. The world will experience a peace never before realized, and all humanity will acknowledge and worship the one true God.[215]

In conformity but contrary to the political undertone of the above mentioned background, the Gospel of Matthew, in particular, presents Christ as the One who has come to fulfill the prophecies of the Old Testament. It is believed that he did not come to abolish the religion of his time to establish a new one, but he intended to enrich it and set it on the path of true salvation, hence he preached and worshipped in the Temple and in the midst of his tribe's men and women. He was indeed loyal to the religious and cultural practices of his time. He understood his mission as purely salvific. That is why he criticized and condemned the religious style and practices of his time, especially the roles of the chief priests and Pharisees. It was indeed a 'patriarchal' domination, which was characterized by all kinds of imposition and maneuvering. He saw the people of his time as living under the 'yoke' of these religious leaders and lords. Their cultural and social life-styles were shaped by this religious attitude. Christ's interest however, was based on the establishment of a kingdom of justice, equality and truth, as means of bringing people to the *Kingdom of God.*

The above social, economic, political and religious backgrounds further conceptualize the grand idea or force behind the mission of Christ: A mission that was directed towards the underprivileged in the society who had records of high rates of infant and adult mortality as consequences of war, famine and disease, and periodic cases of infanticide.[216] A mission, which opposes the unjust structures of inequality, human exploitation and deprivation of basic human needs; a mission that was directed not only to temporal welfare of humanity, but also towards the eschatological partici-

215 Wilson, B., Ibid. p. 60.

216 van der Ven, J.A. et al, Ibid., p. 195.

pation in the Kingdom of God. This Kingdom is said to be a metaphor that refers to a particular kind of power and rule, or in a general sense, a pattern of life.[217] It is indeed a mission that is meant to establish this Kingdom in view of eliciting a peaceful co-existence and equality among peoples irrespective of race, religion and capabilities.

The nature of this Kingdom now opens up the model of the mission of Christ as smacking universal inclusiveness. Even though Christ championed the course of the downtrodden in the society and presented a Kingdom that signals their triumph and occupation of a privileged place, he nonetheless, was always open to the wealthy and powerful and expressed ardent concern for their participation in this Kingdom. His encounter with the rich young man is a typical example of this claim (cf. Matt. 19, 18-21). The young man was indeed a pious fellow, who observed the Torah to the latter, but Christ demanded that he goes an extra mile, by disposing his wealth to the poor and to join his ministry. The story stopped with the young man walking away sad, but did not tell us further what he eventually did. One can envisage that his quest for the Kingdom may have propelled him to do what Christ asked him to do irrespective of the difficulty. This supposition notwithstanding, my interest here is based on the deep concern Christ expressed about the young man and indeed about all who are metaphorically wealthy from the exegetical point of view. In this perspective, I tend towards those who are drawn back from the Kingdom not necessarily by their riches, but by other elements Christ considered as 'idols'. It is good also to remark that Christ used this encounter with the rich young man to give a lesson to his followers who may be considered not wealthy from the formal standard of richness.

On the basis of this universal inclusiveness, Christ opened up a mission of universal justice and love, which accommodates everyone by means of transcending 'ethnic conditioning (the rich alien), political correctness (tax collectors), social respectability (destitutes and prostitutes), and religious community (the Good Samaritan)'.[218] And this is a model of mission J.A. van der Ven, et al, call 'multipolar universality', due to its openness to the participation of all in this universality.

217 Ibid. p. 196.
218 Ibid., p. 210

It is on the above mentioned historical background and conceptualization that Christ established what could be called his mission of liberation – based on the principles of justice and peace. This mission was based on the 'Prophetic' tradition, which concerned him with repentance and salvation for all. This mission of liberation is considered an integral type, in the sense that it embraces all facets of life: spiritual, economic, cultural, social and political. He declared the liberative dimension of his ministry in the following words: "The Spirit of the Lord is upon me. He has appointed me to bring the good news to the poor, to proclaim liberty to captives and new sight to the blind; to free the oppressed and announce the Lord's year of mercy." (cf. Luke 4:16-19). Christ made this declaration while participating in the Sabbath services in the synagogue of his area, Galilee. The passage he read is from the Prophet, Isaiah 61:1-2, where the prophet was referring to his own mission: God had sent him to the Jews in exile to announce that soon God would visit them. Yet his words proved more appropriate in the case of Christ who claimed to be sent by the Father in order to bring real freedom to a people waiting for it. The phrase *to free the oppressed* is not found in Isaiah's text, but is believed that Luke takes it from another text of the same prophet (cf. Is. 58:61) and inserts it here because this expression 'to set free' summarizes better the very essence of Christ's mission.

This 'inaugural' speech of Christ's public ministry announces the reign of God's Kingdom, which is characterized by an introduction of a new era and new order of life in which God becomes present and reconciles people. Every fifty years Israel celebrated a jubilee year during which debts were forgiven and slaves recovered their freedom (cf. Leviticus 25:10). In the same way a *year of mercy from the Lord* is the beginning of liberation and freedom for humankind. It entails liberation and freedom "to the sick who are segregated on cultic and ritual grounds, to the prostitutes and *sinners* who are ostracized on moral grounds and to the tax-collectors who are excluded on religious and political grounds."[219] Christ brings real liberation to all peoples since his deeds urge people to live in truth: "the Son makes you free … the truth will make you free…" (cf. John 8:30).

As earlier mentioned, the Jews were actually looking first and foremost for political freedom, which is part of total human liberation. They eventually

219 Hahn, F., 1965:30, in: Bosch, D., Ibid. p. 27.

were disappointed with Christ's approach and conceptions (especially at his death on the cross), and felt that he was only interested in people's spiritual welfare. The Old Testament foretold that the Messiah would be the Savior of his people and of his race. Nonetheless, his words and deeds were stirring people who had become helpless and were opening the way for human liberation at all levels, but they were like seeds and could not produce immediate fruits. Christ had no intention of joining the fanatics and violent among his people in order to obtain political freedom. He rather witnessed to the truth and, one could say, laid the foundations for all future *liberation* movements. In this sense, Christ becomes the hope of the 'hopeless' and help of the 'helpless' of the society within both the religious and political circles, but not necessarily in the strict modern sense of the word. This notwithstanding, the New Testament presents Christ's work as one of liberation: "God in the fullness of time sent his Incarnate Son into the world to free men from every form of slavery to which they were subject by reason of sin and of human egoism, - from ignorance, destitution, hunger, oppression, hatred or injustice (cf. Galatians 4:4-5)".[220]

Christ's concern for justice and peace could be looked upon as the pseudo-political aspect of his ministry. Even though he seemed not to have talked about the *macrostructure* of his era, it is very clear that he decried the ills and injustices of his time in their respective fashions, and expressed ardent desire for change to a better situation. Declaring liberation for the less privileged, the oppressed and those discriminated against in the society: lepers, tax-collectors, the poor and sinners, was a sign that he calls for justice and peace on behalf of these needy and marginalized groups within the Jewish establishment of his time. This is the reason why the local authorities of his time, comprising of the chief priests and Pharisees, saw him as a threat to their hegemony, up to the point of accusing him before Pilate of disrupting law and order in the society. Bosch's description of the situation is succinct: "Jesus cannot seem politically dangerous to the establishment – and the authorities sense this, far more clearly, in fact, than Jesus' own followers do. In the end he is crucified because of what has been interpreted as his "political" claims."[221]

220 *Justitia et Pax,* No 56.
221 Bosch, D., Ibid. p. 34.

Christ's approach, as depicted above, gives an impression that he did not divorce the call for justice and peace from his mission. He expressed the close link between the evangelistic mission and the societal demands. The prophetic background of his mission played a significant role in this dimension. Irrespective of the latent persecution, he did not hesitate to introduce and establish a mission that was not to compromise the social injustices of the time.

The driving force behind Christ's concern for justice and peace is attributed to 'Love', which eventually was acclaimed to be the greatest and most powerful aspect of his ministry. It is from this backdrop that the duo aspects of his mandate to his disciples, *spiritual* and *social*, emanated. An explanation of these aspects has it that "the first refers to the commission to announce the good news of salvation through Jesus Christ; the second calls Christians to responsible participation in human society, including working for human well-being and justice."[222] Ottmar Fuchs calls our attention in this regard to the true significance of the miracles of Christ. An understanding of this mission on the surface level could be misleading. Hence the miracles of Christ "refer to his praxis of realizing the existence of need, of wanting to communicate with the suffering and to help them as much as possible and to show solidarity with them".[223] In this sense Fuchs opens up for us the *diaconical structure* of Christ's mission, which in essence is of an integral nature and ought to be understood in this direction.

This excursion into Christ's ministry leaves us with no doubt that these two aspects of his mission are and will remain inseparable as far as social justice, peace, which are embedded in the quest for liberation in the mission of the church today, are concerned.

3.2. THE MISSION OF THE CHURCH TODAY

Strictly speaking, it is from the post-resurrection 'Mandate' of Christ that the church's mission took its bearing: "I have been given all authority in heaven and on earth. Go therefore, and make disciples from all nations. Baptize them in the Name of the Father and of the Son and of the Holy

222 Bassham 1979:343, In: Bosch, D., Ibid. p. 403.

223 Ottmar, F., God's People: Instruments of Healing. Peter Lang, Berne, 1993. p. 48.

Spirit, and teach them to fulfill all that I have commanded you. I am with you always until the end of this world." (Matthew. 28:18-20). This mandate commissions the church as a primary agent of evangelization in the footsteps of the 'Master', Christ, hence making evangelization the essential duty of the church.[224] This mandate opens up for the church a liberative model of mission that takes care of material liberation and spiritual liberation of humankind. This aspect would be explicated on in a later part of this chapter.

Meanwhile, it is essential to remark here that evangelization should not just be understood in terms of its popular usage – persuading people to conversion, but most essentially to persuading people to contribute towards the establishment of God's Kingdom and its principles; a Kingdom, where people should be truly equal; a Kingdom of Justice and righteousness. It is the mind of Christ that people should have a foretaste of this Kingdom here on earth by establishing a situation of relative justice and peace, and the eventual eschatological participation in this Kingdom in its fullest sense. Genuine evangelization in this sense entails real liberation. The church can better respond positively to this mandate from this perspective.

The New Testament gives us a very close link between the incentive to mission and the gift of the life-giving spirit that comes from the Risen Lord. In the Gospel according John, it is expressed in the imagery of Christ on Easter Sunday giving the disciples a share in his mission: "As the Father has sent me, so I send you". He enlivens them for this by breathing the Spirit into them (John 20:21-22), just as God breathed into the nostrils of Adam and made him "a living being", according to the Genesis account of creation (Genesis. 2:7). The Acts of the Apostles relates that on the day of Pentecost, the Spirit takes hold of Christ's followers, vanquishes their fears, and sends them out to bear witness to him as "Lord and Christ"(Acts 2:36). They announce the dawning of the New Creation in their Risen Lord (cf. 2 Cor. 5:17-19). As with Christ, so with the church: the Spirit is the dynamic principle, the inner life of mission: "But you will receive power when the Holy Spirit comes upon you, and you will be my witnesses in Jerusalem, throughout Judea and Samaria, and to the ends of the earth" (Acts 1:8).

224 Paul VI, Evangelii Nuntiandi, Vatican City, 1975, no. 59.

The above excursus shows the church's understanding and definition of herself from its earliest days, as missionary by nature and characteristically Christological. Through various means – sacraments, prayers and social services etc., she carries the message to the far corners of the earth. Within the broad sweep of God's salvific mission for the world, the church has an important and irreplaceable role as sacrament and servant of the Reign of God. In acknowledging Christ as Lord , she is to make the mission program Christ announced in Nazareth her own. This program in question is about the all-embracing nature of evangelization, which Paul VI advocates for in the following words:

> In the mind of the Lord the Church is universal by vocation and mission, but when she puts down her roots in a variety of cultural, social and human terrains, she takes on different external expressions and appearances in each part of the world.[225]

In more concrete words, Paul VI goes further to consolidate his recommendation by saying that "Evangelization loses much of its force and effectiveness if it does not take into consideration the actual people to whom it is addressed, if it does not use their language, their signs and symbols, if it does not answer the questions they ask, and if it does not have an impact on their concrete life".[226]

In collaboration with these recommendations, John Paul II expresses that the church promotes love of God, love of neighbor and even love of enemies, when it works for human promotion, justice and peace, care for the sick, relief for sufferers.[227]

The above perspective forms a formidable basis for the church's mission of liberation. This church's mission of liberation is one of the types within the typology by Stephen Bevans and Roger Schroeder, namely: *commitment to liberation and transformation,* which is "a theological perspective that remains centred on the mystery of Christ while always acknowledg-

225 Ibid. no. 62.
226 Ibid. no. 63.
227 John Paul II, Redemptoris Missio, Vatican City, 1990, no. 20.

ing the importance and dignity of the human".[228] Suffice it to say that the first aspect of liberation is linked to the three material stages of liberation: liberation from social, cultural and economic problems. It is within this domain that the church's involvement in human rights issues is evoked. Human rights, as an aspect of social justice, and in its narrow sense, falls within the juridical area, and as such is seemingly diametrically opposed to the spiritual status of the church.

It is earlier mentioned that this diametrical tension between the two realms has provoked some agitating minds to contest the competence and justification of the church to meddle with such socio-political issues as social justice and precisely human rights, albeit its defense and promotion. Opinions are divergent on this point. Some people argue that socio-political sphere should not be the church's domain, while others opine that in virtue of her physical presence in the world, coupled with her vocation, the church cannot afford to close her eyes to the socio-political issues affecting humankind. This latter opinion collaborates with the Vatican II Council Document, *Gaudium et Spes.* To accomplish her evangelical mission for the salvation of mankind, the church has the right, as the Document instructs, "to pass moral judgment, even on matters touching the political order, whenever basic personal rights or the salvation of souls make such judgment necessary".[229] Affirming this stance, document of the 1971 Synod of Bishops clearly states:

> ...of itself it does not belong to the church, in so far as she is a religious and hierarchical community, to offer concrete solutions in the social, economic and political spheres for justice in the world. Her mission (nonetheless) involves defending and promoting the dignity and fundamental rights of the human person.[230]

The above stand of the church, in collaboration with *Gaudium et Spes,* no. 1, which was quoted much earlier, signals a new direction for the church's

---

228 Bevans, S.B., and Schroeder, R.P., Constants in Context. A Theology of Mission Today, Orbis Books, Maryknoll, New York, 2004, p. 63. Next to this type of ecclesiology, which is called "type C", the authors also elaborated on "type A", which is *mission as saving souls and extending the church* (p.36), and "type B", which is *mission as discovery of the faith* (p. 49).

229 GS. no. 76.

230 Document of 1971 Synod of Bishops, *Justice in the World,* AAS LXII (1971), 923-942. Vatican.in: *Justitia et Pax,* no. 44.

mission that involves transcending her traditional borders into the socio-political, economic, and cultural spheres. Even though the church's religious role seems not to have proper mission in the political, social or economic order, she does not consider religion as a private matter because religion and ethics are intrinsically connected (Matt. 25). The church has always attested to this fact: "Thus the church, at once a 'visible organization and a spiritual community', travels the same journey as all mankind and shares the same earthly lot with the world".[231] Meanwhile, "out of this religious and spiritual mission itself comes a function, a light and an energy which can serve to structure and consolidate the human community according to the divine law".[232] Schillebeckx's comment on the above numbers of *Gaudium et Spes,* supports this leap: "In realizing her own purely religious mission the church also performs a humanizing task".[233] In this task of humanization, the church accords humankind the place that is in consonance with its dignity, and impresses the society at large to follow suit. In order to strike a good balance in the church's involvement in worldly affairs, it becomes pertinent to note at this juncture, that the church should not involve herself into excessive intervention in the socio-political arena; neither must she withdraw herself there from. This means in essence that she must operate within the ambient of her mission of liberation as far as her means can afford.

This is where the consideration of human rights from a broad perspective fits in and offers the church the means of doing her liberative mission since this perspective accommodates all aspects of human life. By this means the church must be compelled to present herself to the varied needs of humankind in line with her mission, which strictly speaking has a more religious undertone, but cannot fail to consider humankind in its entirety. If the mission of the church for liberation could be presented in this manner, it then implies that it cannot but engulf the entire humanity and the society. Buhlman places an emphasis on this direction: "Salvation is not purely spiritual in character, but tends to embrace man in his immediate totality as well as in his social and cosmic relations".[234] Dragging this question into the context of social justice, Buhlman continued:

231 GS, no. 40.
232 GS, no. 42.
233 Schillebeeckx, E., The Mission of the Church, New York, 1973, p. 68.
234 Buhlman, W., The Coming of the Third Church, Orbis Books, St. Paul Publications, New York, 1976, p.91.

> Sin is no longer considered predominantly an affair of the individual, but is seen as incarnate in structures and in political and social justice. Consequently salvation in the fullest sense implies also redemption from these injustices; and transformation of the structures towards a better world in the way indicated in the gospel.[235]

This articulation of Buhlman opens up the second aspect of liberation, which has to do strictly with religious dimension of liberation: liberation from sin, from the spiritual and sacramental perspectives. Another dimension of this aspect also opens up a collective dimension of sin, which indicates the participation of individuals therein that invariably results to individual sin. This dimension would be explained further in the next section, especially with regard to the relation of liberation from sin to other aspects of liberation.

The above views offer us the forum to place the mission of the church for liberation, in its global sense, also as the promotion of social justice as a means of defending and safeguarding the dignity of the human person and his/her inviolable and inalienable rights.

3.2.1. The Church's Mission as Liberation-oriented

The above demands from the church indicate that the transition from the popular understanding of evangelization to actual liberation in the mission of the church is a very vital process. This process entails preaching the good news and listening to the social demands of humankind: liberation and freedom from oppression, poverty and social consequences of sin; humanizing the world as much as possible through integral development, constant dialogue, justice and peace, promotion and protection of human rights in general. The duo aspects of the church's mission – eschatological and temporal - are embodied here, taking care of the spiritual and material demands of humanity both individually and collectively. She must, as a matter of fact, permeate into the political, social, economic and cultural spheres of human history in order to bring about this mission in the foot steps of its 'Master'. Lochman beautifully articulates in the following words:

235 Ibid.

> Now, as then, it should make all the difference to society if there is within it a group of human beings who, focusing their minds on the reality of God's reign and praying for its coming, advocate the cause of the poor, serve those on the periphery, raise up the oppressed and broken and, above all, "proclaim the year of the Lord's favor".[236]

The liberative mission of the church, as linked to the mission of Christ, is primarily directed towards liberating humankind from sin, thereby offering us a "more balanced perspective on humanity's nature as both radically sinful and yet fundamentally good".[237] Nonetheless, it must be noted that this perspective should not just be considered from the spiritual aspect only. One also ought to see it from the political, economic, social and cultural aspects. This is so because the separation of the spiritual aspect from the other aspects is simply utopic. If one, for example, is hungry and is denied the means of satisfying his/ her hunger out of no just cause, one of the tendencies will be to steal. In the strict Christian understanding, stealing is basically sinful. So to help the fellow to avoid stealing, the root cause(s) of his/her hunger must be addressed. In the words of Leonardo Boff, the Kingdom of God "is not merely the annihilation of sin; it is also the annihilation of all that sin means: pain, death, blindness, and hunger".[238] Ordinarily speaking, liberation smacks of oppression, servitude and bondage, hence the distinctive character of the Christian liberation stems from the fact that it entails *liberation from* something and *liberation for* something; in other words, liberation *from* injustice and oppression and liberation *for* liberty and love. This view of the Christian liberation forms the two signs of the credibility and legitimation of the church's mission of liberation.

On this note, Boff remarks that there is a spirituality that underlines the theology of liberation: the encounter of the poor with the Lord.[239] The "poor" in this sense are understood as the oppressed and marginalized/ exploited persons in the society. This gives us the idea that the theology of liberation is developed from the reality of misery, which takes various forms: springing from liberation from slavery of sin – personal faults and their inner consequences for the individual, to liberation from objective

---

236 Lochman, J.M., 1986:67, in: Bosch, D., Ibid., p. 34.

237 Bevans, S.B., and Schroeder, R.P., Ibid. p. 62.

238 Boff, L., Jesus Christ Liberator: A Critical Christology for our time, Trans: Patrick Hughes, Maryknoll, Orbis Books, 1978, p. 53.

239 Boff, L., and Boff, C., Salvation and Liberation, Maryknoll, Orbis Books, 1985, p. 2.

forms of oppression that stem from the sins of human beings: sickness, premature death, poverty, devastation, most often coming from those who possess power and hence exploit and oppress the poor unjustly. Continuing, Boff states that "the principal interest of liberation theology is to generate activity on the part of the church that will aid the poor *efficaciously.* Everything must converge toward practice (love)".[240]

The motivation behind this remark is that Boff, in a way, presents the church as tending to be the church *of* the rich *for* the poor. In this sense, he means that the church plays a paternalistic role by assisting the poor with resources of the rich. It has been observed that this did not yield adequate fruit for positive change. The church in her mission of liberation is to place herself at equal service of both the rich and the poor in order to utilize the resources of both classes in instituting a balanced process of change. This articulation evokes the need to institute the triangular shape of the church: the church *for* the poor, the church *with* the poor, and the church *of* the poor. Boff has already given us a clue to how the church can be *of* the poor and *for* the poor. To complete this triangular shape, the church ought also to assume her position as the church *with* the poor by identifying with the cause of the poor and being in solidarity with them.[241] In order to settle the seeming tension between the three sides of this triangle, it is suggested that the image of the church *for* the poor has to be an ethical task of the church; the image of the church *of* the poor implies an ecclesiological approach to the church itself; and the image of the church *with* the poor implies the church's engagement with the poor .[242] Over and above all, the efficacy of Christian love must be made manifest here, which means a better understanding of human reality; for example, "to understand better the mechanisms that produce poverty, and the avenues that can lead its victims away from it".[243] In this way, the potentials embedded in the poor must be given equal consideration with the resources of the rich.

This expresses the Christological aspect of the church's mission of liberation: directed to all – the oppressors and the oppressed. It is aimed at liberating human beings from everything that diminishes them and offends God and humankind. Collaborating with this structure of liberation, the

240 Ibid. p.4.
241 van der Ven, J.A., Ecclesiology in Context, Cambridge, U.K., 1996, p. 514.
242 Ibid. pp. 514 - 515.
243 Boff, L., and Boff, C., Ibid. p.5.

Sacred Congregation for the Doctrine of the Faith remarked that liberation is first and foremost liberation from radical slavery to sin. As a logical consequence, it calls for freedom from many different kinds of slavery in the cultural, economic, social and political spheres, all of which derive ultimately from sin.[244]

To bring about what liberation proposes, Boff employs three mediations[245]: (a) *the Socio-analytical mediation*, which involves radical analysis and criticism of a given situation. This radical analysis and criticism is aimed towards a new form of organization for the whole of society.[246] In other words, it is a type of reading and analyzing social reality of human beings such as suffering and marginalization; (b) *the hermeneutical mediation*, which calls for an interpretation of the situation that should be balanced by faith and reason. This mediation goes to verify the presence or absence of God in such human realities in order to offer a response to God's salvific design or its rejection. For example, where social analysis says "structural poverty", faith will say "structural sin"[247]; and (c) *the pastoral mediation*, which translates into concrete action what has been seen and assessed or judged. This involves action flowing from the functions of the former two mediations. The general rule guiding this mediation is to do what objective conditions of reality permits and not the other way round. Pastoral prudence comes in here, not as a matter of intimidation, but of exercising wisdom with respect to what is feasible and viable.[248]

It is in the above capacities that the church has the duty of acting as agent of liberation if she must carry out well her salvific mission. Boff maintains that "liberation is never merely a matter of intention, aspiration. It is the fruit of a process, in which all must participate; it is not the result of a single stroke of the will".[249] It is interesting to relate the *process* he talks about here as a process that also means *salvation*. Salvation is a process that is to be realized in this process. Affirming the similarity between salvation and

244 Sacred Congregation for the Doctrine of the Faith: Instruction on Christian Freedom and Liberation, Boston: Daughters of St. Paul Publications, 1986, nos. 37-39.

245 I will not go into details about the three mediations of Boff for doing theology of liberation. Further reading could be done In: Boff, L., and Boff, C., Ibid. pp. 5- 12.

246 Ibid. p.8.

247 Ibid. p.9.

248 Ibid. p.11.

249 Ibid. p.12.

liberation, Ignacio Ellacuria remarked that it enhances Christian liberation the chance of evading two dangerous tendencies: the tendency to view liberation as a purely immanent process, and the tendency to view liberation as a purely transcendental process.[250] Boff's comment on this relationship is that the two are without division and also without separation. He also affirms that the two should also be understood without confusion and without any change of one into the other.[251]

Flowing from this reflection, the church's aim towards liberation could to be done in the light of the three *mediations* of Boff, as very essential for this task. As long as the church claims the evangelizing task, she ought to constantly be engaged in the critical and radical analysis and interpretation of the situation of things in the world in order to give adequate and relevant pastoral attention to them.

This brings us further to the integral nature of Christian liberation. From the Christian perspective, liberation is pre-eminently religious; but because it is integral it includes socio-economic and cultural dimensions as well. Its integral nature manifests both the eschatological and temporal dimensions. "Christ's mission of liberation for our salvation is ultimately directed towards our eschatological salvation since eschatological salvation comes by a way of historical liberations".[252] This process continues and imbues the church to demonstrate to the world that her evangelizing task is operative through her works in history; deeds, words and actions, as indispensable in the process of liberation. On the basis of Christological liberation, the church continues to signify the presence of Christ in the world and in history. Nevertheless, "the church will be authentic if she consistently follows the way of her Master, who could be astonished at the faith of people whom others in his culture counted as unreligious and unworthy of notice".[253]

Because mission is the work of the Triune God, and the Spirit blows where it wills, the church carries out her service to the Kingdom in collaboration with other faith communities, all people of good will and with adequate methods/ means proper to it. The metaphors Christ used to describe how

250 Ellacuria, I., Freedom Made Flesh, Maryknoll, Orbis Books, 1976, p.104.
251 Boff, L., and Boff, C., Ibid. p.60.
252 Ibid.
253 Bevans, S.B., and Schroeder, R.P., Ibid. p. 385.

his followers were to relate to the world, calls to mind here: salt, light and leaven. Can the church salten, lighten and leaven the world by means of human rights promotion and protection?

3.3. HUMAN RIGHTS: AN ELABORATION OF THE CHURCH'S MISSION OF LIBERATION

In reaching out to the world to promote greater communion, the church is aware that the Reign of God is a reality more extensive than itself.[254] She rejoices that God's saving presence has been, and continues to be present in history, cultures and religions of all peoples.[255] In the same vein, the church ought to recall that though Christ inaugurated this mission of God's Reign, he did not consummate it. "As we pray "your kingdom come!" we also commit ourselves to initiate, here and now, approximations and anticipations of God's reign. Once again: God's reign *will* come, since it has *already* come. It is bestowal and challenge, gift and promise, present and future, celebration and anticipation".[256] By this 'anticipation', the church realizes herself as still existing and operating in an imperfect world where "injustice has not yet vanished, oppression had not yet been eliminated, poverty, hunger, even persecution were still very much the order of the day".[257]

If the church must remain truthful to her mission of liberation, which entails liberation of humankind from the exigencies of the modern era, she must also employ modern programme in carrying out this task. One of the evocative and effective theories of the modern era for this liberation is development of Human Rights culture and attitudes. (An elaboration on human rights attitudes and human rights culture would be made in later chapters). Since the Universal Declaration of Human Rights in 1948, humankind has been enormously made to be conscious of its roles towards its preservation, promotion and protection. The church is at the same time called upon as an institution that exists within the framework of the so-

---

254 Vatican II Council Document: *Lumen Gentium*, no. 5.

255 John Paul II, Ibid. nos 28 and 29.

256 Boff, 1983:16, In: Bosch, D., Ibid. p. 37.

257 Ibid. p.49.

cial, political, economic and cultural contexts of the modern era, to be part of this task, especially in the light of the ills caused by some major world-changing events.

Over the years, the church has officially and outwardly legitimated her involvements in human rights question by means of some *magisterial* documents.

3.3.1. Legitimation of the Church's Involvement in Human Rights Question

The programme one can claim the church used and is still using to legitimate her engagement in human rights issues is legitimized by the authoritative documents, which bear the church's social teachings and doctrines. The major ones are some of the Encyclicals and Apostolic Letters of her Pontiffs, and the Vatican II Council Documents. These documents go a long way to present the church's teaching and doctrines on social issues. In the words of John Paul II:

> …with respect to this teaching, the church has a mission to carry out; she must preach, educate individuals and collectivities, form public opinion, and offer orientations to the leaders of the peoples. In this way she will be working in favor of society, within which this Christian and evangelical principal will finally bear the fruit of a more just and equitable distribution of good, not only within each nation, but also in the world in general.[258]

He affirmed further by saying: "Christ did not remain indifferent in the face of this vast and demanding imperative of social morality, nor could the church".[259]

This is a re-affirmation of the foundation of the mission of the church on the mission of Christ, especially as it relates to liberation. Nevertheless, it is pertinent to remark that this "teaching" is not meant to be a fixed type. It is said to be *dynamic* and *innovative:*

---

258 cf. Address at the opening of the III General Conference of the Latin American Episcopate, 28 January, 1979, in: Heckel, R., Social Teaching of John Paul II (Pontifical Commission *Justitia et Pax*), Vatican, 1980, p. 28.
259 Ibid.

> The inexhaustible richness of the Gospel and the constant reality of changing situations means that the social teaching of the church is a *dynamic* and *innovative* reality, not to be identified with any standard, but which represents at the very heart of all systems as active criteria for *discernment* and *renewal* and a *guarantee for the authenticity of Christian commitment.*[260]

Without any doubt, these teachings are essentially moral-oriented and are directed towards transforming unjust situations and structures in a design to "liberate and form the constituent facets of the human conscience, and train men and women to be good citizens".[261]

The general expression of these documents is seen in their vehement opposition to the social injustices that are perpetrated all over the world. In the first instance the Papal encyclicals and apostolic letters adopted very strong themes and theories that decry the ills of the times as warranted by the trends of each epoch, while the Vatican II Council Documents corroborated what the papal documents upheld and even goes further to expose the church to a more critical involvement in the quest for social justice in the modern world.

The Pontifical Commission *Justitia et Pax* (1974) is considered a mirror through which the church analyzed herself on issues of human rights and encouraged herself to a self-examination. It is this Commission that also analyzed these magisterial documents in the process and gave reasons why human rights should be an instrument for the church's mission of liberation. These documents would be presented in three parts: pre-Vatican II Council official publications, Conciliar and Post Conciliar Documents, and post-Vatican II Council official publications.

3.3.1.1. Pre-Vatican II Council Official Publications and Human Rights

Papal Encyclicals and Apostolic Letters

Some of the encyclicals and apostolic letters of Popes over the years have also proved the church's supposed adoption of human rights as a way of doing her mission of liberation.

---

260 Ibid. p. 25.

261 Ibid.

Pope Leo XIII is known in this direction with his *Immortale Dei* (November 1, 1885), on the Christian constitution of States – presenting the church's role as a source of prosperity in both spiritual and earthly welfare of humankind; and *Rerum Novarum* (May 15, 1891), on Capital and Labor – precisely the condition of working classes, searching for remedy for the misery and wretchedness pressing so unjustly on the majority of the working class. *Rerum Novarum* ushers in a new beginning in the church's concerns for social questions: "Gratifying itself into a tradition hundred years of old, it signals a new beginning and a singular development of the church's teaching in the area of social matters".[262] This Encyclical addressed the Labour question and in unequivocal terms examines the condition and rights of workers. It lists abnormalities that give rise to social ills in the society by way of denouncing socialism as a solution and precisely expounds in clear words:

> the Catholic doctrine on work, the right to property, the principle of collaboration instead of class struggle as the fundamental means for social change, the rights of the weak, the dignity of the poor and the obligations of the rich, the perfecting of justice through charity, on the right to form professional associations.[263]

The entire church's social doctrine is said to "be seen as an updating, a deeper analysis and an expansion of the original nucleus of principles presented in *Rerum Novarum"*.[264]

Pope Pius XI is famous for his *Quadragesimo Anno* (May 15, 1931), on reconstruction of the social order – written in full support of *Rerum Novarum* of Leo XIII, for the church's effort to guide humanity to not only fleeting and perishable happiness, but to that which is eternal. This Encyclical was published in commemoration of the 40th anniversary of *Rerum Novarum,* as a result of the grave economic crisis of 1929. "The Encyclical warns about failure to respect the freedom to form associations and stresses the principles of solidarity and cooperation in order to overcome social contradictions. The relationship between capital and labour must

---

262 Cf. The Catechism of the Catholic Church, Pauline Pub., 2421.

263 Cf. Congregation for Catholic Education, *Guidelines fo the Study and Teaching of the* Church's *Social Doctrine in the Formation of Priests,* 20, Vatican Polyglot Press, Rome 1988, p.24.

264 Compendium of the Social Doctrine of t he Church, *Compendium of the Social Doctrine of the Church,* Paulines Publications, Africa, 2005, p.51

be characterized by cooperation".[265] Pius XI upholds the Family in this Encyclical by confirming the criteria of paying salaries not only according to the needs of the worker but also to those of his family. The principle of *Subsidiarity,* which eventually became an integral element of the church's social teaching, was strongly proposed in the Encyclical. In a disorganized society, "Pius XI felt the duty and the responsibility to promote a greater awareness, a more precise interpretation and an urgent application of the moral law governing human relations… with the intent of overcoming the conflict between classes and arriving at a new social order based on justice and charity".[266] At the rise of totalitarian regimes in Europe especially the Hitler regime, Pius XI did not hesitate in raising his voice in condemnation of their totalitarian practices, which abused the rights of the populace. He did not favour discrimination by means of his condemnation of anti-semitism.

Pope Pius XII is distinguished by his Messages and Christmas Broadcasts of 1941 and 1942. He pontificated during the terrible years of the Second World War and the difficult years of reconstruction. Through his *Radio Messages,* he identified with the international Order, which had been badly shaken:

> During the war and the post-war period, for many people of all continents and for millions of believers and nonbelievers, the social teaching of Pope Pius XII represented the voice of universal conscience…. With his moral authority and prestige, Pope Pius XII brought the light of Christian wisdom to countless men of every category and social level.[267]

It is further stated that "due to his sensitivity and intelligence in grasping the 'signs of the times', Pope Pius XII can be considered the immediate precursor of Vatican Council II and of the social teaching of the Popes who followed him".[268]

Pope John XXIII was influential with his *Mater et Magistra* (May 15, 1961), on the Church as mother and teacher of humanity – representing the church's two-fold task of giving life to her children and of teaching them and guiding them in life's exigencies such as livelihood, education,

---

265 Cf. Pius XI, Encyclical Letter *Quadragesimo Anno: AAS* (1931), 186-189.

266 Cf. Congregation for Catholic Education, Ibid., p.52

267 Ibid., p.53

268 Ibid., pp.53-54

and general temporal welfare and prosperity. In this Encyclical he "aims at up-dating the already known documents, and at taking a further step forward in the process of involving the whole Christian community".[269] By dwelling on the words, *community* and *socialization*, he called for the church's involvement in the development of humankind in an *authentic communion and dignity* with each other.

In his *Pacem in Terris* (April 11, 1963), on establishing universal peace in truth, justice, charity and liberty – Pope John XXIII clamoured for peace on earth, which every era yearns for. This Encyclical came up in an era of nuclear proliferation. It is said to contain "one of the first in-debt reflections on rights on the part of the Church; it is the Encyclical of peace and human dignity".[270] It is on record that through the *Pacem in Terris*, Pope John XXIII applauded the United Nations for its promulgation of the Universal Declaration on Human Rights[271], thus becoming the first to give such applause.

3.3.1.2 Conciliar and Post Conciliar Documents and Human Rights

It is necessary to first of all note that it was during the 19th century that the magisterium gradually assimilated the theme of human rights, while contemplating the "new freedoms enshrined in the constitutions of modern states, and inspired by the lofty ideals of the French Revolution".[272] Following this trend, the church officially identified with human rights ideals in its classical documents, *The Vatican II Council*. These are explicitly manifested in the "Pastoral Constitution on the Church in the Modern World" *(Gaudium et Spes)*, and the "Declaration on Religious Liberty" *(Dignitatis Humanae)*.

The "Pastoral Constitution on the Church in the Modern World" ***Gaudium et Spes,*** is very much lauded for its anthropological concern. It posits the humankind as its central thrust. It also acclaims the profound vocation of the dignity of humankind and its fundamental rights. Based on the argument of the equality of all men[273], this document solidly affirms that

269 Ibid., p.54

270 Compendium of t he Social Doctrine of t he Church, Ibid., p. 54

271 In: Heckel, R., Ibid., p. 13.

272 *Justitia et Pax*, no. 19.

273 G.S. no 29.

humankind has rights, which are inviolable, universal and inalienable. It hence advocates that with respect to such fundamental rights, every kind of discrimination must be overcome and eradicated as contrary to God's intent.[274] In more unequivocal terms, this document expresses the church's openness to dialogue with the human family in order to address her different problems. The supposed problems of humankind exposes the anguish humanity is plunged into and in the light of this reality this document opened the church to the signs of the times and the need to effect changes in the social order. It explicitly addressed issues of inequalities, on the social, political, economic and cultural levels, in view of bridging the widening gap of the role of the common good of peoples.

In the cultural arena, among other issues, this document expresses the church's recognition of the uniqueness of every culture and approval of peoples' right to their cultures and their implementation. And on this note too this document also expresses the church's readiness to also engage in exchange of values from the world, especially by profiting in the history and development of humankind. In more practical terms, the document vehemently condemns whatever is vigorously opposed to life itself, (both individuals and groups) such as murder, willful self-destruction, genocide, euthanasia, abortion, contraception, and sterilization. The document also condemns whatever violates the integrity of the human person such as mutilation, corporal or mental torture, attempts to coerce the will itself. It also condemns whatever offends human dignity like subhuman living conditions, arbitrary arrests and imprisonment, deportation, slavery, prostitution, the trafficking of women and children, and disgraceful working conditions.[275] A greater emphasis is laid on the fact that human promotion can only be realized through the strong and definite affirmation of fundamental human rights within a civil community, which is organized both judicially and politically.[276]

One can conclude that this document is a clear proof that throughout the universal church, concern with the nature of man, his dignity and his role in the world and in contemporary history has reached a new depth; and new maturity.[277]

---

274 Ibid.
275 Ibid., nos 27, 47, 51, 14.
276 *Iustitia et Pax*, no. 26.
277 *Iustitia et Pax, no. 26.*

Dignitatis Humanae is pastorally motivated and doctrinal in content. Its doctrinal tenets comprise of the ethical doctrine of religious liberty as a human right (personal or collective), political doctrine of religious liberty (concerning functions of government in matters of religion), and the theological doctrine of the freedom of the church as a fundamental principle in what concerns the relations between the church and the socio-political order. This document makes a profound contribution to the development of the church's consistent teaching on human rights, by admitting that "in dealing with this question of liberty, the sacred Council intends to develop the teaching of recent popes on the inviolable rights of the human person and on the constitutional order of society".[278] Precisely the freedom meant here refers to Immunity "from coercion on the part of the individuals, social groups, and every human power so that, within due limits, no body is forced to act against his convictions in religious matters in private or public, alone or in association with others".[279] The Council further emphasized: "This right of the human person to religious freedom must be given such recognition in the constitutional order of the society as will make it a civil right".[280] In this sense, this section is in concrete affirmation of human rights as part of the general order in human society.

One can rightly admit that these documents are clear proofs of great challenge to the church in particular and the world in general, to be concerned with the nature of humankind; its dignity and its freedom.

3.3.1.3 Post-Vatican II Council Official Publications and Human Rights

Other Papal Encyclicals that touched on human rights issues came after the Vatican II Council. One could imagine that they must have been also influenced by the spirit of Vatican II Council. Three prominent figures in this era include Popes Paul VI, John Paul II, and in these latter days Benedict XVI.

Pope Paul VI is known for his *Populorum Progressio* (March 26, 1967), on development of peoples – especially peoples striving to escape from

278 Vatican Council II: *Dignatitis Humanae,* no. 1.
279 Ibid. no. 2.
280 Ibid.

hunger, misery, endemic diseases, ignorance and striving for empowerment of human qualities and complete fulfillment. In this Encyclical, he solemnly proclaims that *Development is the new name for peace*, thereby pointing his major concern towards an integral development of humankind in cooperation with each other. A *transition* he called for "is not limited to merely economic or technological dimensions, but implies for each person the acquisition of culture, the respect of the dignity of others, the acknowledgement of "the highest good, the recognition of God himself, the author and the end of these blessings"".[281] In this same vein, Paul VI, in 1967, instituted the Pontifical Commission *"Iustitia et Pax"* (which has been quoted extensively here). By so doing he fulfilled the wishes of the Council Fathers for establishing an organism of the church for the promotion of God's Justice and Love in the world.[282]

Pope Paul VI's *Octogessima Adveniente* (May 14, 1971), came as a call for action at a time of ideological controversy (the 80th Anniversary of *Rerum Novarum)* – calling for a continued inspiration of action for social justice in response to the changing world. This Encyclical is said to be an update of Pope Leo XIII's *Rerum Novarum:*

> The Pope reflects on post-industrial society with all of its complex problems, noting the inadequacy of ideologies in responding to these challenges: urbanization, the condition of young people, the condition of women, unemployment, discrimination, emigration, population growth, the influence of the means of social communications, the ecological problem.[283]

Pope John Paul II is popular for his numerous struggles in favour of human rights promotion and protection, as depicted in most of his encyclicals, apostolic letters, messages and tours around the countries of the world. The inaugural encyclical of John Paul II *Redemptoris Hominis* reveals his extraordinary and permanent concern for the human person. In this encyclical, he sees the idea of the human person as "the primary and fundamental way for the church".[284] He defined the human person in the context of openness to God: "The human dignity is rooted in being created *in the image and likeness of God* and in being redeemed by Jesus Christ

281 Compendium of the Social Doctrine of the Church, Ibid. P. 57.
282 Ibid.
283 Ibid.
284 Heckel, R., Ibid. p. 5.

who, in a certain way united himself with each man".[285] The dignity of the human person thus became the basis for his concern for human rights promotion and protection.

This special aspect of his works is an important indicator towards the church's understanding of the equality of men and women, and should propel her to propagate this fact in the light of human rights demands. A summary of these demands is mentioned in a part of John Paul II's homily at St. Gregory the Great Parish, Magliana, Rome on 18 February, 1979 states:

> This gives rise to the practical urgency, the permanent and fundamental necessity to strengthen the human person from within.... If within man there is good – a sense of justice, love, ...a wholesome desire for dignity – then good radiates outside, is stamped on families, environments and institutions.[286]

This is simply a call for a positive formation of human rights culture as an essential task of the church.

Worthy of note also are his *Laborem Exercens* (September 14, 1981) on Workers' rights, and *Mulieris Dignitatem* (August 15, 1988), on the dignity of women. His *Laborem Exercens,* which came ninety years after *Rerum Novarum*, dwelt heavily on the rights of workers, especially in the relationship between employers and employees. It elaborates spiritual and ethical guidelines for work, which are deeply rooted in human dignity:

> Work must not be understood only in the objective and material sense, but one must keep in mind its subjective dimension, insofar as it is always an expression of the person. Besides being a decisive paradigm for social life, work has all the dignity of being a context in which the person's natural and supernatural vocation must find fulfillment.[287]

In his *Mulieris Dignitatem,* John Paul II expressed his special interest for the welfare and rights of women. He expressly elevated the dignity of women and their special vocation, especially with regard to the salvation history of humankind. This forms a special particularism in this dimen-

285 Ibid.
286 Ibid. p. 19.
287 Compendium of the Social Doctrine of the Church. Ibid., p.58

sion, among other encyclicals. It forms a formidable background for the concerns of women from the ecclesiastical point of view. No other Pope has given this type of particularism to the women question as he did, and that makes him outstanding in the area of the promotion and protection of women's rights. Hence he challenges the church towards an integral consideration of the role of women within and outside the church.

Pope Benedict XVI, by following the church's *Mission of truth*, toed the footsteps of his predecessors, especially Pope Paul VI (*Populorum Progressio*) and Pope John Paul II (*Solicitudo Rei Socialis*), in addressing the consequences of imperial globalization, which resulted in the 2008 global economic melt down. His recent Encyclical *Caritas in Veritate* (July 2009) vehemently condemned the current economic crisis that holds the whole world, especially the poor nations, in ransom. As a major solution to the crisis, he called for a authentic global solidarity, which points to John Paul II's principle of *Opus Solidaritatis pax* (peace in the fruit of solidarity). Addressing the solidarity question Benedict XVI strongly opined that the human person (as a primary capital) should be at the centre of all the economic and social discussion and endeavours,[288] thus projecting the all important dignity of the human person.

On further analysis of this urgent call to solidarity Benedict XVI cited the extreme dangers of insecurity peoples' lives in many poor countries are exposed to, especially as it regards shortage of food and water. He therefore pointed out that the human rights to food and water "has an important place within the pursuit of other rights, beginning with the fundamental right to life".[289] It is on this basis that the Pope calls for respect for life.

Benedict XVI also addressed the question of religious freedom[290] by condemning the misuse of religion, which in most cases result into the abuse of the right to freedom of belief and worship.

---

288 Benedict XVI, Charity in Truth (Caritas in Veritate), Encyclical Letter to the Bishops, Priests and Deacons, men and women Religious, the lay Faithful and all people of Goodwill on Integral development in Charity and Truth. Published in Washington by the USA Conference of Catholic Bishops, July 2009, No. 25, p. 25.

289 Ibid., No. 27, p. 27.

290 Ibid., No. 29, p. 28.

In the fourth chapter of *Caritas Veritate*, Benedict XVI reflected extensively on the close bond that binds *rights* and *duties* closely to each other. He goes to establish that rights *presuppose duties*:

> Duties thereby reinforce rights and call for their defence and promotion as a task to be undertaken in the service of the common good. Otherwise, if the only basis of human rights is to be found in the deliberations of an assembly of citizens, those rights can be changed at any time, and so the duty to respect and pursue them fades from the common consciousness.[291]

On the basis of solidarity, the Pope calls the humankind to the *duty* of promoting human rights.

Among other ethical norms on this basis of solidarity, the Pope passionately called for a global protection of and care for the environment: "The environment is God's gift to everyone, and in our use of it we have a responsibility towards the poor, towards future generations and towards humanity as a whole".[292] From the above discussion it becomes very clear that for Benedict XVI the human person occupies a central position in the world's duties towards every endeavour in promoting and protecting human rights.

These Pontiffs of the church by means of their encyclicals, letters, messages and activities, vehemently denounced all forms of human rights violations, and gallantly defended the cultural, political, social and economic rights of humankind and suggested workable schemes for the total reconstruction of the human community.

In the ***The New Code of Canon Law*** the church also identified with human rights question as a fundamental aspect of human dignity in both the 1917 Code and the new code. But it is exclusive only to obligations and rights of the Christian faithful of the Catholic Church. This Code however imposes on the church the obligation of defending and promoting human rights.[293]

---

291 Ibid., No. 43, p. 48.
292 Ibid. No. 48, p. 54.
293 Canon 221.

3.4 THE CHURCH'S MISSION OF DIALOGUE

Addressing the various aspects of the Church's mission would not be complete without also pointing to the Mission of Dialogue as fundamental aspect of Christ's mission. Christ introduced his mission in a form of Dialogue. At the age of twelve, his parents found him, after a long search, dialoguing with and answering questions from the elders (Lk. 4:45-50). Dialogue characterized the corpus of Christ's mission to the peoples. He entered into a dialogue even with Satan after his baptism (Mt. 4:3-10). Some elements of dialogue is also observed in the selection of his disciples: some objected to his call based on some reasons, while he objected to others following him. At the wedding in Cana he had a dialogue with his mother, which led to the miracle of Cana (Jn. 2:1). On several occasions he dialogued with the Pharisees and Scribes on matters of faith, custom and ritual practices (Lk. 7:36ff; 13:10ff; Matt. 9:1ff; Jn. 6:28ff; Jn. 8:1-11). Most of his healing and exorcism events are accompanied by dialogues (and in some cases with the unclean spirits that possessed persons) (e.g. in Matt. 8:1ff; 8:5ff; 8:28; 12:9ff; Mk. 1:23ff; 8:22ff). Personal conversations Jesus had with some biblical figures are characterized by dialogue: with Nicodemus (Jn. 3:1); with the Samaritan woman (Jn. 4:1); with the rich young man (Matt. 19:16); with Zacheus (Lk. 19:1); with Pilate (Jn. 18:28ff). As a gesture of respect for the law and custom of the land Jesus had a dialogue with Peter regarding the Temple Tax (Mtt. 17:24). The whole of Jesus ministry and teachings are dotted with various styles of dialogue and as such automatically presupposes its importance in the mission of the church today.

The plurality of testimonies and truth claims causes deep tensions between religions and peoples of diverse beliefs and opinions. It was not different in the time of Christ. He too confronted the tensions that originated from his own proclamation of the *new teachings*. This phenomenon at the same time challenges humanity to find ways and possible structures which enhances a possible peaceful co-existence in dignity and mutual respect. A realistic tool for realizing the goals of this challenge is *dialogue*.

Following the example of her master dialogue becomes an important element of the Church's mission. Special emphasis on dialogue is given in the very important document of the Church – the Vatican II Council document. In the Constitutions *Gaudium et Spes* and *Lumen Gentium* and the

Declaration *Nostra Aetate*, the Church emphasizes the importance of dialogue as a method in her theology and practice. In the declarations of *Nostra Aetate* the Church ushers in a very accommodating language of making herself available in conjunction with peoples of other beliefs and cultures to address the common problems of humankind. Hence disposing herself to the ideas and views of others in such matters:

> The Catholic Church rejects nothing of what is true and holy in these religions. She has a high regard for the manner of life and conduct, the precepts and doctrine which, although differing in many ways from her own teaching, nevertheless, often reflect a ray of that truth which enlightens all men.[294]

The bane of attention here is the common good: promoting peace, liberty, social justice and moral values[295] via dialogue. It took the Church, however, several years to come to this stage of maturity.

Borrowing the description of the Vatican II Council Document Guidelines on *Religious Relations with the Jews*, dialogue in a context of religious pluralism "presupposes that each side wishes to know the other, and wishes to increase and deepen its knowledge of the other. It constitutes a particularly suitable means of favouring a better mutual knowledge and … of probing the riches of one's own tradition. Dialogue demands respect for the other as he is; above all, respect for his faith and his religious convictions".[296] The emphasis here is on mutual understanding and enrichment in total witness to truth and respect for freedom.

Several reasons are responsible for the call to dialogue. The core factor that motivates and, one could also say, constrains the Church to engage in dialogue with peoples of other beliefs is the urgent need for unity of the human family in the biological and theological perspectives (which forms the basic concept of Christ's mission). This need is underlined by the final goal of humankind in this present life and the hereafter. Dialogue in this sense is seen as "a means of collaboration in the salvific action of God

294 *Nostra Aetate* (Declaration on the Relation oft he Church to non-Christian Religions), No. 2, Vatican II Council Document, St. Paul's Edition, 2001, p. 654
295 Ibid. No. 3
296 Ibid., Guidelines on Religious Relations with the Jews (N.4). p. 658

for persons and human communities in their pilgrimage through life".[297] Bringing in Charity and Christ into the question of dialogue Zago Marcello went on to write: "Dialogue is an expression of charity towards all human beings. Charity is sharing in the Trinitarian love; it is a fundamental command of Christ and as such it is the driving force of mission".[298] In this spirit of charity, respecting, challenging, confronting and collaborating with one another form good basis for a successful dialogue among peoples. The *diaconical* dimension of Ottmar Fuchs could still be connected to this aspect. That means dialogue in this connection is meant to have a diaconical function since "diaconia are not only the immediate giving of help and the reduction or removal of suffering, but at the same time the search for the political conditions and structural origins which create suffering and the resulting socio-political and economic position".[299] On this level the church is to collaborate with other institutions in healthy dialogue in searching for and rooting out the *political conditions and structural origins* that result in perpetual suffering of the underprivileged. More on this aspect would be highlighted in the chapter five.

As means of realizing the goals of dialogue based on mutual understanding and respect, the Church's document *Dialogue and Proclamation* sums up the major forms of dialogue:[300]

a. The *dialogue of life*, where people strive to live in an open and neighborly spirit, sharing their joys and sorrows, their human problems and concerns.

b. The *dialogue of action*, in which Christians and others cooperate with each other for integral development and liberation of peoples.

c. The *dialogue of theological exchange*, where specialists seek to deepen their understanding of their respective religious heritages and to appreciate each other's spiritual values.

---

297 Zago, Marcello, "Interreligious Dialogue", in: *Following Christ in the Mission*, Ibid. p.104.

298 Ibid.

299 Ottmar, Fuchs, Ibid. pp. 56-57.

300 Cf. DP 42, 45, 46.

d. The *dialogue of religious experience*, where persons, rooted in their own religious traditions, share their spiritual riches, for instance with regard to prayer and contemplation, faith and ways of searching for God and the Absolute.

e. The *dialogue of culture*, which relates to the various ways in which culture and religions are linked.

f. And finally the *internal religious dialogue*, which enables believers to evaluate their own faith in the light of the culture in which they live.

In the above sense the Church emphasizes and demands the moral quality of imagining the other, but without loss of one's identity. In this connection *Redemptoris Missio* gives us some conclusive words on dialogue:

> Those engaged in this dialogue must be consistent with own religious traditions and convictions, and be open to understanding those of the other party without pretence or close-mindedness, but in truth, humility and frankness, knowing that dialogue can enrich each side. There must be no abandonment of principles or false irenicism, but instead a witness given and received for mutual advancement on the road of religious inquiry and experience, and at the same time for the elimination of prejudice, intolerance and misunderstandings. Dialogue leads to inner purification and conversion which, if pursued with docility to the Holy Spirit, will be spiritually fruitful.[301]

Summary

This chapter has extensively presented the various sides of the mission of the church. Central to these sides is the mission of Christ who is the founder of the church. The Chapter further focused on the liberative aspect of Christ's mission as the central aspect of his mission as far as the underprivileged persons in the society are concerned. It is on this basis that the church's mission of liberation is proposed to focus on the demands of the modern era, which is depicted in matters of human rights. By discussing the legitimation of the church's involvement in human rights issues, this

301 *Redemptoris Missio*, No. 56.

Chapter addresses also the magisterial documents that form the 'context of legitimation', in view of evoking a better response to the human rights demands by the church.

However, taking cognizance of the above mentioned aspects of the church's legitimation for her engagement in human rights issues, I am compelled to recall the three *mediations* of Boff for doing theology of liberation: *socio-analytical, hermeneutical and pastoral practice.* There is no doubt that the church has not done well yet on the first two mediations. But as far as human realities are concerned, the church still have a lot of hurdles to jump with regard to the third mediation. This is the stage it encounters all kinds of problems and conflicts with the world she evangelizes. It is on this note that the ills of the times, especially the violations of human rights, which motivated the development of these instruments above, challenges the church still to throw further into the 'deep' in order to stimulate the search for a more just and humane societal structures; and continuously struggle with the current day *counter-forces and destructive forces of alienation and of human rebellion.*[302] The church, however, must carry on with this mission through the guidance of the Holy Spirit and the Light of the Word, to venture out beyond her own confines as a visible, historical reality, until the complete communion of our human family is achieved in the banquet of the Reign of God (cf. Isaiah 25:6; Matt. 8:11).

With special respect for the role of the Holy Spirit, the church's mission of Dialogue comes into the discussion of this chapter. Following the example of her Master, the church makes herself available to the values and traditions of peoples of other beliefs and practices. She can succeed in this aspect of her mission by not holding claims to the absolute truth or interpretation of her religious practices. This calls for the practicability of the demands and suggestions of the Vatican II Document. She is called to bear witness to Humility as a virtue.

But, if evangelization and proclamation of the good news remain the fundament of the mission of the church for liberation, care for and use of human rights as a veritable tool cannot but form an indispensable part of this great task. It is one of the effective means the church can better do this mission in order to be in touch with the realities of human rights vio-

302 Boff, 1983:16, in: Bosch, D., Ibid. p. 49.

lations and also be relevant to the modern world she claims to evangelize. Nevertheless if the instruments mentioned above as means of the church's engagement in human rights question, are not properly translated into action (as is sometimes the case), then her quest for liberation could be only as good as the papers on which these instruments are written. Recalling John Paul II's *Mulieris Dignitatem,* for instance, one would immediately expect the church's immediate application of this third mediation, as far as women's position in the church in many parts of the world is concerned. This leads us to the next question: "how far does the church contribute effectively to human rights issues in practical terms?"

CHAPTER FOUR

EMPIRICAL RESEARCH IN RELIGION AND HUMAN RIGHTS IN NIGERIA

Introduction

Up until this point, I have tried to present the possibility of a church as an institution that is capable of promoting and protecting human rights by means of her mission. If this mission is to be truly rooted in the mission of liberation, which her founder Jesus Christ, preoccupied himself with, then the church ought to, as a matter of mandate, to be faithful to this mission in words and in practice.

The church's history over the centuries, especially in her attitude towards human rights issues, leaves no doubt that she has not been an institution of human rights (as formerly indicated). Events such as the Crusades that were propagated by and within the church are not indeed good events to recall because of the extent of violations of fundamental human rights it perpetrated. However, there is the possibility that the church ought to be an institution for human rights, by virtue of her mission.

In the previous chapter, I mentioned some of the instruments the church has used over the centuries and still uses to legitimize her promotion and protection of human rights. Unfortunately some aspects of her structural arrangement seem to give a different impression. In view of Johannes van der Ven "the … Church is known for its outspoken protests against violations of human rights in any society on any continent. Yet within its own structure, which reminds one of the feudal system of pre-modern times, human rights like the rights to freedom of speech, freedom of religion and cultural identity – all of them established human rights – are not structurally implemented".[303] The Vatican II Council, among other aims, aimed at preparing the church to throw open her windows to let in fresh air from the realities of the world around her (Aggiornamento). This gives

303 van der Ven, J.A., et al, Is there a God of Human Rights: Ibid., p.477.

the impression of a new progressive church. This development influenced the church in some parts of the world, and led to the introduction of all kinds of theologies like theology of Inculturation (for Africa), theology of Liberation (in Latin America) and theology of Dialogue (for Asia)[304]. Nevertheless, this is not completely the case since some of the church's structural arrangements remain rigid and do not offer adequate answers to some of the existential and contextual problems the world is facing today. The issue of women's equality, for example, is still a nagging issue that the world beckons the church to recognize in her structural arrangement. Let us not loose attention to the mission of her founder who did not allow any form of discrimination within his mission. One can notice the Jewish cultural influence over some of the church's attitude as far as patriarchy is concerned. Other established rights like freedom of speech, freedom of religion and cultural identity are yet to receive realistic structural attention. Not measuring up as expected in these areas leaves the church still wanting in terms of human rights issues in its strict sense, and as far as her critics are concerned.

This chapter is to question by means of empirical research the effectiveness of the church's engagement in human rights issues, and to investigate to what extent the instruments of legitimation of her involvement in human rights matters as mentioned earlier, are and could be effective. The chapter will dwell essentially on the responses of my questionnaire respondents, especially as it regards their attitudes towards religion (using the church as a bearing point), and human rights in Nigeria, anchored on theoretical and empirical perspectives. The correlation between these attitudes will close the chapter with an evaluation.

4.1 FUNDAMENTAL CLARIFICATION TO SOME OF THE RESEARCH QUESTIONS AND ATTITUDES

Before going into the empirical research presentation and analysis, some clarification is necessary as regards the research method. Firstly my questionnaire items were basically concentrated on finding out the religious at-

304 The mentioned Theologies were developed originally in the interest of the mentioned continents but not exclusive to them since they could also be applied to other contexts. That is why some scholars prefer to call them (in a singular form) Contextual Theology.

titudes and practices of my respondents; and their attitudes towards human rights. Secondly the data were collected from a total number of 609 senior secondary school students of Christian and Muslim backgrounds across the three major geographical-political parts of Nigeria: Eastern (Okigwe and Uturu), Western (Lagos), and Northern (Abuja). The students filled in their answers in a strictly academic (school) environment.
Some preliminary data from this total population are as follows: firstly, gender, secondly, age; thirdly, political and religious orientations; and fourthly, their attitudes towards values.
A total of 379 male students (62,2%) and 230 female students (37,8%) participated in the exercise (Table 4.1.1). The age range of the population runs from 13 to 23, with the following age categories as indicated in the Table 4.1.2.

Table 1

q1 What is your gender

		Frequency	Percent	Valid Percent	Cumulative Percent
Valid	1 male	379	62.2	62.2	62.2
	2 female	230	37.8	37.8	100.0
	Total	609	100.0	100.0	

Table 2

q2 What is your age?

		Frequency	Percent	Valid Percent	Cumulative Percent
Valid	13	2	.3	.3	.3
	14	47	7.7	7.7	8.1
	15	149	24.5	24.5	32.6
	16	182	29.9	29.9	62.5
	17	145	23.8	23.8	86.3
	18	51	8.4	8.4	94.7
	19	20	3.3	3.3	98.0
	20	11	1.8	1.8	99.8
	23	1	.2	.2	100.0
	Total	608	99.8	100.0	
Missing	System	1	.2		
Total		609	100.0		

The majority of this population (75,9%) indicated that political matters are sometimes spoken about in their homes, while 18,8% indicated political matters as often spoken about in their homes, and 5,3% indicated that political matters are never spoken about in their homes. On religious matters majority of the population (70,4%) indicated that religious matters are often spoken about in their homes, while 28,3% indicated as sometimes and 1,3% as never. In other words, religion plays major role in the family life and environment of the respondents, and politics to an extent.

Table 3

q7 Are political matters spoken about at home?

		Frequency	Percent	Valid Percent	Cumulative Percent
Valid	1 Never	32	5.3	5.3	5.3
	2 Sometimes	459	75.4	75.9	81.2
	3 Often	114	18.7	18.8	100.0
	Total	605	99.3	100.0	
Missing	System	4	.7		
Total		609	100.0		

Table 4

q8 Are religious matters spoken about at home?

		Frequency	Percent	Valid Percent	Cumulative Percent
Valid	1 Never	8	1.3	1.3	1.3
	2 Sometimes	172	28.2	28.3	29.6
	3 Often	428	70.3	70.4	100.0
	Total	608	99.8	100.0	
Missing	System	1	.2		
Total		609	100.0		

On questions regarding Values my respondents indicated strong inclinations towards 'Study' (98,9%), 'Family' (96,2%), 'Career' (93,3%), 'Religion or World View' (92,6%), and 'Having time for oneself' (91,5%). Besides, other values that got serious attention are as follows: 88% of the population placed much importance on 'being in a good financial situation'. 87% indicated special interest in 'getting on in life'. 81,7% support 'promoting greater equality in society'. 80,7% of the respondents like 'experiencing new events', while 80,5% indicated that 'living for their family' is important to them. Other values included in the questioner, 'being Married', 'contributing to existing income differences', 'enjoying life', 'Having children and raising them', 'having fun', 'deciding for oneself what is allowed and what is not', 'not being tied to rules', 'breaking through the existing relations of power', 'practicing an occupation', and 'being independent of anyone', did not get adequate attention as others mentioned above and in the Tables below did. This approach is also a pointer that would be highlighted on in the course of this chapter.

Table 5

q10_1 my study

		Frequency	Percent	Valid Percent	Cumulative Percent
Valid	1 not important at all	3	.5	.5	.5
	2 not important	2	.3	.3	.8
	3 I am not sure	2	.3	.3	1.1
	4 important	602	98.9	98.9	100.0
	Total	609	100	100	

Table 6

q10_8 my family

		Frequency	Percent	Valid Percent	Cumulative Percent
Valid	1 not important at all	3	.5	.5	.5
	2 not important	6	1.0	1.0	1.5
	3 I am not sure	14	2.3	2.3	3.8
	4 important	586	96.2	96.2	100.0
	Total	609	100.0	100.0	

Table 7

q10_4 my career

		Frequency	Percent	Valid Percent	Cumulative Percent
Valid	1 not important at all	2	.3	.3	.3
	2 not important	4	.7	.7	1.0
	3 I am not sure	35	5.7	5.8	6.7
	4 important	567	93.1	93.3	100.0
	Total	608	99.8	100.0	
Missing	System	1	.2		
Total		609	100.0		

Table 8

q10_9 my religion or world view

		Frequency	Percent	Valid Percent	Cumulative Percent
Valid	1 not important at all	2	.3	.3	.3
	2 not important	4	.7	.7	1.0
	3 I am not sure	39	6.4	6.4	7.4
	4 important	563	92.4	92.6	100.0
	Total	608	99.8	100.0	
Missing	System	1	.2		
Total		609	100.0		

Table 9

q10_10 having time for myself

		Frequency	Percent	Valid Percent	Cumulative Percent
Valid	1 not important at all	3	.5	.5	.5
	2 not important	15	2.5	2.5	3.0
	3 I am not sure	34	5.6	5.6	8.5
	4 important	557	91.5	91.5	100.0
	Total	609	100.0	100.0	

Table 10

q11_10 Being in a good financial situation

		Frequency	Percent	Valid Percent	Cumulative Percent
Valid	1 not important at all	8	1.3	1.3	1.3
	2 not so important	16	2.6	2.6	3.9
	3 I am not sure	49	8.0	8.1	12.0
	4 important	535	87.8	88.0	100.0
	Total	608	99.8	100.0	
Missing	System	1	.2		
Total		609	100.0		

Table 11

q11_2 Getting on in life

		Frequency	Percent	Valid Percent	Cumulative Percent
Valid	1 not important at all	5	.8	.8	.8
	2 not so important	11	1.8	1.8	2.6
	3 I am not sure	60	9.9	9.9	12.5
	4 important	531	87.2	87.5	100.0
	Total	607	99.7	100.0	
Missing	System	2	.3		
Total		609	100.0		

Table 12

q11_6 Promoting greater equality in society

		Frequency	Percent	Valid Percent	Cumulative Percent
Valid	1 not important at all	12	2.0	2.0	2.0
	2 not so important	19	3.1	3.1	5.1
	3 I am not sure	80	13.1	13.2	18.3
	4 important	495	81.3	81.5	99.8
	5 very important	1	.2	.2	100.0
	Total	607	99.7	100.0	
Missing	System	2	.3		
Total		609	100.0		

Table 13

q11_15 Experiencing new events

		Frequency	Percent	Valid Percent	Cumulative Percent
Valid	1 not important at all	8	1.3	1.3	1.3
	2 not so important	22	3.6	3.6	4.9
	3 I am not sure	87	14.3	14.3	19.3
	4 important	490	80.5	80.7	100.0
	Total	607	99.7	100.0	
Missing	System	2	.3		
Total		609	100.0		

Table 14

q11_9 Living for your family

		Frequency	Percent	Valid Percent	Cumulative Percent
Valid	1 not important at all	7	1.1	1.2	1.2
	2 not so important	18	3.0	3.0	4.1
	3 I am not sure	93	15.3	15.4	19.5
	4 important	486	79.8	80.3	99.8
	5 very important	1	.2	.2	100.0
	Total	605	99.3	100.0	
Missing	System	4	.7		
Total		609	100.0		

The next range of questions suggests the sincerity of the respondents, and indicates the level of authenticity of their answers to the questions. These are not all the questions they were asked in this domain, but I selected these ones for the purpose of showing the extent of their sincerity. The Tables below present to us this measurement:

Table 15

q13_7 Have you ever blamed someone for doing something you knew was really your fault?

		Frequency	Percent	Valid Percent	Cumulative Percent
Valid	1 yes	330	54.2	55.2	55.2
	2 no	268	44.0	44.8	100.0
	Total	598	98.2	100.0	
Missing	System	11	1.8		
Total		609	100.0		

Table 16

q13_10 Have you ever taken anything (even a pin or button) that belonged to someone else?

		Frequency	Percent	Valid Percent	Cumulative Percent
Valid	1 yes	401	65.8	66.3	66.3
	2 no	204	33.5	33.7	100.0
	Total	605	99.3	100.0	
Missing	System	4	.7		
Total		609	100.0		

Table 17

q13_17 Have you ever cheated at a game?

		Frequency	Percent	Valid Percent	Cumulative Percent
Valid	1 yes	362	59.4	59.9	59.9
	2 no	242	39.7	40.1	100.0
	Total	604	99.2	100.0	
Missing	System	5	.8		
Total		609	100.0		

Table 18

q13_19 Have you ever taken advantage of someone?

		Frequency	Percent	Valid Percent	Cumulative Percent
Valid	1 yes	367	60.3	61.0	61.0
	2 no	235	38.6	39.0	100.0
	Total	602	98.9	100.0	
Missing	System	7	1.1		
Total		609	100.0		

The answers given to the above mentioned questions (as indicated in the Tables), which are typically personal in nature, suggest the openness of the respondents thereby making us confident of their reactions to the themes of the empirical research.

It is however necessary to note that gaining access to the Muslim respondents was not an easy task. Typical Muslim school authorities did not allow us any form of access to their students. The exercise was viewed with suspicion and distrust. Even an Education Ministry in the capital city of Nigeria denied us a written permission to having access to a government-run school in the city. The Muslim students we could reach are those in public (in Lagos) and private mixed schools of Christians and Muslims, rich and poor alike. The denial of access into Muslim schools has a negative indication, which deserves special comment at the latter part of this chapter and in the following chapter.

4.1.1 Theoretical conceptualization and empirical methods

An empirical research of this nature can be better approached with clear conceptualization and methods in order to realize a clearer focus into the relationship of the realities of theory and practice. To that effect, the theoretical conceptualization and empirical methods that will be employed here are those developed by Johannes van der Ven, et al[305]. The results of the empirical research by means of questionnaire as mentioned above will be extensively made use of. It is more or less, a search into the relationship between human rights and specific aspects of religious identity, practice and structure, in view of investigating into the aspects that are likely to promote the desired human rights culture[306]. It is aimed to find out to what extent the attitudes of these future leaders of Nigeria towards religion and its practices influence their attitudes towards human rights. The result of this investigation will be presented as a stimulant towards the Church's missionary strategy in this contemporary era.

As a result of the limited nature of this work and for the purpose of the theoretical conceptualization and empirical methods, the Catholic Church as a religious institution will be the bearing point of the said attitudes of the respondents towards religion in finding out the influence of the former on their attitudes towards human rights. 59,4% of the population profess the Christian faith. Out of this population, 21,7% preferred seeing themselves as 'Catholic', 2,5% as 'Pentecostal', 2,3% as 'Anglican', ,5% as 'Protestant', whilc ,2% as 'other Christian tradition'. The majority, however, see themselves as 'Christian'. Among the 31,3% of the respondents from the Islamic faith, ,2% see themselves as 'Sunnite', and ,2% as Shiite. The majority prefer to see themselves as 'Islamic'. Then the remaining 9,5% of the population see themselves as 'religious', without any particular faith indication.

305 Johannes Van der Ven and his team of researchers have been since several years ago into empirical researches in Religion and Human Rights. Their theoretical conceptualization and empirical methods will be extensively (but not exclusively) used because of their suitability in this empirical research.

306 Human Rights in this regard is considered as a pattern of life, and as such is being addressed in this context as a culture.More insight on the Human Rights Culture will be given in the following chapter.

Table 19

q15 How do you see yourself? Please, make sure that you mark only one answer.

		Frequency	Percent	Valid Percent	Cumulative Percent
Valid	1 religious	58	9.5	9.5	9.5
	2 Christian	196	32.2	32.2	41.7
	3 Catholic	132	21.7	21.7	63.4
	4 Protestant	3	.5	.5	63.9
	5 Anglican	14	2.3	2.3	66.2
	6 Pentecostal	15	2.5	2.5	68.6
	7 other Christian tradition	1	.2	.2	68.8
	8 Islamic	188	30.9	30.9	99.7
	9 Sunnite	1	.2	.2	99.8
	10 Shiite	1	.2	.2	100.0
	Total	609	100.0	100.0	

The respondents also expressed their religiosity by expressing the influence their religion wields in their lives. An overwhelming majority of the respondents indicate the significant influence and importance their religion or worldview has in their lives, as regards their daily living, taking important decisions and other aspects of their lives. The tables below give us a detailed analysis of these indications:

Table 20

q18_1 My religion or worldview has great influence on my daily life

		Frequency	Percent	Valid Percent	Cumulative Percent
Valid	1 I totally disagree	14	2.3	2.3	2.3
	2 I disagree	8	1.3	1.3	3.6
	3 I am not sure	28	4.6	4.6	8.2
	4 I agree	163	26.8	26.8	35.0
	5 I fully agree	396	65.0	65.0	100.0
	Total	609	100.0	100.0	

Table 21

q18_2 If I have to take important decisions, my religion or worldview plays a mayor part in it

		Frequency	Percent	Valid Percent	Cumulative Percent
Valid	1 I totally disagree	9	1.5	1.5	1.5
	2 I disagree	16	2.6	2.6	4.1
	3 I am not sure	65	10.7	10.7	14.8
	4 I agree	207	34.0	34.0	48.8
	5 I fully agree	311	51.1	51.2	100.0
	Total	608	99.8	100.0	
Missing	System	1	.2		
Total		609	100.0		

Table 22

q18_3 My life would be quite different, had I not my religion or worldview

		Frequency	Percent	Valid Percent	Cumulative Percent
Valid	1 I totally disagree	24	3.9	3.9	3.9
	2 I disagree	26	4.3	4.3	8.2
	3 I am not sure	119	19.5	19.5	27.8
	4 I agree	147	24.1	24.1	51.9
	5 I fully agree	293	48.1	48.1	100.0
	Total	609	100.0	100.0	

In other words, all the respondents profess to be religious, and as the above analyses indicate, all the respondents regard religion as an important value in their lives. Their collective views of religion will be utilized as an instrument of evaluation with regard to the church as a religious institution. Apparently their views about religion and religious practices could also be synonymous with their views about the church, or what they expect from the church with regard to the Muslims or non-catholic respondents.

4.2 ATTITUDES TOWARDS THE CHURCH (RELIGION)

This section is precisely meant to investigate the attitudes of the respondents towards the church (as a religious institution), and their expectations of the church as an institution for human rights. It involves both theoretical and practical aspects. Meanwhile, a brief historical overview of the church's relationship to human rights in Nigeria is necessary as conceptual basis for a better understanding of the respondents' attitudes towards the church and towards human rights.

4.2.1. The Church in Nigeria and Human Rights

A significant attention has already been given in chapter two about Christianity in general and human rights in Nigeria. As a follow-up to that history chapter three gave specific attention to the mission of the Catholic Church and human rights. Following that direction the Church is being referred to in this context as the Catholic Church that established the catholic faith in the Eastern part of Nigeria. It is a church transported and planted in this part of the world firstly by the Holy Ghost Fathers from France, who landed at the Onitsha Wharf on December 5, 1885[307]. With Onitsha as their base, these missionaries under very difficult circumstances spread the Good News to all the nooks and crannies of this part of the country. This gives us a glimpse of the preponderant role Europe played towards the introduction of Christianity to Africa and Eastern Nigeria in particular, about 125 years ago. The missionaries came to the region with the intention of leading its people into the caravan of 'the Family of God' – the church, in order that they may experience God's salvation. To a reasonable extent, their activities were warmly accepted. From some other points of view, some of their activities were incompatible to the lives of the folks.

307 It is necessary to note that the Christian story of Igboland began in 1857 with the arrival on the shores of the River Niger of the London-based Church Missionary Society (CMS), the missionary arm of the Church of England. The Catholic presence in Igboland began in 1885 with the arrival of the Holy Ghost Fathers, who were mostly French. But from about 1900 politcal expediency saw the gradual replacement of French Holy Ghost Fathers by their Irish colleagues. These Irish Holy Ghost Fathers are recorded till this day as the group of missionaries that left a lasting missionary legacy in Igbo land. From Igbo land they paved their way into the non-Igbo speaking parts of eastern Nigeria. The missionary endeavours of today's Igbo Church are greatly influenced by their missionary strategy and methods.

The successes and failures that came with the establishment of the Catholic faith in eastern Nigeria are said to have had, and in some cases, are still having some positive and negative effects on human rights issues, both at its infant stage and at the present time. The possibility of a zero effect in some aspects may not be overlooked.

4.2.1.1. Positive Effects on Human Rights

The positive effects of the said establishment are noticed in the immense concern for human dignity promoted by the church. This concern led to the extermination of some of the inhuman practices and cultures of that period such as killing of twin babies, slave trade, some degrading treatments to women such as female circumcision,[308] and infant betrothal and child marriages.[309] Christianity also condemned the taking of Ozo[310] title and other similar titles because they tend to promote division between the slave and the free-born and also keep alive the oppression of the poor.[311] Some forms of discrimination were condemned by the church such as Osu and Ohu[312]. These were sort of castes stigmatized in a socio-psychological way as slaves dedicated to deities and slaves bought and maintained by wealthy masters.[313] They were discriminated against on these grounds. These practices were more or less legitimatized by the African Traditional religion, which dominated the region at the time. In the present day, the church in Nigeria is still poised to eliminate all those inhuman and degrading cultural practices.

---

308 Obi, C.A., (ed.), A Hundred Years of the Catholic Church in Eastern Nigeria (1885-1985), Africana-Fep Publishers, Lagos, 1985, p.295.

309 Ibid. p.147.

310 The "Ozo" title is a special honour reserved for men of integrity and impeccable charachter in the commuities. They must be honest and straight-forward people, who are expected to contribute immensly towards a peaceful and harmonious living in Igbo communities. The members hold to each other in manner of a secret cult. Unfortunately this cultural institution suffered a terrible abuse in the course of time, which striped it of its revered charachter.

311 Obi, C.A., Ibid. p. 147.

312 "Osu" and "Ohu" are forms of caste system. These names refer to people regarded as Outcastes in the communities, and as such do not enjoy equal rights with the so-called "Free borns".

313 Obi, C.A., Ibid., p.116.

Another positive dimension of the faith establishment is depicted in the area of education for emancipation and empowerment, and other social developments. The church was actively engaged in the educational programs in order to teach people how to read and write,[314] on the levels of primary, post primary, secondary and Teachers' Training. This aspect of her mission remains a very important mandate till the present day. Her educational involvements are regarded as one of the best in the country.

The church was also very much concerned about the people's healthcare by establishing hospitals and clinics (popularly known as Health Centres). In this connection her impact was felt in the area of providing food, medicine, clothing and shelter, especially to hundreds of thousands of refugees and the sick and other victims of the Nigeria – Biafra civil war. The church is still very vibrant today in this regard. There is no doubt that these services contributed immensely to the promotion of human rights and improvement of the folks' standard of living. Some successful politicians and business people in Nigeria today proudly and gratefully relate their success to the efforts and contributions of the church, especially in educational endeavors.

4.2.1.2. Negative Effects on Human Rights

The positive effects notwithstanding, the establishment of Christianity in Eastern Nigeria also had negative effects towards human rights. The most outstanding violation of human rights legitimated (knowingly or unknowingly) by the church was with regard to cultural rights. The superiority complex and a sort of triumphalist attitudes of the missionaries led them to the condemnation of the local cultural practices and ethos as paganish, primitive and barbaric. This attitude towards the local culture led to the extinction of some of the cultural values and identity of the Easterners. There was a form of colonization of the minds of the local people to regard their culture as evil. And this is one of the problems the church is facing in that part of the world with regard to the introduction of the Theology of Inculturation. Reviving those values is now a difficult task since most of them have been termed evil by the indigenes themselves. Some of these cultural values are still not structurally accepted.

314 Ibid., p. 36

In a similar dimension, the church also fouled the right to religious freedom by its total condemnation of the Traditional Religion of the people. The missionaries persuaded the people to abandon their traditional religious practices and convert to Christianity. Converts surrendered their worshipping instruments, which the church term "idols", for destruction.[315] However it is ironical to see the 'destruction' of those items in their conveyance into Europe, and made good enough for exhibition in Museums (often called African Museums)[316]. This is indeed a deplorable violation of cultural and religious rights. One cannot be far from the truth to conclude that people were indirectly induced to convert to the church by means of gifts and social services/ facilities.[317]

I cannot deny the positive aspects of the missionaries' evangelizing efforts, as I mentioned earlier, but at the same time, they must have been done also under guise for conversion to Catholicism. This conclusion is drawn from the triumphalist attitude noticed in the missionary methods of the church, especially with regard to their struggle with other Christian denominations and traditional religion for conversion. This triumphalist tendency is still latent within the church in Nigeria today in her missionary methods, especially with regard to conversion and spread of the Good News of the Gospel.

A similar side of the coin regarding conversion is that the church did not offer her converts the freedom of expression and to choose their life-styles. They were meant to live in a community where they are compelled to live according to the dictates of the authorities. Celestine Obi reported extensively on this matter:

Ordinarily, living in a community has got some unpleasant sides to it. You cannot choose who your immediate neighbors will be. It imposes rules and regulations. Life in the Christian village was additionally difficult since it made so many demands on the people. It was very monastic and by their understanding of life, both inhuman and detestable. Christians in the Christian village were strictly secluded from the world and had to live in

315 Ibid. p. 46.

316 A typical example of the so-called African Museum is the African Museum in The Netherlands, which I personally visited. Most of these rare artefacts are ostensibly displayed in glass cases of course with their historical facts.

317 Obi, C.A., Ibid., p. 29.

a world of their own. Daily attendance at morning Mass was compulsory, so were night prayers and the recitation of the rosary in common. Every Christian villager was bound to work very hard in the farms, orchards and plantations, often under supervision and had to be of impeccable character under fear of expulsion from the village.[318]

I recall at this point that the church condemned and helped to exterminate slavery, but one cannot but look at this report as a neo-colonialism and semi-slavery of human beings. Irrespective of the church's good intention for making this type of structure, it points directly to violations of fundamental rights of the people.

The above structure of the church's control over her adherents, which gives latency to the violations of fundamental human rights, continues today in different forms. The church is accused of perpetrating such neo-colonialism and semi-slavery as seen in most cases, through the church's insistence on some of her doctrines and practices that do not offer concrete solutions to human realities. The church's reluctance to allow her members to participate in some traditional feasts and festivals is a clear example of this fact.

As I mentioned earlier in chapter one, some members of the church do not feel very free to express themselves on controversial religious matters, mostly under the fear of being denied one sacrament or the other, or in extreme cases, denial of membership. The church's religious formation houses like seminaries and convents are not free of such violations. Despite the seeming air of freedom that circulates in such houses, a deeper look leaves one with the conclusion that much is yet to be done. Most inmates of such houses are trained under fear of being punished or in some cases, dismissed there from. The tendency is for them to hide their true behavior while in formation, and disclose same after ordination or religious profession.

There is no doubt that the church promotes human dignity by not allowing discrimination, as depicted by her roles towards slaves and outcasts in the society, and HIV/AIDS patients. Nonetheless, there is another form of discrimination the church is said to be guilty of. This is mainly noticed in

318 Ibid., p. 53.

her attitudes towards women. The church definitely condemns degradation of women in general, but the place of women within her structures is still heavily influenced by the Jewish background of Christianity and African patriarchal mentality. I can vividly recall that some years ago, women were not allowed entrance into the sanctuary inside the church buildings. Canon 813 (1) of the 1917 Code of Canon Law even supported this prohibition at that time. They had no 'voice' or 'say' in church's important matters. They were made to accept total and presumably sheepish obedience to their husbands, following the one-sided interpretation of admonitions of St. Paul (Ephesians 5:21). Though there has been a remarkable improvement and canonical change in this regard, but one can claim that there are still some elements of discrimination against women when it comes to leadership and ministerial roles in the church. The church is still reluctant to accord women such opportunities. If the church does not accord such a pride of place to women, the secular society may not do so as well.

4.2.1.3. Zero Effects on Human Rights

Apart from the positive and negative effects of the church's presence in Igbo land on human rights, there is also an aspect of zero effect that is noticed. There isn't much to comment on in this aspect. However, it suffices it to remark that there are some people who did not heed to the church's evangelizing mission. This set of people is found among the African traditional religionists. They openly opposed the church and her doctrines and accused her of thwarting the traditional customs and cultures of Igbo people. The African traditional religion is significantly known for its discrimination against women. The patriarchal nature of its structures relegates women to the position of second class citizens. Some inhuman practices warranted by some of the traditional practices (as earlier mentioned) militate against the promotion of human rights. Since this people refused to heed to the church's missionary activities, invariably their attitude towards these aspects of human rights violation could not have changed in any way, hence giving us a possibility of a zero effect of the church's mission on human rights. In other words, the church's activities did not have any effect on their normal behavior, especially as it relates to their human rights understanding.

In the strict understanding, these attitudes pose a threat towards the transformational expectations of the church and hence of the research population.

4.2.2 Theoretical Perspective

With the above brief presentation of some historical and current facts regarding the church and human rights in the Nigerian context, I can now go further to investigate ecclesiastic (religious) attitudes of the respondents and the effects of these attitudes on their human rights attitudes. The major question of this investigation dwells on the attitudes of the respondents towards religion (invariably towards the church as a religious institution).

This investigation will be approached methodologically from theoretical and empirical perspectives. The former is taken from the ecclesiological reflections given earlier (in the historical analysis), while the latter will aim at finding out whether these attitudes in the theoretical domain are in consonance with the empirical data collected from the research questions. For the purpose of conceptualization and reflection of these attitudes four categories will be employed: Religious Practices, Religious Convictions, Cultural Openness and Democratic Openness.

Religious Practices and Convictions are closely interrelated. In most cases they have to do with the daily rituals, practices and convictions that form an individual's religious background. People talk about being religious, Christian, Islamic, catholic, protestant, etc. The religious practice of a Christian could be very different from that of a Muslim; as well as that of a catholic from a protestant or Pentecostal. People's religious convictions to a great extent determine the devotedness of their religious practices, and also to a great extent determine their ways of life. People often talk about the influence their religious practices and convictions play in their daily lives, as well as by some decision-making. For many they are inseparable from their lives. In other words, they exhibit their religiosity in all facets of their lives. That is why someone's religious affinity could be told from the person's single act. At various levels and places people trace their successes in life and career, their goodness, their behavioral tendencies and even their level of endurance and tenacity to their religiosity. People's religious convictions are also reflected in their attitudes towards God; and in cases of

Christians and Muslims, towards Jesus Christ and Mohammed. The quest here is to present the religious practices and convictions of the respondents and eventually to determine to what extent these practices and conviction affect their attitudes towards the church as a religious institution.

Cultural Openness is employed here in order to know whether it is necessary for the church to keep in touch with her cultural environment and engage in dialogical communication about what she does, or whether she should isolate herself from cultural trends and movements by maintaining her own stance and views.[319] As a religious institution that is built on traditions, the church's flexibility and dynamism in matters of her faith and doctrines do not sometimes match with the demands of the realities of life. The attitudes of my respondents to this regard are expected to tell us to what extent the church is or ought to be open to reforms and re-figurations due to the changing realities around her.

Democratic Openness in this context has to do with the ability of church members to participate actively in the affairs of the church – with regard to the church's administrative matters and ideological stances. Arendt's 'Power-in-common-with' and 'Power-over' could enhance an elaboration in this regard. The former reflects a participatory concept of power, whereby every individual has the right to responsibly participate in decision making in a given community. While the latter reflects a concentration of power in the hands of one person or a few persons who are meant to hold on to power, dominating those who have to abide by their decisions and measures.[320] In most cases the centralization of the church's authority does not allow its lay members to contribute very effectively in administrative and ideological matters. This attitude widens the gap between the authorities of the church and other members. It paints a picture of "you are there and we are here" structure. Do the attitudes of my respondents approve of this or not?

The picture of the church presented above is that with hierarchical and paternalistic tendencies. This forms the basis for the first attitude of my respondents towards the church. This hierarchical consciousness of the church's structure has been questioned by majority of the church members,

319 Yinger: 1970, in: van der Ven, J.A., et al, Ibid., p. 497.
320 van der Ven, J.A., et al, Ibid., p. 496.

especially her lay members because of the growing latency for domination and in some cases, autocracy. It is regrettable to note that this tendency has not augured well with the church and her affairs in most parts of Nigeria. It has resulted into conflicts between the lay faithful and ministerial authority holders in the church, even among the ministerial authorities themselves. Protests from parishioners often lead to forceful ejection of priests from rectories. In most cases, these protests reflect decry of violation of rights, restriction of freedom and lack of 'due process' or inadequate recourse. An excessive use of power and unnecessary rigidity by some authority holders in the church are also contributive to this problem. As a result the religious practices and convictions of the respondents could be adversely affected, since there are already elements of mistrust and suspicion.

Going by the above situational description, one expects that majority of the research respondents would express their dissatisfaction with the trend and indicate progressive and transformational expectations from the church in many administrative and structural matters. However, the empirical perspective that follows will give us better practical insight and determines the extent of correctness in the theoretical judgment.

4.2.3 Empirical Perspective

It is already earlier mentioned that the empirical aspect of the research respondents' attitude is to find out whether the suppositional attitudes displayed in the theoretical domain are in consonance with the data collected from the research questions. This process involves, so to say, operationalizing the four categories described in the last section. The empirical question is still the same with the theoretical question. The operationalization will be done in tabular forms. Meanwhile, note should be taken that the cells in the following Tables contain the average values of human religious (ecclesiastic) attitudes among the respondents on a five-point scale stretching from 1 (I totally disagree), 2 (I disagree), 3 (I am not sure), 4 (I agree) to 5 (I fully agree). The Constructs with one Variable would be summarized, hence forming the calculation for "Total Statistics", and as such Reliability analysis is not necessary. In this respect their correlations tables would be given.

These tables with the frequencies of the various items in regard to Religious Practices and Convictions, Cultural Openness and Democratic openness will be given below, together with their Histograms. These Histograms give us the Frequency distribution of the Mean of items, which will be used for the construct analysis, as way of exploring whether these three concepts corresponded to the respondents' consciousness structure. The Reliability Analysis attached to the major Tables is made in order to explain the Constructs in question. At the end of the statistical presentations a collective interpretation of their mean will be made.

4.2.3.1 Attitudes towards the Church: Empirical Perspective.

4.2.3.1.1RELIGIOUS PRACTICES (q18):

Table 23: My religion has great influence on my life

Item-Total Statistics

	Scale Mean if Item Deleted	Scale Variance if Item Deleted	Corrected Item-Total Correlation	Cronbach's Alpha if Item Deleted
q18_1 My religion or worldview has great influence on my daily life	8.39	2.542	.469	.457
q18_2 If I have to take important decisions, my religion or worldview plays a mayor part in it	8.59	2.374	.502	.403
q18_3 My life would be quite different, had I not my religion or worldview	8.82	2.233	.324	.690

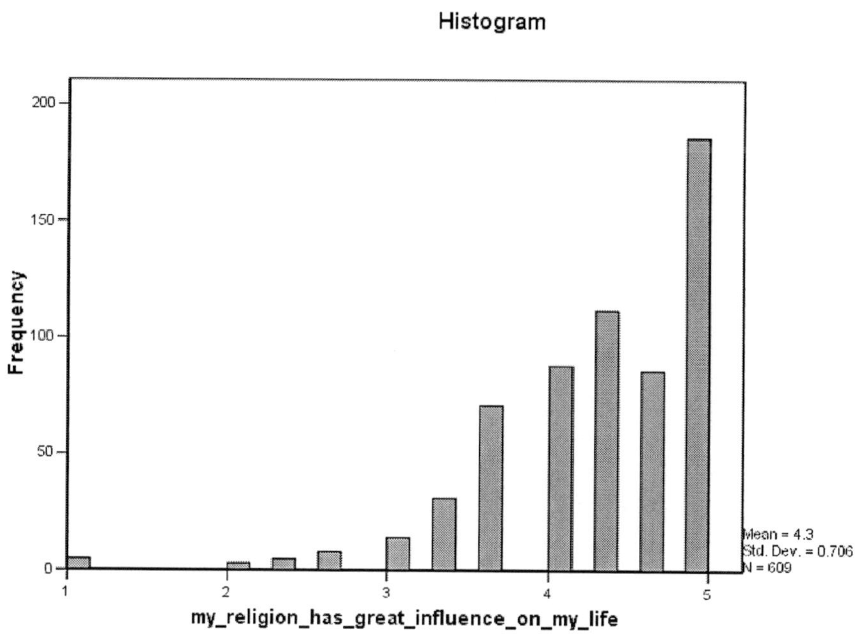

4.2.3.1.2 RELIGIOUS CONVICTIONS:

4.2.3.1.2.1 God (q25):

Table 24: God is near

Item-Total Statistics

	Scale Mean if Item Deleted	Scale Variance if Item Deleted	Corrected Item-Total Correlation	Cronbach's Alpha if Item Deleted
q25_2 I trust God never to abandon me	22.67	8.163	.596	.787
q25_3 When people are friendly that is God's love at work	23.04	7.605	.515	.808
q25_4 I experience Gods goodness in the peace of nature	22.77	8.161	.557	.794
q25_5 When people live in friendship, Gods love is present	22.83	7.629	.624	.779
q25_6 God knows and understands me	22.73	7.857	.649	.775
q25_8 I experience Gods presence in the beauty of nature	22.79	7.779	.576	.790

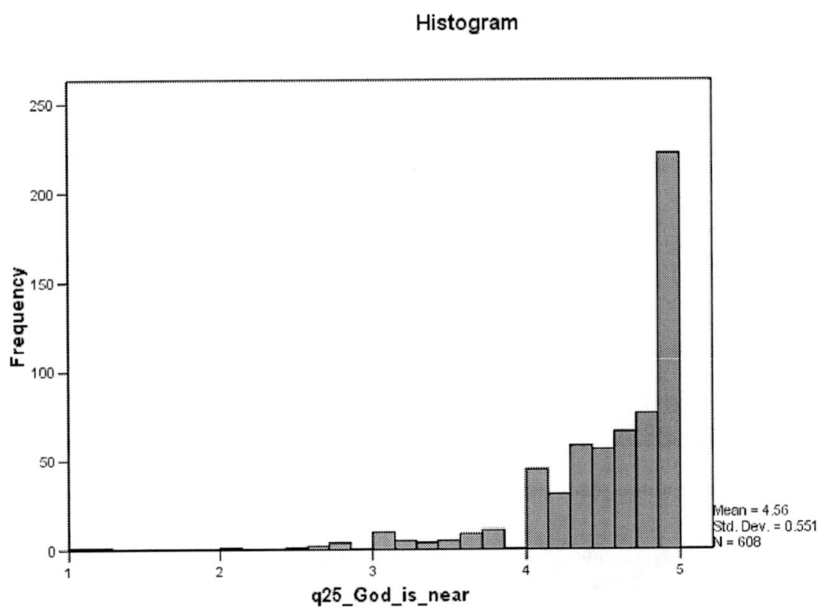

Table 25: God is far away

Correlations

			q25_7 God got the world going and left the responsibility for it to humans
Spearman's rho	q25_1 God set the world in motion and left it to humans to take care of it	Correlation Coefficient	.570
		Sig. (2-tailed)	.000
		N	607

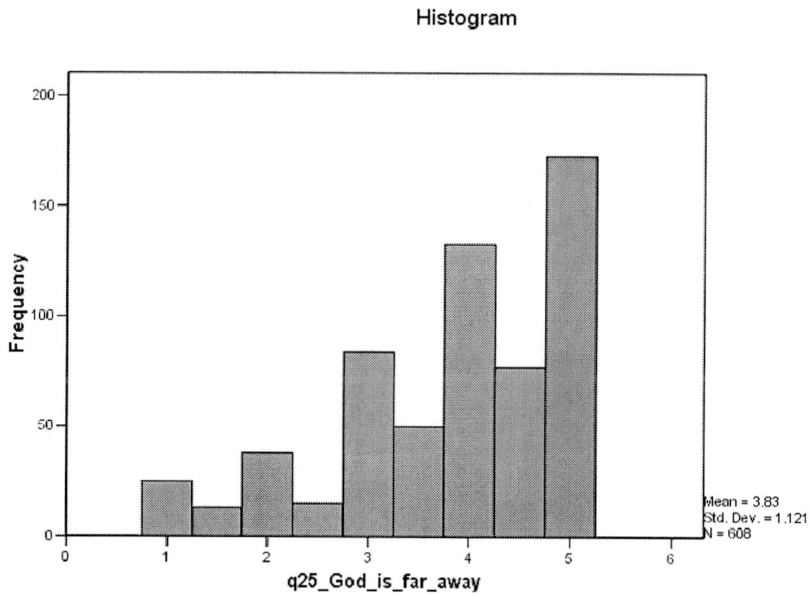

4.2.3.1.2.2 Jesus (q27):

Table 26: Jesus has a special relationship to God

Item-Total Statistics

	Scale Mean if Item Deleted	Scale Variance if Item Deleted	Corrected Item-Total Correlation	Cronbach's Alpha if Item Deleted
q27_1 God sent his son Jesus to earth	16.53	10.849	.687	.792
q27_2 Jesus was a unique prophet, as Gods Spirit of mercy directed his work and deeds	16.54	12.723	.556	.828
q27_5 Jesus is the God-man who existed with the father from the beginning	16.87	10.816	.671	.797
q27_12 Before Jesus came to earth he had lived with the father from the beginning	16.84	10.749	.673	.797
q27_13 Jesus was a unique teacher, as Gods Spirit of love was in him	16.58	12.188	.630	.810

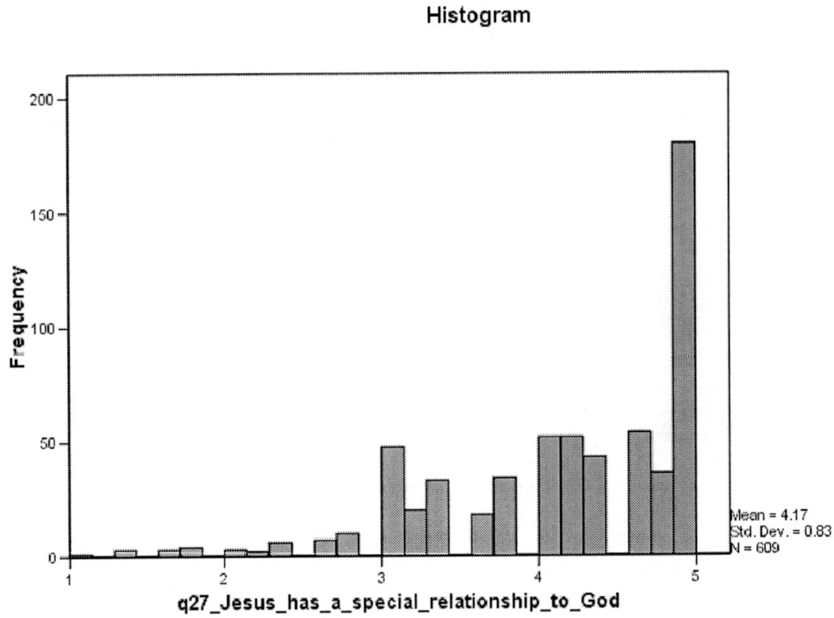

Table 27: Jesus is concerned about human welfare

Item-Total Statistics

	Scale Mean if Item Deleted	Scale Variance if Item Deleted	Corrected Item-Total Correlation	Cronbach's Alpha if Item Deleted
q27_3 Jesus works among the marginalised in their struggle for liberation	25.31	19.368	.515	.853
q27_4 Jesus has shown us how to live in solidarity with others	24.89	18.929	.687	.830
q27_6 Jesus guides the oppressed to the land of justice and peace	24.93	18.257	.722	.823
q27_7 Through his life Jesus showed us what it is like to be a loving human being	24.84	18.690	.671	.831
q27_9 Jesus was a unique servant, as Gods Spirit of compassion animated his life and words	25.19	18.435	.550	.850
q27_11 Jesus was a real example of caring for everybody in need	24.81	18.717	.679	.830
q27_15 Jesus supports the poor by liberating them from injustice	25.03	18.989	.575	.844

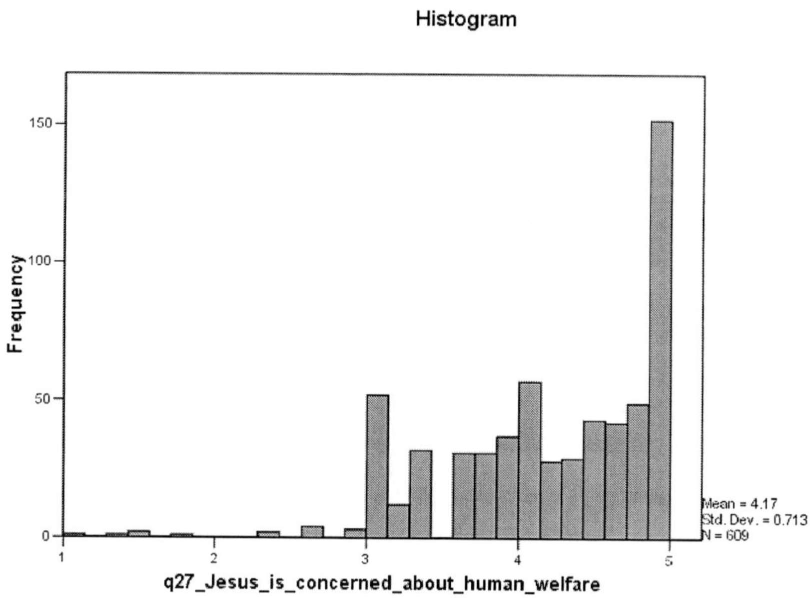

Table 28: Jesus is just a historical figure

Item-Total Statistics

	Scale Mean if Item Deleted	Scale Variance if Item Deleted	Corrected Item-Total Correlation	Cronbach's Alpha if Item Deleted
q27_8 Jesus only significance is that he started an important historical movement	6.83	5.557	.452	.632
q27_10 Jesus was a special person, no more	6.85	4.788	.479	.599
q27_14 Jesus is no more than just one of the great figures in human history	7.04	4.312	.548	.502

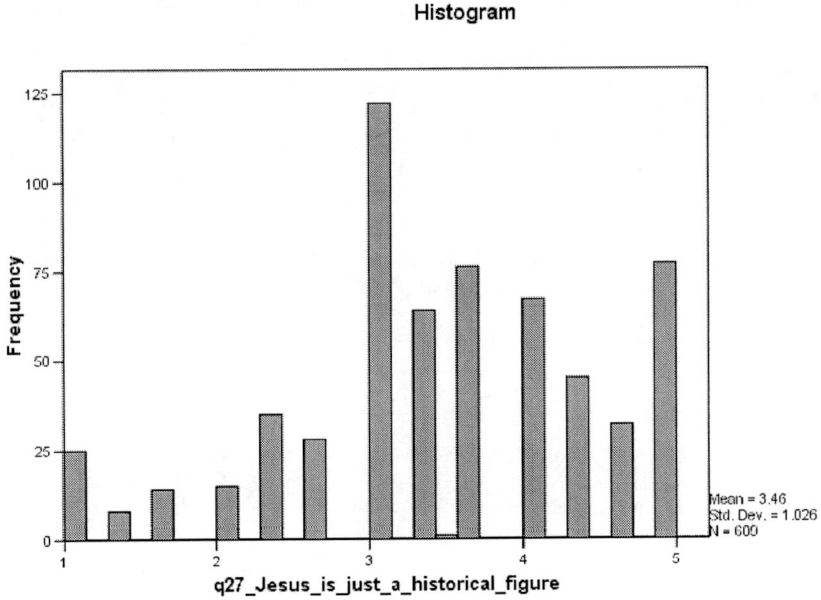

4.2.3.1.2.3 Mohammed (q28):

Table 29: Mohammed has a special relationship to God

Item-Total Statistics

	Scale Mean if Item Deleted	Scale Variance if Item Deleted	Corrected Item-Total Correlation	Cronbach's Alpha if Item Deleted
q28_1 Muhammad received special revelations which led him to announce Gods message	27.69	64.406	.849	.953
q28_2 Muhammads journey to, and union with, God is absolutely unique	27.78	64.607	.866	.952
q28_3 Muhammads union with God is the perfect model for everyones journey to God	27.87	65.076	.863	.952
q28_6 Muhammad was called to preach Gods teachings about faith and ethical demands	27.79	65.603	.843	.953
q28_8 Muhammad teaches us how to walk our spiritual path to God	27.78	64.514	.871	.952
q28_11 Muhammad was sent by God as his prophet in order to proclaim his message	27.80	65.498	.819	.955
q28_13 Muhammads religious experiences inspire and motivate our striving for union with God	27.80	65.058	.862	.953
q28_7 No one can ever replicate Muhammads mystical experience	27.92	66.742	.773	.957
q28_12 No one can ever copy Muhammads divine revelations.	27.95	66.731	.728	.959

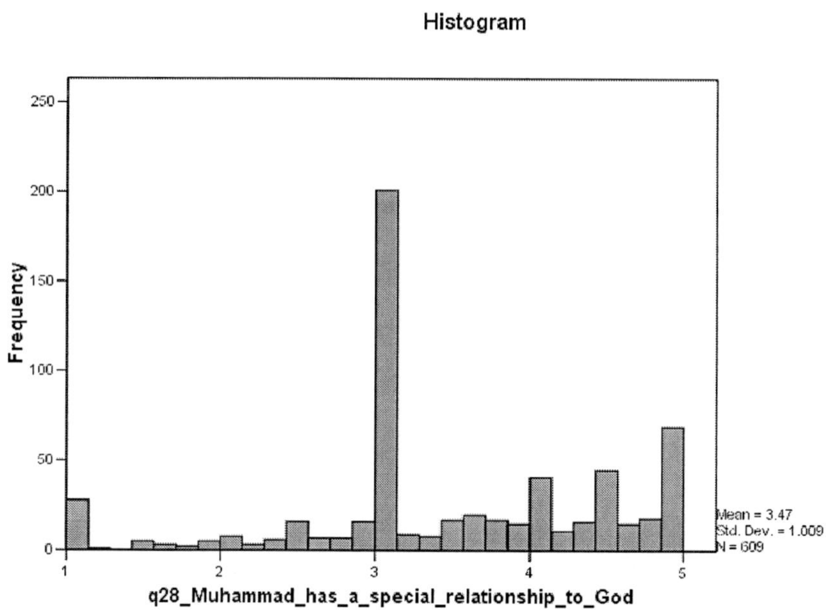

Table 30: Mohammed is concerned about human welfare

Item-Total Statistics

	Scale Mean if Item Deleted	Scale Variance if Item Deleted	Corrected Item-Total Correlation	Cronbach's Alpha if Item Deleted
q28_4 Muhammad motivates us to maintain and strengthen our bond with fellow human beings	7.10	4.584	.780	.846
q28_9 Through Muhammad we learn to strive for the common good of society as a whole	7.16	4.553	.768	.856
q28_14 Muhammad teaches us to care for everybody in need and distress	6.99	4.521	.802	.826

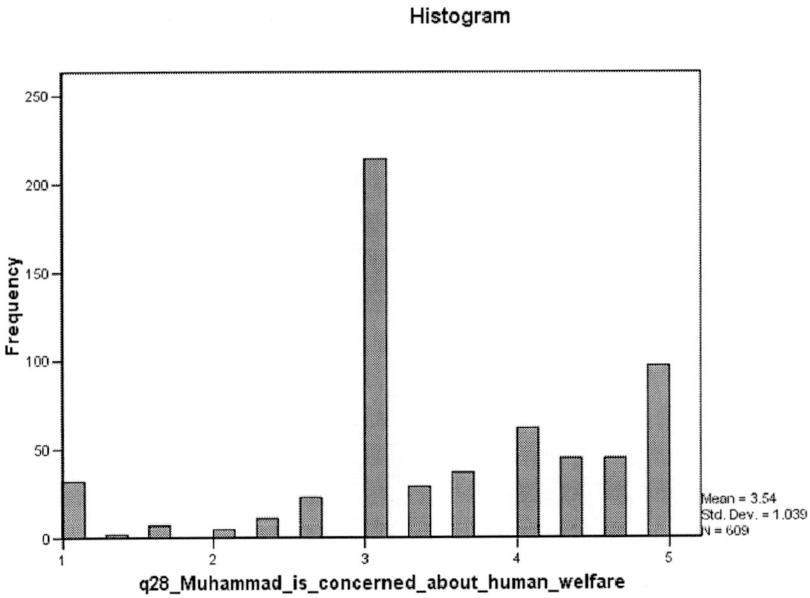

Table 31: Mohammed is just a historical figure

Item-Total Statistics

	Scale Mean if Item Deleted	Scale Variance if Item Deleted	Corrected Item-Total Correlation	Cronbach's Alpha if Item Deleted
q28_5 Muhammads only significance is that he started an important historical movement	6.69	4.174	.599	.747
q28_10 Muhammad was a special person, no more	6.81	3.803	.640	.704
q28_15 Muhammad is no more than just one of the great figures in human history	6.76	3.789	.654	.688

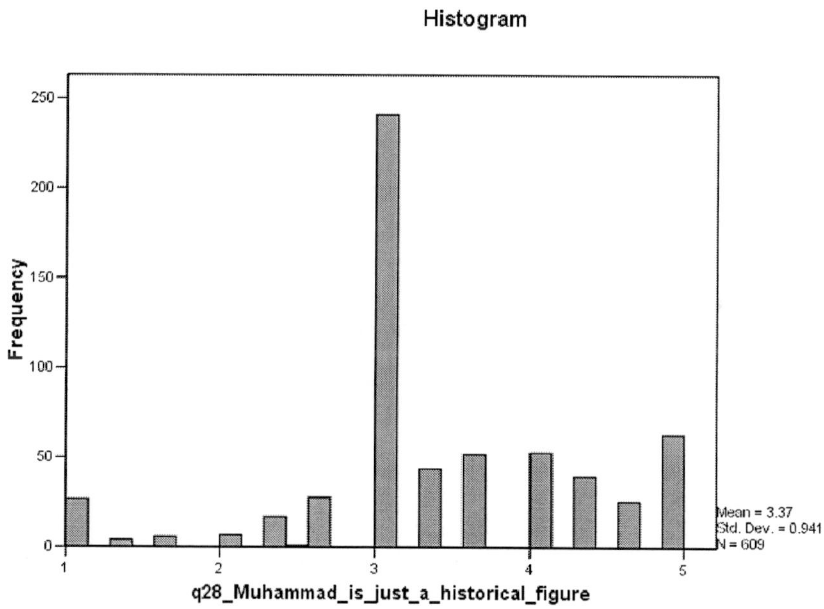

4.2.3.1.3 CULTURAL OPENNESS: Religious Communities (q29)

Table 32

Item-Total Statistics

	Scale Mean if Item Deleted	Scale Variance if Item Deleted	Corrected Item-Total Correlation	Cronbach's Alpha if Item Deleted
q29_1 Religious communities should publicly stand up for the underclass	36.67	33.833	.371	.842
q29_2 Religious communities should join in new trends in society as far as possible	36.62	33.078	.508	.828
q29_5 Religious communities should get enough knowledge to speak sensibly about social issues	36.32	32.878	.622	.819
q29_6 Religious communities should publicly discuss social problems people are subjected to	36.46	32.712	.585	.821
q29_7 Religious communities should go along with changing ideas in society	36.61	32.570	.509	.828
q29_10 Religious communities should get enough information to deal with social problems effectively	36.47	32.429	.614	.819
q29_11 Religious communities should publicly denounce social abuses people suffer	36.50	32.500	.549	.824
q29_12 Religious communities should always keep up with current social trends	36.77	32.049	.530	.826
q29_14 Religious communities should strive to influence peoples attitudes towards social issues	36.58	32.636	.537	.825
q29_15 Religious communities should get sufficiently /qualified to speak authoritatively about social problems	36.46	32.592	.564	.823

Histogram

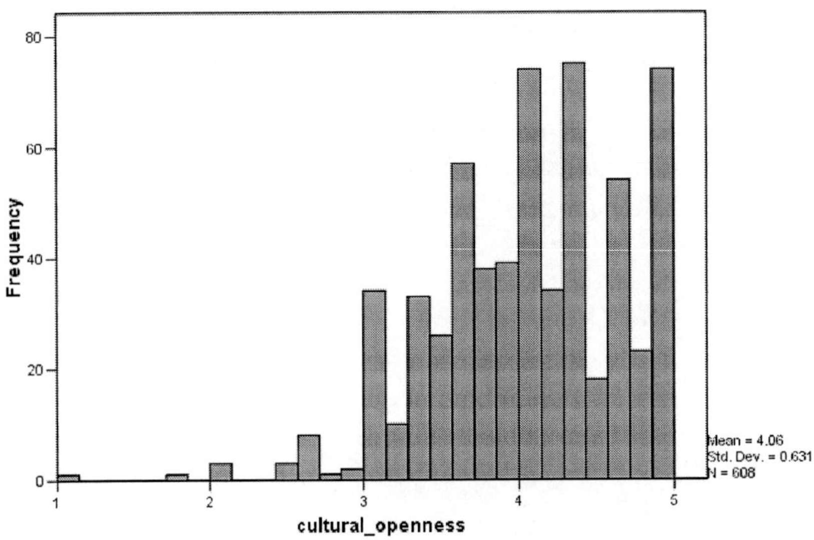

4.2.3.1.4 DEMOCRATIC OPENNESS: Religious Communities (q29)

Table 33

Item-Total Statistics

	Scale Mean if Item Deleted	Scale Variance if Item Deleted	Corrected Item-Total Correlation	Cronbach's Alpha if Item Deleted
q29_3 Religious communities should never reject people who want to become members	8.10	2.883	.401	.557
q29_8 Everyone should be able to join a religious community	8.33	2.405	.506	.403
q29_13 Anyone should be able to participate in a religious community without preconditions	8.54	2.423	.386	.590

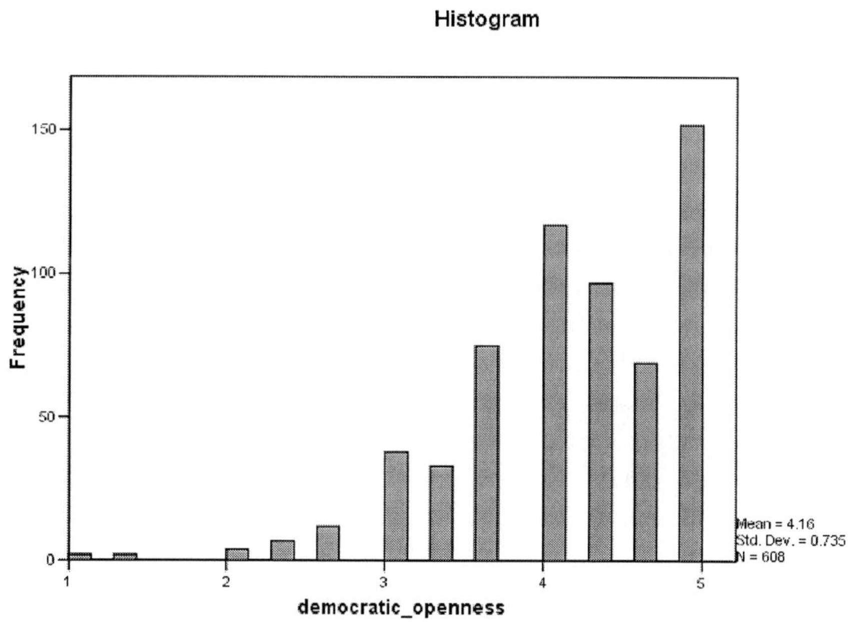

4.2.4 Interpretation

From the above histogramic charts the empirical perspective has eventually given us some answers to the investigation into the attitudes of the respondents towards religion (the church). The research population indicated to a great extent that their religion has great influence on their lives (mean 4.3). At the same time, this population remarkably shows their conviction that God is near (4.58); and at a lesser degree to the former, that God is far away (3.83). Their conviction about Jesus special relationship to God is on a higher mean (4.17); and at the same degree (4.17) they manifested strong conviction that Jesus is concerned about human welfare. At a bit lower mean, the respondents indicated that Jesus is just a historical figure (3.46). With regard to Mohammed, the respondents agreed that Mohammed has special relationship to God (3.47). Almost with similar degree they agreed that Mohammed is concerned about human welfare (3.54). Finally on Mohammed, the respondents agreed to a lower degree that Mohammed is just a historical figure (3.37). On the two final items, the respondents showed significant acceptance of cultural openness (4.06), and democratic openness (4.16).

From this brief interpretation, one discovers that there is a very close agreement between the theoretical suppositions and empirical results. In other words we do not have any complications as such. The religious convictions of the respondents to a great extent determine their religious practices and vice versa. All the same there is need to offer some brief explanation to the items that have lesser degrees of agreement in comparison to others.

The first item with a lesser degree of agreement is the conviction about God being far away. The clear tendency of this mean is that of 'not being sure'. Nevertheless, as far as all the respondents presented themselves as religious (in one way or the other) there is the supposition that they regard God as a personal God, who stays with His people, to guide, protect and bless them in their daily activities. This explains the higher degree of agreement in the previous item of God being near. I however tend to read a tendency of 'uncertainty' from this result[321]. Another item with lesser degree of agreement is the conviction that Jesus is just a historical figure

321 By tendency of "uncertainty" here I mean their not being perhaps not fully in grasp of the teachings of their faith. This calls attention to a more intensive religious teaching.

(q27). Generally Christians believe that Jesus is the son of God, who came in the world to show the humankind the way to righteousness and peace. So regarding him as just a historical figure could not be welcomed by majority of the Christian respondents. I therefore suppose that greater degree of agreement could have been indicated by most of the Muslim respondents, which reflects what they believe about Jesus. This does not indicate any problem since people are free to their right of belief and practices. Nevertheless, the result tends towards uncertainty.

There is a general supposition to the explanation on why items on Mohammed have lesser degree of acceptance as compared to that of Christ. The first explanation to this is simply because of the fact that the minority of the respondents are Muslims (31.3%). A similar explanation to the question 27 on Jesus could be applicable to the question 28 on Mohammed being just a historical figure. Majority of Muslims have also special regard for Mohammed, and they believe that his presence is still being felt in their religious world-views and practices. Holding him as just a historical figure could be absurd. I also suppose that majority of the Christian respondents could have responded either negatively or merely ambivalently to this item.

With regard to cultural openness, the research population agrees to a great extent with the church's openness to reforms and re-figurations (4.06). This is a remarkable sign that the majority of them have progressive and transformative aspirations towards the church in the 21st century.

From the result of the democratic openness, it is then not a surprise that the majority of the respondents indicate their interest in seeing a church that is open to democracy (4.16). I tend to suppose that this democratic tendency could not be in its absolute manner, but in a more positive participatory way, as described by Arendt.

To a great extent, the empirical results have proved the suppositions in the theoretical domain right. However the search continues: to determine to what extent the attitudes of my respondents towards religion (the church) influence their attitudes towards human rights. The correlation will eventually offer us an adequate conclusion.

4.3 ATTITUDES TOWARDS HUMAN RIGHTS

The formation of a human rights culture is the basis of all my concern regarding the church's structural arrangement. This culture must be part of this arrangement for it to be truly addressed to the church's promotion and protection of human rights in its entire ramification. However, the acquisition of the right attitude towards human rights is a very necessary condition for the right formation of a human rights culture. If the attitude is not positive, in the sense of being directed towards the welfare and liberation of human beings, it will simply be worthless. Hence, "if human rights are not rooted in a positive attitude, a positive mind-set, positive engagement on the part of those who have to realize a human rights culture, then the entire culture of critical reflection that forms the core of it is illusory".[322]

This calls for an investigation of the attitudes of the research respondents towards human rights. It is a search to find out to what extent their attitudes towards the church contribute to their attitudes towards human rights. A number of factors will be involved here. So the question is whether and to what extent the respondents' attitudes towards each of the four categories in the ecclesiastic (religious) attitudes affect or influence their human rights attitudes. This will be based on the three generations of human rights – first generation: civil, political and judicial rights (the blue rights); second generation: socio-economic rights (the red rights); and third generation: collective (environmental) rights (the green rights).

The first generation rights are Western-oriented rights, which originated out of liberalism invoked to ensure that the state implements a hands-off policy towards citizens. This refers to the first element of the famous slogan of the French Revolution – 'Liberty, Equality and Brotherhood'. The second generation rights originated from socialism, more especially the former socialist Eastern bloc. They are sometimes called rights of credit, since they imply an active role for the state, and they refer to the second element of the French Revolution slogan – 'Equality'. The third generation rights evolved mainly out of interests of developing countries, and they refer to the third element of the Revolution – 'Brotherhood'.[323] A brief

322 van der Ven, J.A., et al, Ibid., p. 96.

323 Ibid. p. 97.

review of these generations of human rights and their categories suffices here in order to decipher attitudes towards human rights as they refer to the three generations.[324]

(i) First Generation Rights

Civil rights, which forms the first category of this generation of human rights is made up of liberties, and was developed between the 17th and 18th centuries. They are very interrelated to each other and are considered to be natural rights since the people possess them 'by nature'. They comprise of such rights like: freedom of speech, freedom of the press, freedom of lifestyle, freedom of conscience, freedom of religion and the right to own property. They should not be tampered with by the state, they are people's birthright. They are often associated with human rights with focus on a capacity or a legal competence. These rights form the basis of the Universal Declaration of Human Rights of 1948, of which article three reads: "Everyone has the right to life, liberty and security of person". With regard to exploitative conditions, article four reads: "No one shall be held in slavery or servitude; slavery and slave trade should be prohibited in all their forms". These liberties were eventually codified in the International Covenant on Civil and Political Rights in 1966, and article 6 of this Covenant reads: "Every human being has the inherent right to life. Thus right shall be protected by law. No one shall be arbitrarily deprived of his life. … In countries which have not abolished the death penalty, sentence of death may be imposed only for the most serious crimes in accordance with the law in force at the time of the commission of the crime…." These themes also form the basis for the Constitution of the Federal Republic of Nigeria, chapter IV, sections 33 to 44, on fundamental human rights.

Political Rights, which is the second category of the first generation rights, was formed in the early 19th century. It was formed in consonance with the formation of civil human rights, and they meant an extension of the existing rights, especially of the aristocracy in England, to other sections of the population. On this theme, article 24 of the Universal Declaration of Human Rights of 1948 emphatically states: "Everyone has the right to take part in the government of his country, directly or through freely

324 This review of the three generations of human rights will be based on the analysis of van der Ven, J.A., et al, Ibid. pp. 97 – 105.

chosen representatives". Article 25 of the International Covenant on Civil and Political Rights collaborated: "Every citizen shall have the right and the opportunity… to take part in the conduct of public affairs, directly or through freely chosen representatives". The Nigerian Constitution explicated this in chapter VI, section 40, which allows freedom of peaceful assembly and association.

Judicial Rights, which is the third category of the first generation rights points to the right to justice and equality before the law. This involves both the vertical relation between the citizens and the government, and horizontal relation between citizens. Backing this theme, article 9 of the Universal Declaration of Human Rights of 1948 declares: "no one shall be subjected to arbitrary arrest, detention or exile". Article 14 of the International Covenant on Civil and Political Rights supports: "All persons shall be equal before the courts and tribunals". The Nigerian Constitution beautifully toed this line in the Chapter VI, sections 35, 36 and 46. Sections 35 and 36 advocates for right to liberty and right to fair hearing in court respectively, while section 46 offers citizens the freedom to apply to the High Court in any State for redress of alleged violations of the provisions of the said chapter.

(ii) Second Generation Rights

The second generation of human rights comprise of economic, social and cultural rights. They are said to have been formulated in the course of the 20th century. Of significance importance here is the establishment of the International Labor Organization in 1919. The first formal definition of these rights was done in the Universal Declaration of Human Rights in 1948, and the preamble readily indicates the aspiration "to promote social progress and better standards of life in larger freedom". This is enlarged in succeeding articles into the right to work (article 23), to rest and leisure (article 24), "to a standard of living adequate for the health and well-being of himself and his family, including food, clothing, housing and medical care and necessary social services, and the right to security in the event of unemployment, sickness, disability, widowhood, old age or other lack of livelihood in circumstances beyond his control" (article 25), "the right to education" (article 26), and the right freely to participate in the cultural life of the community" (article 27).

The International Covenant on Economic, Social and Cultural Rights of 1996 implanted these rights in international law, clearly specified as the right of all "to the enjoyment of just and favorable conditions of work which ensure, in particular: remuneration which provides all workers, as minimum, with "fair wages … (and) a decent living for themselves and their families …" (article 7).

In the 1999 Constitution of the Federal Republic of Nigeria, these rights are designated in Chapter Two, section 16, under Fundamental Objectives and directive Principles of State Policy. Part of the number 1 of this section on economic welfare reads, "The State shall direct its policy towards ensuring that suitable and adequate shelter, suitable and adequate food, reasonable national minimum living wage, old age care and pensions, and unemployment, sick benefits and welfare of the disabled are provided for all citizens". On Social order, the number 3 of the same section reads: "the State shall direct its policy towards ensuring that (a) all citizens, without discrimination on any group whatsoever, have the opportunity for securing adequate means of livelihood as well as adequate opportunity to secure suitable employment. (b) Conditions of work are just and humane, and there are adequate facilities for leisure and for social, religious and cultural life". This aspect also covers health and medical care of citizens, protection for children and young persons against any form of exploitation and neglect, and evolution and promotion of family life.

It is very striking and worrisome to observe that these rights are not categorized under the fundamental human rights. They are also designated as objectives and directive principles of State policy. My interpretation of this placement is that of little regard for these rights as rights very fundamental to human beings. I may be wrong about this conclusion, but that it the signal it gives me.

(iii) Third Generation Rights

As earlier mentioned, third generation rights are collective rights, designated as such by the former director of the Division of Human Rights and Peace of UNESCO, Karl Vasak. He said that they are meant to augment the first and second generations rights. He classified them as: rights to development, the right to a healthy environment, the right to peace, the right to co-ownership of the common heritage of humankind, and the right to communicate.

Since then the Advisory Committee of 1995 has clarified the various subjects and addressees of collective rights. These categories are then said to be very fundamental to humankind. But J. van der Ven points out some problems with regard to denoting the holders of collective rights. These rights are rendered less practicable because of the harmony that is noticed in some cases between Subject and Addressee. The State, for example, is seen as subject and at the same time Addressee of collective rights like, right to peace and right to co-ownership. This is so because the State is the Addressee of all human rights, in either negative sense or positive sense. With regard to the complications embedded in peoples being holders of collective rights, J. van der Ven concluded that "indigenous peoples and cultural minorities may also be regarded as subjects of collective rights, again with the state as addressee".[325]

He also noted that there is contention in this area between proponents and opponents. "The claims made by these communities may be legitimate, it is argued, but that does not mean that they need to be formulated as collective rights".[326] The logic behind this claim is that other existing human rights may cover the claims being made in this regard, such as the right to enjoy culture, language and religion.[327] Others argue for providing a scope for collective rights, especially for cultural minorities on the basis of the principle of equality.

It is however pointed out that the Universal Declaration of Human Rights of 1948 offers little or no basis for such a move. The emphasis the declaration made is on the individual person, hence: "everyone has the right …" Reclusive allusion is made to 'the community', in the manner that "everyone has duties to the community in which alone the free and full development of his property is possible" (article 29) – but there is no mention of any community right as such.

325 Ibid. p. 105.
326 Ibid.
327 Donders 2002, 327 –345, In: van der Ven, J.A., et al, Ibid.

Legitimation of the idea of collective rights in the official documents is found in the first articles of both the International Covenant on Civil and Political Rights of 1966 and the International Covenant on Economic, Social and Cultural Rights of 1966. Both of them uphold nations' right to self-determination: "All peoples have the right of self-determination" (article 1). An allusion is made to the rights of members of minorities also in the International Covenant of Civil and Political Rights of 1966: "In those states in which ethnic, religious or linguistic minorities exist, persons belonging to such minorities shall not be denied the right, in community with the other members of their group, to enjoy their own culture, to profess and practice their own religion or to use their own language" (article 27). Another example may be seen in the UNESCO Declaration on Race and Prejudice of 1978, where it is declared: "all individuals and groups have the right to be different, to consider themselves as different and to be regarded as such" (article 1).

The Nigerian Constitution of 1999 also placed these collective rights under the Fundamental objectives and directive principles of State policy. Again, I am not comfortable with this placement in so far as these rights are also very fundamental to humanity. Nonetheless, these collective rights are found in the Chapter Two of the Constitution, especially in sections 18 and 20. Section 18 articulated on human development, especially as it regards eradication of illiteracy: "Government shall direct its policy towards ensuring that there are equal and adequate educational opportunities at all level". Section 20 states that "the State shall protect and improve the environment and safeguard the water, air and land, forest and wildlife of Nigeria". An aspect of collective rights that is categorized under fundamental human rights in the Nigerian Constitution is with regard to minority rights. Section 42, Article 1 of this category states that "a citizen of Nigeria of a particular community, ethnic group, place of origin, sex, religion or political opinion shall not, by reason only that he is such a person: be subjected … to disabilities or restrictions to which citizens of Nigeria of other communities, either ethnic groups, places of origin, sex, religious or political opinions are not made subject". Though this section broadly speaking is for right to non-discrimination, but it is not devoid of an expression of concern for minority rights, especially making mention of restrictions against any ethnic, religious or political group.

The above overview of the three generations of human rights points out to us that all those rights in their various categories belong to all citizens as well as all human beings.[328] Having attempted the establishment of that fact, I will go further to investigate the attitudes of the research respondents towards human rights in the following specific rights that represent the three generations: civil rights (liberal attitudes and traditionalism), right to life (abortion and euthanasia), political rights (right to protest and refugees' freedom), Judicial rights (rights of terrorists and mass murderers), Socio-economic rights (children's' rights, women's rights and right to decent standard of living), and environmental rights (state responsibility and individual responsibility). These will also be approached from theoretical and empirical perspectives.

4.3.1 Theoretical Perspective

In investigating the attitudes of the research respondents towards these three generations of human rights, I have created room for divergences in character as described above. This implies that the measuring instruments have to be modeled in a suitable way for this study. The instrument used for measuring the first generation centers strictly on the legal character of the individual rights; the instrument for the second generation rights dwells on the legal character of the state's obligation; and on the instrument for third generation rights attention is focused on moral obligations, especially those of individuals and the State; for example, their awareness, appreciation, action and readiness to make sacrifices for the sake of the environment. The central theoretical question here is to find out to what extent the attitudes of the research respondents towards the church contribute to or influence their attitudes towards these rights.

Their attitude towards civil rights will be expected from six liberties known as "negative rights" or "rights to negative actions". They are: freedom of speech, freedom of the press, freedom of assembly, right to privacy, freedom of lifestyle and freedom of religion. They are referred to in this context as 'liberal attitudes' and 'traditionalism'. Woman's right to obtain legal abortion and euthanasia will be used to determine their attitude towards right to life. Political rights are expected to show their attitudes with

328 van der Ven, J.A., et al, Ibid., p. 105.

regard to rejection of political oppression, active political participation and passive political participation. Judicial rights are meant to show their attitudes regarding equality before the law and adequate legal protection of people. Socio-economic rights are meant to manifest their judgment regarding children's rights (against exploitation and neglect), women's rights (equality) as well as the State's duty to provide essential needs for the society such as: employment, health care and decent standard of living. And finally their judgment on environmental rights will be shown in items regarding the State's and individual's responsibilities respectively towards a healthy environment.

For the theoretical supposition of the human rights attitudes of the respondents, permit me to use the same problems and conflicts I pointed out in the historical sketch and facts I presented earlier in this chapter regarding the relationship between human rights and the church in Nigeria. Going by those problems and conflicts and the eventual reactions of the respondents, I also expect that their attitudes to human rights issues will be a progressive and transformational kind. The empirical perspective will tell us more about the extent of the agreement between the two domains.

4.3.2 Empirical Perspective

Going by the same method I used for the empirical perspective of the attitudes of the respondents towards the church, I will also operationalise the various aspects of human rights already mentioned in the theoretical perspective. The aim is to also find out the corroboration between the theoretical perspective and empirical perspective. The cells in the tables below contain the average values of human rights attitudes among the respondents on a five-point scale stretching from 1 (I totally disagree), 2 (I disagree), 3 (I am not sure), 4 (I agree) to 5 (I fully agree), for all the items. It is also to be noted that some Constructs with one Variable would be summarized, hence forming the calculation for "Total Statistics", and as such Reliability analysis is not necessary. In other words, their correlations tables would be given. As by the former empirical analysis, the Reliability Analysis will be attached to the major Tables as part of explaining the Constructs in question.

The Histograms will be presented alongside the Tables. An interpretation of each theme will be made.

4.3.2.1 CIVIL RIGHTS

Table 34: Liberal Attitudes

Item-Total Statistics

	Scale Mean if Item Deleted	Scale Variance if Item Deleted	Corrected Item-Total Correlation	Cronbach's Alpha if Item Deleted
q31_17 Prayers in public schools should be forbidden	47.07	58.040	.479	.773
q31_3 Making fun of religious people in cabinets is a legally protected right	46.57	58.302	.530	.768
q31_12 Making fun of atheists in public meetings is permissible	46.28	60.187	.511	.770
q31_2 In regard to euthanasia politicians should decide irrespective of any religious leaders will	46.13	61.113	.472	.774
q31_18 Inflicting severe physical suffering on potential terrorists is prohibited	46.19	61.292	.401	.780
q31_11 In regard to abortion politicians should take decisions independently of religious leaders	46.19	60.506	.447	.776
q31_13 Children should be free to discuss all moral ideas and subjects in schools, no matter what	45.45	65.482	.265	.790
q31_14 A cabinet minister should allow his striking officials to meet in a ministerial building	45.75	62.838	.460	.776
q31_15 TV journalists with radical ideas have a civil right to employment	45.69	63.864	.371	.783
q31_9 Imposing inhuman mental treatment on people accused of mass murder is forbidden	45.82	63.621	.342	.785
q31_5 Minority groups should be free to use the town hall to hold protest meetings	45.62	63.354	.445	.778
q31_6 Newspaper columnists should be free to express radical convictions	45.57	65.329	.307	.787
q31_4 The communitys moral standards should be critically debated in schools	45.55	64.365	.331	.785
q31_10 Any form of sexual relations between adults should be their individual choice	45.90	62.404	.361	.784

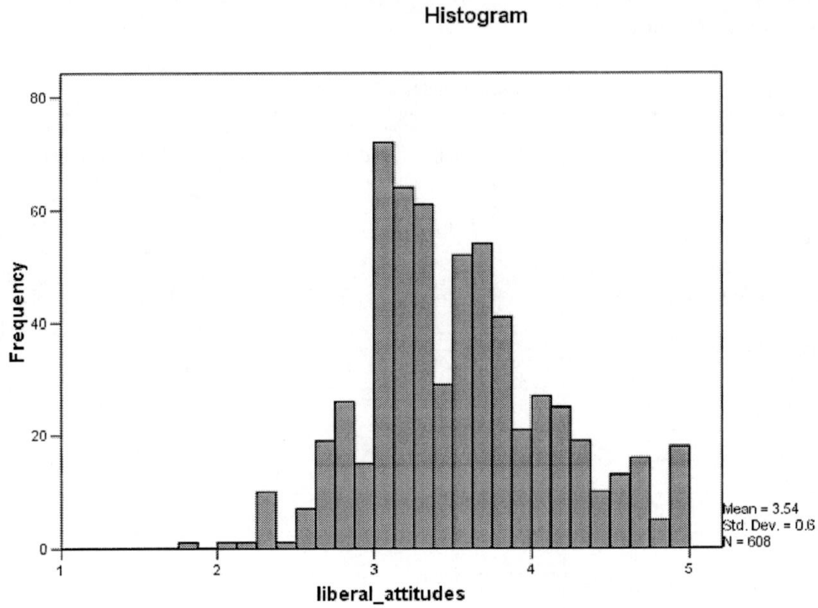

Interpretation

The 'liberal attitudes' border on five liberties – freedom of lifestyle, freedom of religion, freedom of speech, freedom of assembly and freedom of the press. The above Histogram gives us a positive attitude of the respondents towards these liberties. This result presents a picture of a progressive generation of future leaders. This reaction goes against the traditional current in the Nigerian society, whereby such liberal issues are seen as being too progressive hence dangerous for the upbringing of youths as well as for the values of the society. It is a sign that these future leaders do no longer accept the extreme conservative attitude or trends of adult class both in families and in the society at large. This tendency could also explain further why the Islamic school Authorities did not allow us access to their students, perhaps for fears of instigating anti-Islamic-values tendency in their youth.

However, the influence of the religious background of the respondents is also very visible here. It borders mainly on the first question of this domain on forbidding prayers in public schools. The respondents rejected this suggestion. This indicates the strong influence their religious attitudes have over their attitudes towards civil matters. We have here a picture of a progressive generation with strong religious inclination. In other words, their progressive attitudes have religious undertone.

Table 35: Traditionalism

Item-Total Statistics

	Scale Mean if Item Deleted	Scale Variance if Item Deleted	Corrected Item-Total Correlation	Cronbach's Alpha if Item Deleted
q31_16 The police are only allowed to inspect peoples cars under strict judicial conditions	11.18	7.120	.263	.592
q31_8 Politicians are not allowed to interfere with religious communities	11.20	6.258	.419	.469
q31_7 Police searches of private homes without a search warrant are prohibited	11.04	6.265	.411	.476
q31_9 Imposing inhuman mental treatment on people accused of mass murder is forbidden	11.17	6.874	.377	.506

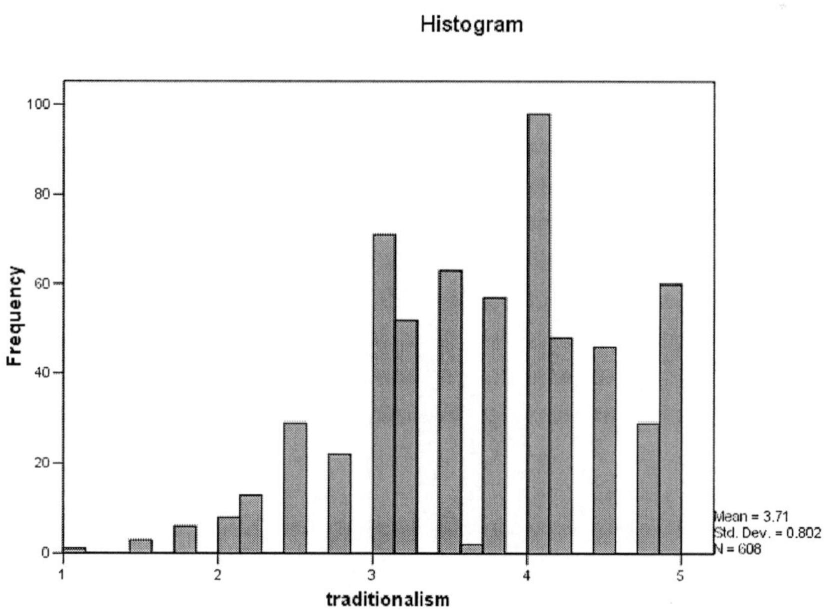

Interpretation

'Traditionalism' represents the freedom of privacy and human dignity, especially as it regards police search and inspection of homes and people's cars, interference with religious communities by politicians and imposition of inhuman mental treatment on people accused of mass murder.

Two of the questions were presented in negative forms and the other two had conditions attached thereto. This method of presentation is to make the intensity of the themes clear enough to the respondents so as to enable them make clearer judgment on the themes in question. The above Histogram shows the acceptance of the respondents that the police could search and inspect homes and cars only on the conditions of possessing genuine search warrant and under strict judicial conditions. Their acceptance that politicians are not allowed to interfere with religious communities is clearly explained by their strong religious inclinations. The respondents' clear acceptance that imposing inhuman mental treatment on people accused of mass murder should be forbidden is also a positive sign of the acceptance of human rights culture as it pertains to the respect of the human dignity. It shows also their level of understanding of the law, that an accused remains innocent until proved guilty. These are positive and transformative attitudes in this domain of traditionalism.

4.3.2.2 RIGHT TO LIFE

Table 36: Abortion

Item-Total Statistics

	Scale Mean if Item Deleted	Scale Variance if Item Deleted	Corrected Item-Total Correlation	Cronbach's Alpha if Item Deleted
q32_1 There is a strong chance of serious defect in the baby	9.91	9.656	.576	.749
q32_2 Economically she cannot afford any more children	10.17	9.223	.645	.713
q32_3 The womans own health is seriously endangered by the pregnancy	9.70	10.315	.546	.763
q32_4 Psychologically she cannot afford any more children	10.04	9.576	.626	.724

Histogram

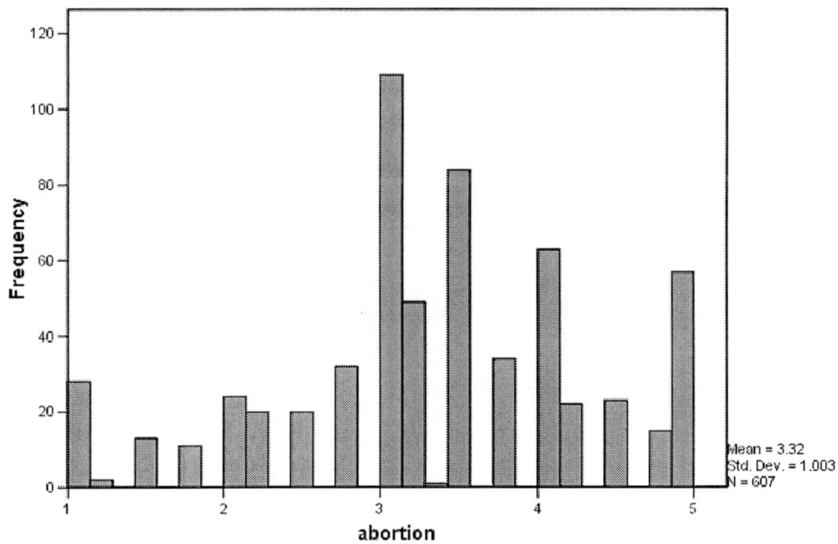

Table 37: Euthanasia

Correlations

			q33_2 The doctor is allowed to do this, only if palliative care is exhausted
Spearman's rho	q33_1 The doctor is allowed to do this	Correlation Coefficient	.614
		Sig. (2-tailed)	.000
		N	608

Histogram

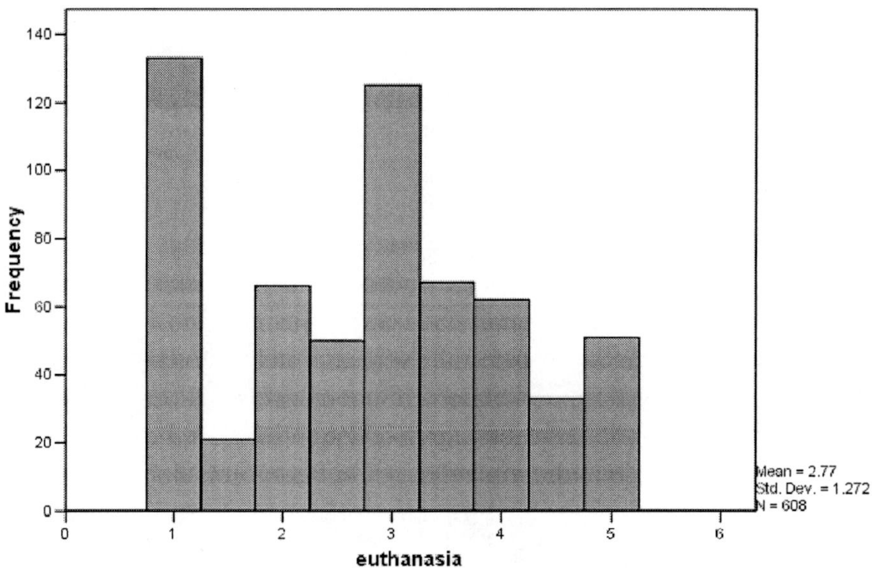

Interpretation

The questions in this domain border on the right of a woman to commit legal abortion under health, economic and psychological conditions; and the voluntary request for the termination of life by someone who is at the final stage of an incurable disease. The first question receives a positive ambivalence from the respondents, while the latter on euthanasia got negative ambivalence.

This is indeed a delicate area. The conditions given for obtaining legal abortion in this situation could be seen as morally and psychologically considerable. For example the outcome of the defect in a baby could be also considered to be detrimental to the health of the mother. Moreover bringing a physically and possibly, mentally disabled child in the world could be a grave psychological trauma for the family and eventually for the child in question. The respondents could have tended towards this positive ambivalence as a result of these health and psychological reasons. I presume that economic consideration could not have played any major role in their judgment because of the spirit of communalism in the Nigerian society context. This is one of the values of the African people I discussed in chapter two. The respondents' reaction to this aspect is progressive despite their ambivalent tendency.

It is not surprising that the respondents responded negatively ambivalent to the question of termination of life. Africans in general believe that life is a gift from God and only God has the right to take it away from a living person. This belief is also not only African, but also has Christian and Islamic characters[329]. So this religious conviction must have contributed immensely to the respondents' rejection of termination of life irrespective of the conditions.

I could add to their reaction: no condition is morally acceptable for the termination of life. The African value of the sacredness of life (in chapter two) explains this attitude better.

329 The incessant violent termination of life in Nigeria as a result of religious and ethnic crises is opposed to this beautiful African cultural value. It therefore calls for special attention.

4.3.2.3 POLITICAL RIGHTS

Table 38: Protest is allowed; Refugee's Freedom

Correlations

Correlation Coefficient

		q34_1 The police should not use force against political demonstrators	q34_2 The government is obliged to guarantee political refugees freedom to travel	q34_3 The government should not pass a law forbidding all forms of public protest	q34_4 The government is obliged to provide a decent standard of living for political refugees
Spearman's rho	q34_1 The police should not use force against political demonstrators	1.000	.389	.433	.333
	q34_2 The government is obliged to guarantee political refugees freedom to travel	.389	1.000	.392	.363
	q34_3 The government should not pass a law forbidding all forms of public protest	.433	.392	1.000	.398
	q34_4 The government is obliged to provide a decent standard of living for political refugees	.333	.363	.398	1.000

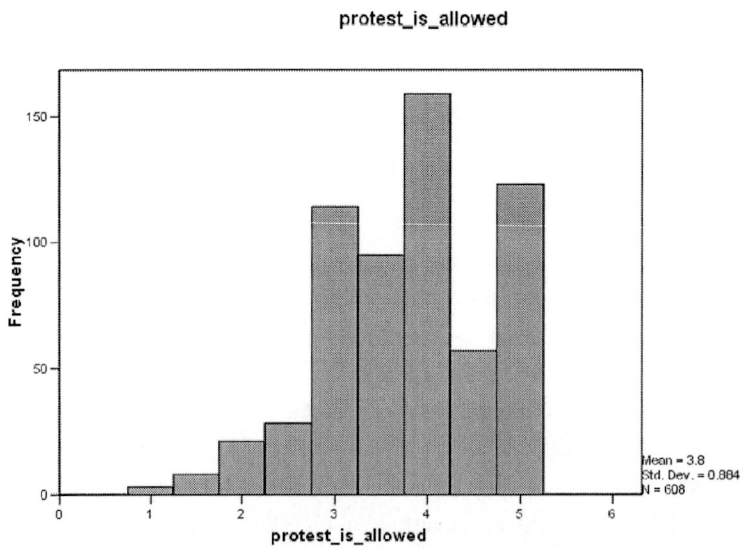

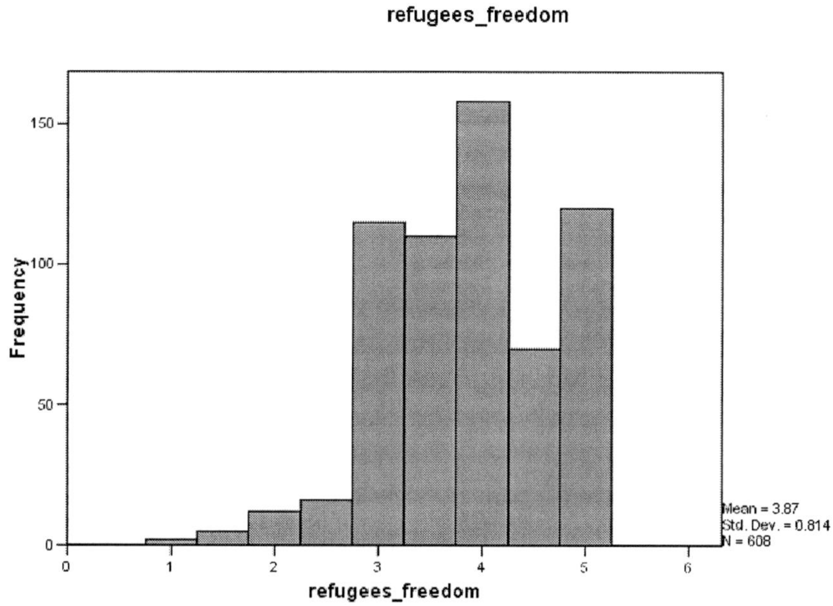

Interpretation

Political rights domain represents two themes: allowing protest and refugee's freedom. The questions asked on political oppression came in a negative formula, as the above table shows. The questions on refugee's freedom were presented as obligations. The respondents responded positively to these themes thereby rejecting political oppression and accepted the government's obligation to grant political refugees travel freedom and decent standard of living.

Political oppression is almost a daily occurrence in Nigeria, and has received the disapproval of every peace-seeking person in the country. This gives us an explanation for the rejection expressed by the respondents. Their positive attitude towards refugees could be based on the special attention strangers generally receive in Nigeria. Africans in general are known for their hospitality, especially to strangers. So this cultural value could have contributed immensely to the respondents' positive attitudes towards refugees whom they regard as strangers. In these two themes we see progressive and transformational attitudes of the respondents towards right to protest and love for the stranger. They are attitudes rooted in transformation trends and cultural values.

4.3.2.4 JUDICIAL RIGHTS

Table 39: Rights of terrorists and mass murderers

Correlations

			q35_2 A mass murderer should be informed of his,her right to keep silent before the court
Spearman's rho	q35_1 Guaranteeing terrorists access to a lawyer is necessary to protect their individual rights	Correlation Coefficient	.316
		Sig. (2-tailed)	.000
		N	607

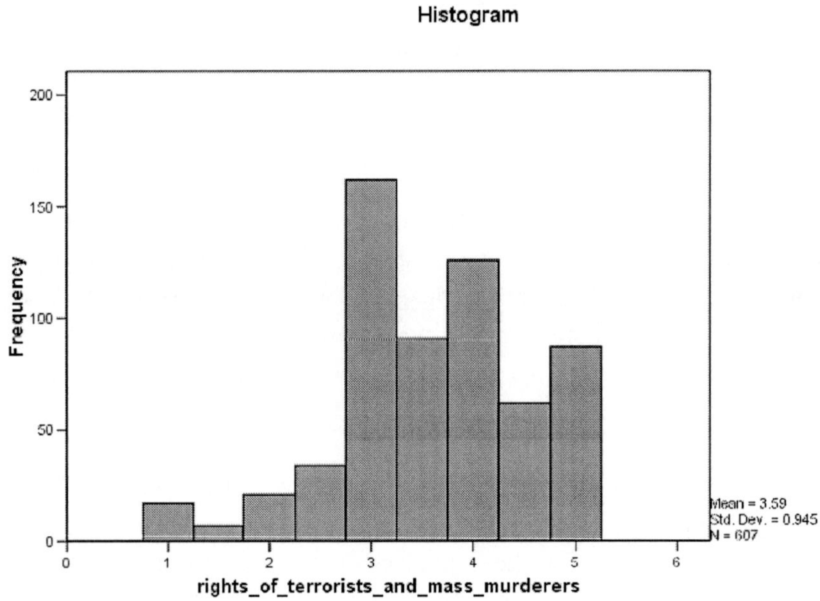

Interpretation

Judicial rights represent the rights of terrorists and murderers. The above table gives us a positive correlation between the two themes: guaranteeing terrorists access to a lawyer being necessary to protect their individual rights correlates with mass murder being informed of his/ her right to keep silent before the court. The respondents responded positively to this attitude.

The judicial system in Nigeria is generally poor, as was discussed in the first chapter. Corruption and lack of just handling have contributed to the mess the Nigerian judicial system finds itself into. Innocent persons have in most cases suffered unjustly in the judicial process because they do not have the means of buying their way through the process. This positive reaction of the students is a positive indication that they understand to a reasonable extent due process in law. It is a transformative and progressive tendency.

4.3.2.5 SOCIO-ECONOMIC RIGHTS

Table 40: Children's rights

Correlations

			q36_8 The state is obliged to protect childrens right to engage in play and recreational activities
Spearman's rho	q36_3 The state is obliged to protect children from neglect or negligent treatment	Correlation Coefficient	.493
		Sig. (2-tailed)	.000
		N	607

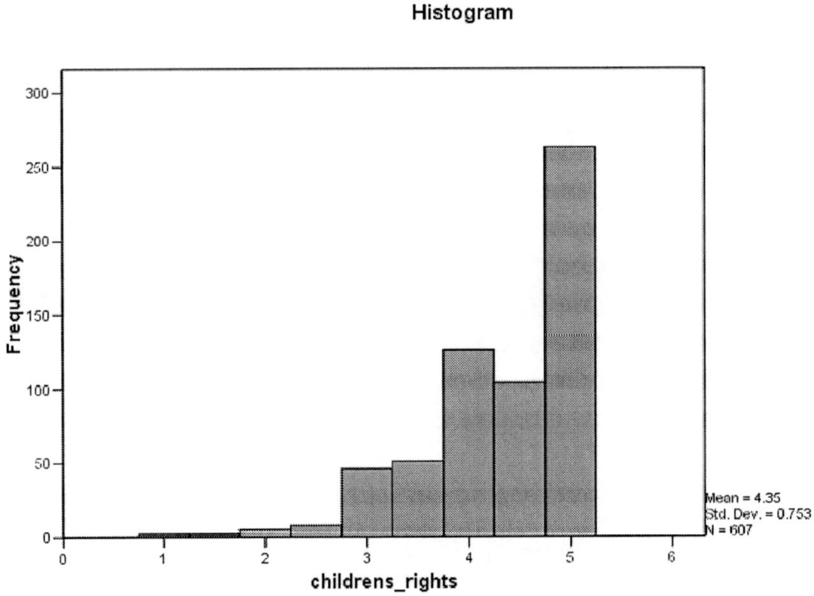

Table 41: Women's rights

Correlations

			q36_7 The state should protect womens right to adequate job opportunities
Spearman's rho	q36_4 The state should protect womens right to ac/quire and administer property	Correlation Coefficient	.556
		Sig. (2-tailed)	.000
		N	607

Histogram

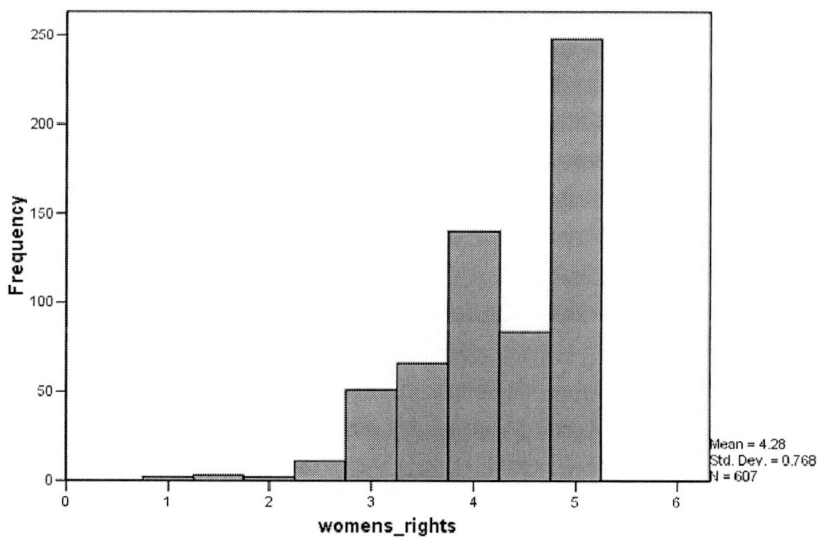

Table 42: Right to decent standard of living

Item-Total Statistics

	Scale Mean if Item Deleted	Scale Variance if Item Deleted	Corrected Item-Total Correlation	Cronbach's Alpha if Item Deleted
q36_1 The government should provide a job for everybody who wants one	8.66	2.382	.389	.685
q36_5 The government should provide a decent standard of living for the old	8.54	2.265	.535	.486
q36_6 The government should provide a decent standard of living for the unemployed	8.65	2.322	.506	.524

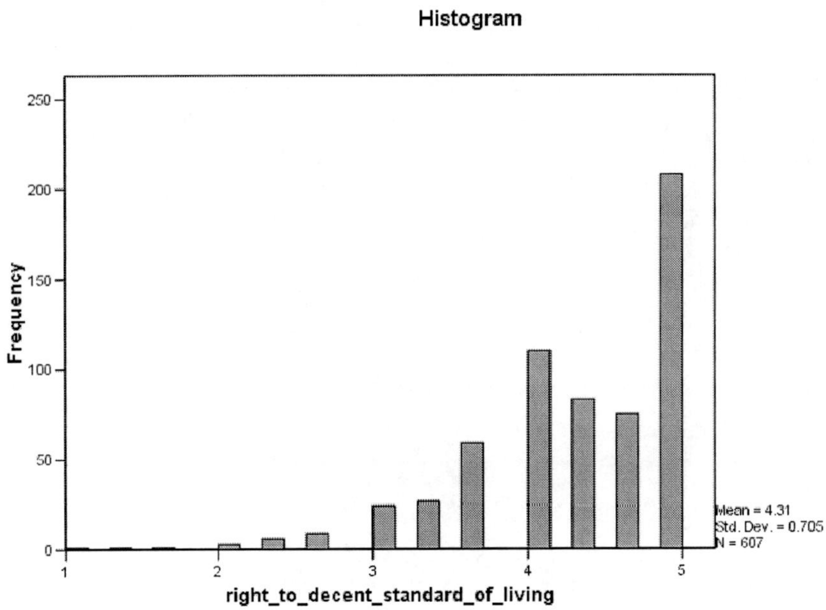

Interpretation

The themes of socio-economic rights dwell on children's right, women's right and right to decent standard of living. These themes received outstanding positive attitudes. Some factors could be responsible for these special tendencies.

The attitudes of the respondents towards state's obligation to protect children from neglect or negligent treatment correlated with their opinion that the State is obliged to protect children's right to engage in play and recreational activities. The positive attitude towards the children's rights shows the respondents' interest in the protection of the rights of the child since the child is considered very delicate and as such should be assisted in his/ her growth and formation. Unfortunately the Nigerian society and government has been widely accused of neglecting their obligation towards the rights of children. Chapter one has already some information in this area. Then most of these youths (respondents) just passed the childhood stage (as their age range in Table 2 indicates). So it is presumed that their childhood experiences of neglect from the adults could still be very fresh in their memories. And as such they indicate a rejection of such neglect for the coming generation of children. We see here a very strong transformative and progressive attitude.

In the same direction, the theme of women's right received yet another significant positive attitude. The respondents' opinion that the State should protect women's right to acquire and administer property correlates with their attitudes towards State's protection of women's right to adequate job opportunities. In the section on Women's Rights in chapters one and two, some descriptions were made regarding the violation of women's rights in Nigeria on religious and cultural grounds respectively. They are often looked upon as the inferior sex and are often discriminated against on matters of equality. Those violations could better explain the positive indication of the respondents towards the two themes in question. Those violations form the daily lives of women. These youths (respondents) are witnesses of same in public and private spheres. They therewith indicate their willingness to raise the dignity of women when it comes to family roles, economic and other similar societal matters.

The gender percentage (as Table 1 shows) indicates that majority of the respondents are male students. And going by the strong positive indication in this aspect, it is worthy to note that the male students strongly reject the traditional relationship between males and females in the traditional set-up in Nigeria. Hence a positive and transformative sign of behavior change in the male domain. These set of positive attitudes give us positive signals for changing mentality among the Nigerian youths.

The attitude of the respondents towards the next theme on right to decent standard of living indicates their rejection of the present status quo in Nigeria. The economic gap between the rich and poor has remained so wide that the poor gets poorer and the rich richer. The fact of more than 65% of the Nigerian population living below one Dollar per day explains the support of the respondents for the government's provision of job for everybody who wants to work. Welfare of the aged and unemployed is closely tied to this aspect of welfare. In other words the respondents support a social welfare that is all-inclusive: young and old, employed and unemployed. This attitude is a significant call for bridging the gap for the purpose of bringing about the welfare of all.

4.3.2.6 ENVIRONMENTAL RIGHTS

Table 43: State's responsibility

Correlations

			q37_3 The state should reduce air pollution by industry by imposing legal limits
Spearman's rho	q37_1 The state should protect unspoiled nature	Correlation Coefficient	.380
		Sig. (2-tailed)	.000
		N	607

Histogram

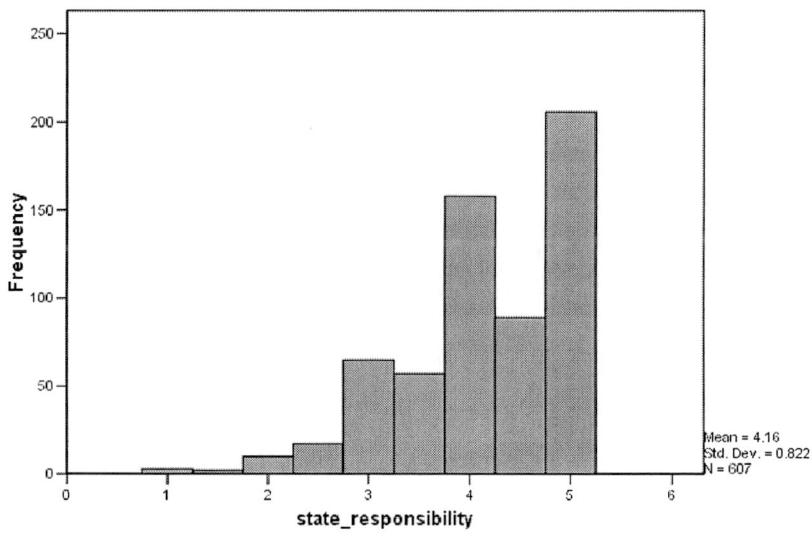

Table 44: Individual's responsibility

Correlations

			q37_4 I am willing to pay higher prices for products if that would mean less industrial pollution
Spearman's rho	q37_2 I am willing to make certain sacrifices for the sake of more beautiful environment	Correlation Coefficient	.340
		Sig. (2-tailed)	.000
		N	606

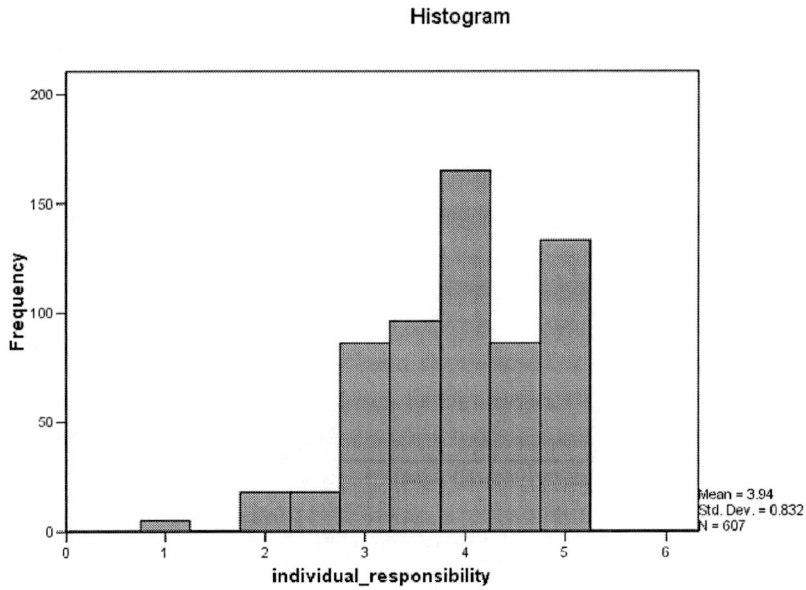

Interpretation

The question on environmental rights is divided into State responsibility and individual responsibility. These two aspects receive yet another significant positive response.

The respondents' attitudes towards the State's protection of unspoiled nature correlated with their opinion that the State should reduce air pollution by industries by imposing legal limits. In chapter one I discussed the violation of environmental rights in Nigeria extensively. Those violations have caused so much damage to the Nigerian society at large. The art of oil exploration by most of the oil companies in Nigeria do not deserve any approval. The international community has condemned this radical behavior and has often called on the Nigerian government to get into the matter through legal methods. This explains why the questions were formulated from the point of view of State obligation. There is no doubt that the Nigerian government has failed her citizens in this regard. Therefore it explains why the respondents opine that the government should indeed play a major role in protecting the environment.

On individual responsibility the respondents also indicated their readiness to contribute towards a healthy environment. Their attitude towards willingness to make certain sacrifices for the sake of more beautiful environment correlated with their readiness to pay higher prices for products if that would mean less industrial pollution. Although their level of agreement is high, their expectation on the state's obligation is higher. In other words, they expect the state to take the lead and thereby motivate private concerns and individuals. Over and above all, we see here a significant positive sign for the protection of the environment among Nigerian youths.

Having giving the general analysis of both the empirical attitudes of the respondents towards the church (religion) and towards human rights, it now becomes necessary to present the correlations between these two attitudes of Nigerian youths in order to finally determine to what extent their attitudes towards the church(religion) influence their attitudes towards human rights.

4.4 CORRELATIONS BETWEEN ATTITUDES TOWARDS THE CHURCH AND ATTITUDES TOWARDS HUMAN RIGHTS

The presentation of the research themes from the theoretical and empirical perspective has been successfully completed. The results of the collaboration show significant agreement between the theoretical and empirical domains. Despite the positive results we got from the analysis above, we do not yet have the end result as to draw our conclusion. That calls for the present exercise: making a general analysis of the entire themes by means of Correlation.

Employing the means of correlation in our context is to find out the extent of relationship between the themes on religious practices, religious convictions and religious communities with the themes on human rights. With this exercise we get the answer to my central questions: what is the influence of the religious (ecclesiastical) attitudes of the respondents towards their human rights attitudes? What message do these youths want to communicate to the church in Nigeria through this exercise?

We have three possibilities for a correlation between attitudes towards the church and attitudes towards human rights. First is the possibility of a positive correlation. Second is the possibility of a negative correlation. And third is the possibility of a zero correlation. Positive correlation is observed as far as an item in the religious (ecclesiastical) attitudes increases to the same extent as a theme on human rights increases. A negative correlation is found as far as an item of religious (ecclesiastical) attitudes increases to the same extent as a theme on human rights attitudes decreases. Correlation becomes zero when there is no correlation at all. It is also necessary to mention that a positive correlation could be either strong or weak. This deserves also an explanation where such is found.

The following correlations tables will present how the two attitudes stand towards each other: the themes on religious attitudes towards the themes on human rights attitudes (as the immediate table shows). Each of the tables will be interpreted respectively.

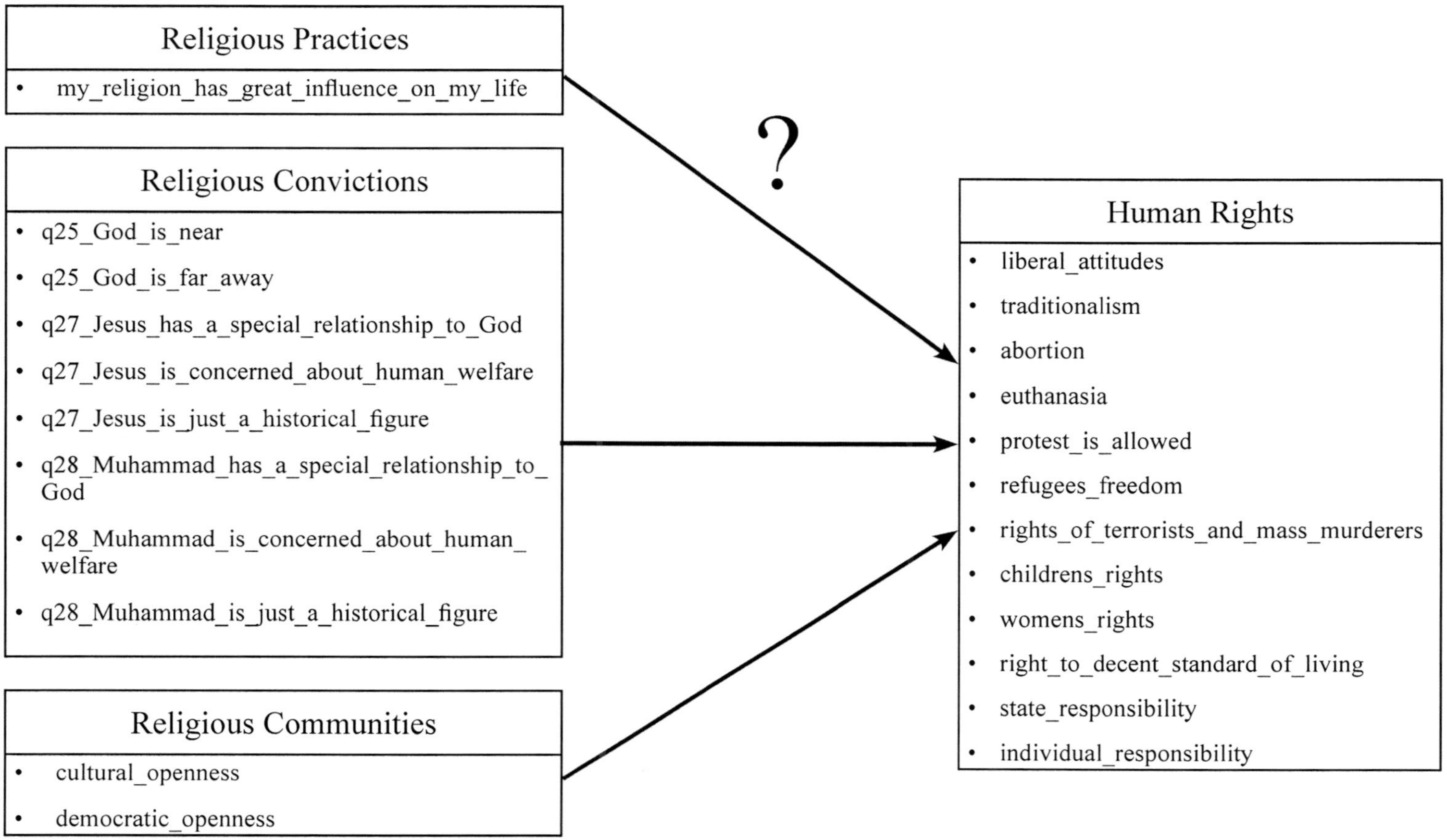
Religious Practices
• my_religion_has_great_influence_on_my_life
Religious Convictions
• q25_God_is_near
• q25_God_is_far_away
• q27_Jesus_has_a_special_relationship_to_God
• q27_Jesus_is_concerned_about_human_welfare
• q27_Jesus_is_just_a_historical_figure
• q28_Muhammad_has_a_special_relationship_to_God
• q28_Muhammad_is_concerned_about_human_welfare
• q28_Muhammad_is_just_a_historical_figure
Religious Communities
• cultural_openness
• democratic_openness
?
Human Rights
• liberal_attitudes
• traditionalism
• abortion
• euthanasia
• protest_is_allowed
• refugees_freedom
• rights_of_terrorists_and_mass_murderers
• childrens_rights
• womens_rights
• right_to_decent_standard_of_living
• state_responsibility
• individual_responsibility

Table 45: liberal_attitudes

Correlations

	Spearman's rho		
	liberal_attitudes		
	Correlation Coefficient	Sig. (2-tailed)	N
my_religion_has_great_influence_on_my_life	.060	.139	608
q25_God_is_near	.168	.000	607
q25_God_is_far_away	.191	.000	607
q27_Jesus_has_a_special_relationship_to_God	.134	.001	608
q27_Jesus_is_concerned_about_human_welfare	.187	.000	608
q27_Jesus_is_just_a_historical_figure	.323	.000	608
q28_Muhammad_has_a_special_relationship_to_God	.318	.000	608
q28_Muhammad_is_concerned_about_human_welfare	.277	.000	608
q28_Muhammad_is_just_a_historical_figure	.307	.000	608
cultural_openness	.352	.000	608
democratic_openness	.337	.000	608

Interpretation

In the correlations table on liberal attitudes we found no negative correlations but we have one zero correlation between the first item on reli-gious attitudes ("my religion has great influence on my life") and the liberal attitudes. This means that no relationship exists between these two attitudes, and as such demands an explanation: It has been previously established that all our respondents have claims to being religious and also attest to the influence their religion has on them. That notwithstand-ing, the zero correlation between this religious influence and the liberal attitude indicates that their religion do not determine their attitudes towards the civil rights of freedom of speech, freedom of the press, freedom of assembly, right to privacy, freedom of lifestyle and freedom of religion. That gives us an impression of two separate 'worlds'. All other themes on religious attitudes correlated with all the themes on liberal attitudes. We found strong positive correlations between religious attitudes and liberal attitudes in the following areas: 'Jesus is just a historical figure', 'Muhammad has a special relationship to God', and 'Muhammad is just a historical figure ', 'cultural openness and democratic openness'. In other words this latter result is an indication that the religious attitudes of the respondents corroborated very strongly with their human rights attitudes on liberal rights.

Table 46: traditionalism

Correlations

	Spearman's rho		
	traditionalism		
	Correlation Coefficient	Sig. (2-tailed)	N
my_religion_has_great_influence_on_my_life	.109	.007	608
q25_God_is_near	.173	.000	607
q25_God_is_far_away	.148	.000	607
q27_Jesus_has_a_special_relationship_to_God	.127	.002	608
q27_Jesus_is_concerned_about_human_welfare	.186	.000	608
q27_Jesus_is_just_a_historical_figure	.127	.002	608
q28_Muhammad_has_a_special_relationship_to_God	.161	.000	608
q28_Muhammad_is_concerned_about_human_welfare	.153	.000	608
q28_Muhammad_is_just_a_historical_figure	.164	.000	608
cultural_openness	.301	.000	608
democratic_openness	.256	.000	608

Interpretation

There are no negative or zero correlations found in the table on traditionalism. The respondents' attitude on religious themes correlated positively to their attitudes towards civil rights on traditional rights regarding privacy and human dignity. In addition we found a strong positive correlation in the domains of 'cultural openness' and 'democratic openness', thereby indicating an extra interest of the respondents in this domain.

Table 47: abortion

Correlations

	Spearman's rho		
	abortion		
	Correlation Coefficient	Sig. (2-tailed)	N
my_religion_has_great_influence_on_my_life	.006	.877	607
q25_God_is_near	.089	.029	606
q25_God_is_far_away	.120	.003	606
q27_Jesus_has_a_special_relationship_to_God	.084	.038	607
q27_Jesus_is_concerned_about_human_welfare	.117	.004	607
q27_Jesus_is_just_a_historical_figure	.292	.000	607
q28_Muhammad_has_a_special_relationship_to_God	.190	.000	607
q28_Muhammad_is_concerned_about_human_welfare	.142	.000	607
q28_Muhammad_is_just_a_historical_figure	.192	.000	607
cultural_openness	.197	.000	607
democratic_openness	.194	.000	607

Interpretation

No negative correlation is found in this domain. But a zero correlation is found between the first item on religious attitudes ("my religion has great influence on my life") and human rights attitudes towards 'abortion'. The 'health' and 'psychological' consequences of this item (as already ex-plained in the empirical perspective on religious attitudes) may have contributed greatly to this development. Positive correlations are found between other themes on religious attitudes and themes on human rights attitudes towards right to life. Then a strong positive correlation is found between the item on religious attitude ('Jesus is just a historical figure') and the right of a woman to abortion.

The question on the right of a woman to obtain legal abortion was pre-sented on three conditions: when there is a strong chance of serious de-fect in the baby; economically she cannot afford any more children; if the woman's health is seriously endangered by the pregnancy; and if psychologically she cannot afford more children. As I already explained earlier, the respondents' positive reaction to this aspect could have been based on the conditions given, especially as it pertains to the woman's health and psychology. It however shows a sympathetic and progressive generation of Nigerian youth.

Table 48: euthanasia

Correlations

	Spearman's rho		
	euthanasia		
	Correlation Coefficient	Sig. (2-tailed)	N
my_religion_has_great_influence_on_my_life	-.116	.004	608
q25_God_is_near	-.025	.539	607
q25_God_is_far_away	.010	.812	607
q27_Jesus_has_a_special_relationship_to_God	-.107	.008	608
q27_Jesus_is_concerned_about_human_welfare	-.133	.001	608
q27_Jesus_is_just_a_historical_figure	.181	.000	608
q28_Muhammad_has_a_special_relationship_to_God	.271	.000	608
q28_Muhammad_is_concerned_about_human_welfare	.249	.000	608
q28_Muhammad_is_just_a_historical_figure	.236	.000	608
cultural_openness	.053	.194	608
democratic_openness	.036	.372	608

Interpretation

We notice a change in the correlations of the religious and human rights themes in this aspect of right to life. We have negative correlations between three of the themes: 'my religion has great influence on my life', 'Jesus has a special relationship to God', and 'Jesus is concerned about human welfare'. Four items on religious attitudes ('God is near', 'God is far away', 'cultural openness', and 'democratic openness') have zero correlations with the right to obtain Euthanasia. Then we found strong positive correlations between the remaining items on religious attitudes ('Muhammad has a special relationship to God', 'Muhammad is concerned about human welfare', and 'Muhammad is just a historical figure') to the human rights item.

We found in this domain a mixed reaction of the respondents: Their re-li-gious practices do not approve of euthanasia in any given condition at all. Then their religious convictions on certain themes (as named above) show no relationship at all between them; and then the remaining themes indicate strong relationship between the items. We see in this domain an extensive tendency of 'uncertainty', and is perhaps explained by the in-ter-pretation of Table 37 in the Empirical perspective on religious atti-tudes. The questions also presented the health and psychological conse-quences of allowing a woman in the final stage of an incurable disease to obtain a painless termination of her life. It is presumed, based on the moral implications of taking away life that most of the respondents may have agreed to this on sympathetic ground, when the doctor must have exhausted all palliative care.

Table 49: protest_is_allowed

Correlations

	Spearman's rho		
	protest_is_allowed		
	Correlation Coefficient	Sig. (2-tailed)	N
my_religion_has_great_influence_on_my_life	.162	.000	608
q25_God_is_near	.226	.000	607
q25_God_is_far_away	.160	.000	607
q27_Jesus_has_a_special_relationship_to_God	.113	.005	608
q27_Jesus_is_concerned_about_human_welfare	.171	.000	608
q27_Jesus_is_just_a_historical_figure	.082	.043	608
q28_Muhammad_has_a_special_relationship_to_God	.239	.000	608
q28_Muhammad_is_concerned_about_human_welfare	.184	.000	608
q28_Muhammad_is_just_a_historical_figure	.146	.000	608
cultural_openness	.335	.000	608
democratic_openness	.260	.000	608

Interpretation

This is the domain of political rights. All the religious themes correlated positively to the political rights themes on the freedom to protest. Two items on religious attitudes ('cultural openness' and 'democratic open-ness') even have strong positive relationship to the human rights item. The respondents thereby indicate that their religious convictions and practices condemn police use of force against political demonstrators, and that the government should not pass a law forbidding all forms of public protest. This tendency thereby projected towards freedom of speech and participatory democracy.

Table 50: refugees_freedom

Correlations

	Spearman's rho		
	refugees_freedom		
	Correlation Coefficient	Sig. (2-tailed)	N
my_religion_has_great_influence_on_my_life	.113	.005	608
q25_God_is_near	.153	.000	607
q25_God_is_far_away	.173	.000	607
q27_Jesus_has_a_special_relationship_to_God	.086	.033	608
q27_Jesus_is_concerned_about_human_welfare	.127	.002	608
q27_Jesus_is_just_a_historical_figure	.143	.000	608
q28_Muhammad_has_a_special_relationship_to_God	.193	.000	608
q28_Muhammad_is_concerned_about_human_welfare	.181	.000	608
q28_Muhammad_is_just_a_historical_figure	.148	.000	608
cultural_openness	.348	.000	608
democratic_openness	.335	.000	608

Interpretation

Freedom of refugees is part of the political rights. Just like in the former, all religious themes correlated positively with the political rights of refu-gees to be guaranteed the freedom to travel and access to a decent stand-ard of living. 'Cul-tural openness' and 'democratic openness' also show strong positive correlation between the items. The respondents regard these as the government's obligations.

Table 51: rights_of_terrorists_and_mass_murderers

Correlations

	Spearman's rho		
	rights_of_terrorists_and_mass_murderers		
	Correlation Coefficient	Sig. (2-tailed)	N
my_religion_has_great_influence_on_my_life	.090	.027	607
q25_God_is_near	.075	.065	606
q25_God_is_far_away	.136	.001	606
q27_Jesus_has_a_special_relationship_to_God	.029	.478	607
q27_Jesus_is_concerned_about_human_welfare	.027	.501	607
q27_Jesus_is_just_a_historical_figure	.128	.002	607
q28_Muhammad_has_a_special_relationship_to_God	.274	.000	607
q28_Muhammad_is_concerned_about_human_welfare	.218	.000	607
q28_Muhammad_is_just_a_historical_figure	.223	.000	607
cultural_openness	.261	.000	607
democratic_openness	.198	.000	607

Interpretation

In the domain of judicial rights, especially as it pertains to rights of terrorists and mass murderers to be given access to lawyer and freedom of keeping silent before the court respectively, we found zero correlation between three items on religious attitudes ('God is near', 'Jesus has a special relationship to God', and 'Jesus is concerned about human wel-fare') and human rights attitudes on. Other items on religious attitudes corroborated positively with the items on human rights attitudes, even with strong positive correlation between 'Muhammad has a special relation to God', Muhammad is concerned about human welfare', and 'cultural openness', and human rights items. The respondents exhibit a high level of understanding regarding due process in law.

Table 52: childrens_rights

Correlations

	Spearman's rho		
	childrens_rights		
	Correlation Coefficient	Sig. (2-tailed)	N
my_religion_has_great_influence_on_my_life	.206	.000	607
q25_God_is_near	.323	.000	606
q25_God_is_far_away	.144	.000	606
q27_Jesus_has_a_special_relationship_to_God	.253	.000	607
q27_Jesus_is_concerned_about_human_welfare	.358	.000	607
q27_Jesus_is_just_a_historical_figure	.063	.119	607
q28_Muhammad_has_a_special_relationship_to_God	.051	.207	607
q28_Muhammad_is_concerned_about_human_welfare	.040	.322	607
q28_Muhammad_is_just_a_historical_figure	.049	.225	607
cultural_openness	.401	.000	607
democratic_openness	.322	.000	607

Interpretation

In the first theme of socio-economic rights, children's rights, we found zero correlations between the themes on religious attitudes ('Jesus is just a historical figure', 'Muhammad has a special relationship to God', 'Mu-hammad is concerned about human welfare', and 'Muhammad is just a historical figure') and children's' rights. Other items on religious attitudes show positive correlation between the two themes, and again strong positive relationship on the items: 'God is near', 'cultural openness', and 'democratic openness'. The respondents regard it as the State obligation to protect children from neglect or negligent treatment and protecting children's right to engage in play and recreational activities.

Table 53: womens_rights

Correlations

	Spearman's rho		
	womens_rights		
	Correlation Coefficient	Sig. (2-tailed)	N
my_religion_has_great_influence_on_my_life	.256	.000	607
q25_God_is_near	.305	.000	606
q25_God_is_far_away	.180	.000	606
q27_Jesus_has_a_special_relationship_to_God	.262	.000	607
q27_Jesus_is_concerned_about_human_welfare	.335	.000	607
q27_Jesus_is_just_a_historical_figure	.090	.026	607
q28_Muhammad_has_a_special_relationship_to_God	.089	.029	607
q28_Muhammad_is_concerned_about_human_welfare	.069	.088	607
q28_Muhammad_is_just_a_historical_figure	.085	.035	607
cultural_openness	.401	.000	607
democratic_openness	.313	.000	607

Interpretation

We also observe in this category of socio-economic rights, on women's rights, another positive correlation between the religious themes and hu-man rights themes, and even a strong positive corroboration between 'God is near', 'Jesus is concerned about human welfare', 'cultural open-ness', and 'democratic openness' with women's rights. A zero correla-tion is found only between 'Muhammad is concerned about human wel-fare' and women's rights. The respondents thereby opine that the State should protect women's right to acquire and administer property, and women's right to adequate job opportunities. In other words, they re-spond very positively to uplifting the welfare of women in the Nigerian society.

Table 54: right_to_decent_standard_of_living

Correlations

	Spearman's rho		
	right_to_decent_standard_of_living		
	Correlation Coefficient	Sig. (2-tailed)	N
my_religion_has_great_influence_on_my_life	.242	.000	607
q25_God_is_near	.350	.000	606
q25_God_is_far_away	.146	.000	606
q27_Jesus_has_a_special_relationship_to_God	.257	.000	607
q27_Jesus_is_concerned_about_human_welfare	.352	.000	607
q27_Jesus_is_just_a_historical_figure	.115	.004	607
q28_Muhammad_has_a_special_relationship_to_God	.075	.064	607
q28_Muhammad_is_concerned_about_human_welfare	.071	.079	607
q28_Muhammad_is_just_a_historical_figure	.051	.208	607
cultural_openness	.343	.000	607
democratic_openness	.318	.000	607

Interpretation

In another aspect of the socio-economic rights, right to decent standard of living, we found yet positive correlations between the themes on reli-gious attitudes and themes on human rights attitudes, and again strong positive relationship exists between 'God is near', 'Jesus is concerned about human welfare', 'cultural openness', and 'democratic openness' and right to decent standard of living. Zero correlations are found between 'Muhammad has a special relationship to God', 'Muhammad is concerned about human welfare', and 'Muhammad is just a historical figure' and item on human rights attitudes. The respondents indicate openness to the government's provision of job for everybody who want to work, provision of decent standard of living for the old and the unemployed. They thereby request for an organized and proper social welfare in Nigeria.

Table 55: state_responsibility

Correlations

	Spearman's rho		
	state_responsibility		
	Correlation Coefficient	Sig. (2-tailed)	N
my_religion_has_great_influence_on_my_life	.195	.000	607
q25_God_is_near	.280	.000	606
q25_God_is_far_away	.102	.012	606
q27_Jesus_has_a_special_relationship_to_God	.261	.000	607
q27_Jesus_is_concerned_about_human_welfare	.314	.000	607
q27_Jesus_is_just_a_historical_figure	.054	.183	607
q28_Muhammad_has_a_special_relationship_to_God	.128	.002	607
q28_Muhammad_is_concerned_about_human_welfare	.112	.006	607
q28_Muhammad_is_just_a_historical_figure	.082	.044	607
cultural_openness	.303	.000	607
democratic_openness	.202	.000	607

Interpretation

Finally we come to the domain of environmental rights. The respondents' religious attitudes correlates positively with their human rights attitudes as it regards the State's responsibility towards protecting unspoiled na-ture and reduction of air pollution by industries by imposing legal limits. Therein is also an indication of strong positive correlation between 'God is near', 'Jesus is concerned about human welfare', and 'cultural open-ness' and the human rights item. A zero correlation is found between 'Jesus is just a historical figure' and the State's responsibility towards a good environment. This positive response of the respondents shows their interest in promoting a healthy environment.

Table 56: individual_responsibility

Correlations

	Spearman's rho		
	individual_responsibility		
	Correlation Coefficient	Sig. (2-tailed)	N
my_religion_has_great_influence_on_my_life	.116	.004	607
q25_God_is_near	.209	.000	606
q25_God_is_far_away	.116	.004	606
q27_Jesus_has_a_special_relationship_to_God	.081	.047	607
q27_Jesus_is_concerned_about_human_welfare	.139	.001	607
q27_Jesus_is_just_a_historical_figure	.076	.063	607
q28_Muhammad_has_a_special_relationship_to_God	.255	.000	607
q28_Muhammad_is_concerned_about_human_welfare	.230	.000	607
q28_Muhammad_is_just_a_historical_figure	.190	.000	607
cultural_openness	.256	.000	607
democratic_openness	.217	.000	607

Interpretation

The respondents also responded positively to their individual readiness to contribute towards a healthy environment, with strong positivity on items: 'Muhammad has a special relationship to God', and 'cultural openness'. A zero correlation is found between 'Jesus is just a historical figure' and the human rights item. This result shows that the religious attitudes of the respondents correlated to great length positively with their individual willingness to make sacrifices for the sake of more beau-tiful environment and to pay higher prices for products if that would mean less industrial pollution.

4.4.2 General Analysis

From the correlations tables we observe a generally significant positive correlation between the items on religious attitudes and items on human rights attitudes. Negative correlations were only found between some items on religious attitudes with the human rights item regarding euthanasia. We see in this domain mixed reactions and tendencies. The interpretation given to this regard directs our attention to a possible sympathetic future generation. The zero correlations do not give us a significant attention in comparison to the much positive relationship that exists between the two attitudes. Meanwhile, the respondents, who are the future leaders of Nigeria, have made their positions clear, not only to the Church in Nigeria, but also to the civil authorities. They have generally exhibited transformative and progressive tendencies towards the establishment of a human rights culture in Nigeria. They expect a transformative and progressive church as regards her mission and structure.

This indication takes me back to chapter three, where I presented the divergent opinions about the church's engagement in human rights matters. A school of thought holds that the church is strictly an eschatological organization that should not meddle with socio-political matters or matters of jurisprudence like human rights. Another schoold of thought is of an opposite view of what the former holds. This disagreement notwithstanding, the respondents express an ardent desire for a church that would proclaim the good news of the gospel and live same out in practical ways by providing relevant and realistic answers/solutions to the questions and demands of the 21st century. In other words, the respondents indicate that the spiritual welfare of humankind ought not to be separated from her social, political and economic welfare. A proper handling of the temporal aspect leads to a fruitful realization of the spiritual aspect. This collaborates with the discussion on the integral nature of the church's mission of liberation (discussed in chapter three).

The church's structural character is another area of concern exhibited by the respondents. The church is highly hierarchically structured. This structure is in most cases characterized by over centralization, which leads to autocracy. In some cases such over centralization tends to place the church behind the shadows of human rights issues, but being excluded from the reality. The implication is that this structure feels threatened when the reality is exposed. Such human rights themes like equality, freedom of expression, freedom of religion and freedom of life-style could be considered very threatening to the integration of the church's hierarchy.

The respondents therefore express statistically here their expectation of a church that becomes more accommodating and open to criticisms and genuine contributions towards her growth. This is not new or absurd taking cognizance of the church's official documents (already cited in the previous chapter), which call the attention of the church towards opening up to construction criticisms. This call beckons on the church to concentrate on what she can really show in concrete terms that she is the Healing (Hope) for the world.[330]

It is not however surprising that the respondents indicated transformative and progressive attitudes towards human rights question. The level of injustice and violation of human rights in Nigeria are enough to dispose any well meaning Nigerian to support and contribute to a better society. Our youth call for a generational change.

In a nutshell, this exercise beckons on the church in Nigeria to open up herself to and include human rights question into her mission agenda, otherwise her quest for integral liberation of the human person will remain utopic, and then put her missionary endeavor to a big question of relevance. What then could be done to bridge this gap? The following and concluding chapter of this research work is an attempt to answering this question, which makes some proposals about what the church can do in relation to human rights question in Nigeria.

330 Ottmar, F., Heilen und befrien: *Der Dienst am Nächsten als Ernstfall von Kirche und Pastoral.* 1990, Patmos Düsseldorf. p. 82. The word in brackets is mine.

CHAPTER FIVE

TOWARDS A CHURCH FOR HUMAN RIGHTS IN NIGERIA

Introduction

A central question has constantly revolved around each of the previous chapters: what the church in virtue of her evangelizing mission owes human rights as a human and societal phenomenon? The answer has also continuously remained: recognition, preservation, promotion and protection of fundamental rights and integral dignity of humankind. The Vatican II Council document *Gaudium et Spes* Remarks nodded to this: "In virtue of the Gospel entrusted to it, the Church proclaims the rights of man: she acknowledges and holds in high esteem the dynamic approach of today which is fostering these rights all over the world".[331] The church's 'mirror', *Justitia et Pax,* also corroborated with this line of thought: "It is the mission of the hierarchy to be a source of inspiration, support and guidance in the struggle for human rights. If her evangelical mission is to be effective, the Church must first and foremost stimulate in the world the recognition, observance, protection and promotion of the rights of the human person..."[332] All these expectations imposed on the church by herself and realities around her pose big challenges to her to avoid a falsification of her mission, especially as it concerns integral liberation.

This mission of integral liberation has its subsistence of course in the 'evangelising' aspect of the church's life, and evangelisation in turn finds its meaning in the three key functions of the church: koinonia, martyria and diaconia[333]. Ottmar Fuchs, whose Pastoral Theology stems from Theology of Vatican II beautifully coined the indispensable bond that holds these three functions of the church together. He is of the opinion that 'martyria' and 'diaconia' reflect the Christological character of the church's evangelization differently from 'koinonia', but they cannot pull together

331 G.S., no. 41.

332 *Justitia et Pax,* no. 62.

333 *Koinonia* has to do with the communal spirit within the church. *Martyria* concerns the verbal and sacramental preaching of the love of God, while *diaconia* through service manifests the love of neighbour.

without 'koinonia'. Hence "the church has the character of being service for the sake of the relationship of God and Mankind and for the sake of improving relationships within mankind. Koinonia can only do this when it is determined in its purpose-related structure by martyria and diaconia. …However, koinonia must be more closely defined by the condition that it realizes the martyria and diaconia authentically".[334] The Christological character of the church's evangelizing mission finds its root in these three functions, and as such propels her actions and service for the integral concern of humankind, in which recognition, promotion and protection of human rights culture is an indispensable aspect of.

By fostering human rights culture, the church serves a yawning community of humankind and acts as a watchdog to oppressive structures that grind human freedom and rights in a crucible of tyranny and dehumanization. In the same manner, the church, by doing so, strives to correct scandals caused by an unjust society. Gradually, she works towards a community of peace, and fraternity and by so doing, she prepares humankind mentally, physically, spiritually and psychologically to respond actively and promptly to the divine invitation to liberation.

The introduction to Gaudium et Spes, (which I already quoted), opens the church to the need to identify with victims of violations of human rights and other human and natural disasters. It is a clear expression of sentiments of unalloyed solidarity with the grieved and anguished the voiceless and less privileged. It remains a starting point for the church in her quest to bring about an integral liberation of humankind. But how can she do this further? This forms the central question of this last chapter. What are the church's obligations and responsibilities towards the promotion and protection of people's rights as far as her evangelizing mission of liberation is concerned? My focus here will be mainly on the church in Nigeria. Meanwhile, the chapter will focus on the church's mission in promotion and protection of human rights, especially from the point of view of liberation, and the challenges of human rights to the Nigerian church, especially as a possible carrier of human rights culture.

334 Ottmar, Fuchs: God's People: Instruments of Healing, p. 114 - 115.

5.1 CHURCH'S MISSION IN THE PROMOTION AND PROTECTION OF HUMAN RIGHTS

In chapter three, I attempted to establish the legitimation of the church's engagement in human rights as an intrinsic part of her mission. All said and done, this mission and its methods ought to be pastorally focused in order to achieve its desired goal – integral liberation of humankind. Being essentially a religious body and serving as a praying organization that matches hopefully towards her eschatological end as a pilgrim church, the church's approach needs to touch the lives of people in an integral manner. According to the Pontifical Commission Justitia et Pax, "the way in which the church carries out this mission, through the collaboration and prayers of every member of the People of God, is commonly called "pastoral". … Pastoral activity to protect and promote human rights among the People of God can be developed in many ways. It is helpful to be aware of them".[335]

A thousand and one avenues are available for the church to dispense this duty. To be relevant, these avenues ought to be directed towards practical goals. This reminds me once again of the methodology of Boff for doing theology of liberation, especially the third mediation. It is good to recall also that the general rule guiding this mediation is to do what objective conditions of reality permits and not the other way round. The application of pastoral prudence in this case is not for purposes of manipulation or deceit, but concretely of 'exercising wisdom with respect to what is feasible and viable'. One of the most sincere exercises of this wisdom is total commitment towards bringing about an integral liberation of the human person.

5.1.1 Liberation

I mentioned earlier that liberation presupposes oppression and bondage. In the face of the numerous records of human rights violations in our world today, one cannot contest the legitimacy of the church's mission to liberate the numerous victims of these violations. More so, by virtue of the foundation of her evangelizing mission, this liberation ought to be Christological

335 *Justitia et Pax,* no. 61.

orientated mission. In other words it means doing mission in the footsteps of Christ. The 'mirror' of the church succinctly made this connection in the following words:

> To imitate Christ and to be his true continuation in the world, the Church as a whole, like every Christian community, is called to work for the dignity and rights of man, both individually and collectively; to protect and promote the dignity of the human person; and to denounce and oppose every sort of human oppression.[336]

Donal Dorr gives us two aspects of liberation: as a dismantling instrument with which the church challenges and unmasks the evils in our world that have become embodied in most traditions and institutions in the world today; and as constructive, which is as a result of the former, meant for the transformation of these traditions and institutions that have become evil in practice.[337] Dorr succinctly remarked that an authentic struggle for liberation tends not just to convert individuals, but to transform or bring about changes in the very fabric of society.

This is a good pointer to the integral dimension of liberation, which ought to aim at the liberation of the human person in his/ her entirety. It is pertinent to refer to this question of liberation once again as far as the findings in the empirical research (in the last chapter) are concerned. It calls for an integral nature of the evangelizing task of the church – to bring about the end-purpose of human existence by way of preparing him/her in this temporal existcncc for the eschatological existence. All possible means ought to be employed to make this preparation worthwhile; spiritual, political, social, economic and cultural means. Human life is not devoid of any of these dimensions as far as the human complexities are concerned. It is only total liberation that can meet the demands such complexities make of humankind. It is an eloquent means through which the church can properly identify with the marginalized and oppressed in the society.

5.1.1.1 Liberation from Human Rights Violations

The oppressed and marginalized in the society are most of the time, the direct victims of human rights violations all over the world. One may not be

336 Ibid., no. 58.
337 Dorr, D., Mission in Today's World, Orbis Books, New York, 2000, p. 113.

mistaken to remark that these violations of their fundamental rights hinder them from responding freely to the divine invitation towards participating in a new life with God. There are some popular sayings in Nigeria that: 'a hungry man is an angry man'; 'a hungry man cannot chant alleluia'. These sayings point to the fact that other aspects of hardship invariably lead to spiritual hardship and hence block the way to God. This reminds us of the integral nature of the mission of Christ manifested in the miracle of the loaves. Christ fed the hungry and afterwards told them about the food that will give them eternal life. The crowd could yearn for this eternal food only when they had eaten the physical and temporal food. The blind man who was healed of his blindness could ask Christ to allow him be with him only when he regained his sight.

By following the footsteps of Christ, the church's mission of liberation must be integral. By virtue of her mission, the church ought to work tirelessly towards the alleviation of human problems, which deny humankind most of its fundamental rights. Liberation is a gift of Christ, and every promotion and protection of human rights is a thrust to liberation. The dramatic Exodus event of the Israelites from the Egyptian slavery is a practical testimony of God's solidarity with the oppressed and marginalized. Yahweh lamented: "I have seen the affliction of my people, who are in Egypt; and I have heard their cry to be free from their task masters. I know their sufferings, and I have come down to deliver them out of the hands of the Egyptians". (Exodus 3:7-8).

It is this divine task of liberation that Christ entrusted to the church in an unprecedented manner. Today's victims of human rights violations are the 'Israelites' under the 'Egyptian' bondage. They are always in need of liberation in order that they might enjoy the privileges of being human.

The privileges of being human call my attention to social aspect of human rights, which are more or less, very direct to every day living of peoples. Outside the guarantee for political freedom and legal equality, people are also entitled to a decent existence, to work, to a minimum income, to health, to education, and to exercise as minority groups.[338] As part of its response to this dimension, article 23 of the Universal Declaration on Hu-

338 Borgman, E., van Dijk, B., and Salemink, T., *Roman Catholic Tradition and Human Right,*. In: Stichele, V. C., et al, Ibid., p. 30.

man Rights (1948), mentions the universal right to work. In recognition of the basic nature of these rights, it is noted that Karl Marx remarks that there is no gain if people acquire political freedom but die of famine, as was often the case in his European days and is still the case in many third world countries today.[339]

The above mentioned reality ultimately implies engagement with these victims and not for them. This aspect has to be lived out in practical terms. In most cases, it implies disengagement with power and privileges and engaging with these needy in our society. It has a lot of implications for, and poses a serious challenge to the church in Nigeria.

5.2 THE CHALLENGES OF HUMAN RIGHTS TO THE NIGERIAN CHURCH

The church in Nigeria is part of the Universal Roman Catholic Church. By virtue of this stand, she is also same with the universal church in faith and doctrines. Significant differences could be noticed in political, economic, social, and cultural aspects of her life. So in some respects, the peculiar challenges facing her from the perspective of human rights could also be shared with the church in some other parts of the world.

Meanwhile, suffice it to say that after more than fifty years of political independence, human rights question in Nigeria is still far below the international standard. The high rate of violations of human rights in the country leaves one with an impression of a hopeless situation. One wonders about the essence of the beautiful lines of the Constitution, which creates a yawning disparity between what is written and what is obtainable in reality. They seem to be good only on the paper they are written on. The question now is about how this disparity between words and action could be reconciled in the Nigerian sad situation. Who can clean up the mess?

I mentioned at the General Introduction that every other sector in Nigeria have almost failed to salvage the situation. The church is looked upon as a kind of panacea for remedy. The Nigerian church up to this day enjoys

339 Ibid.

a privileged position, which she can employ to influence a lot of positive changes in the whole system. So in this regard, cleaning up the mess becomes a challenge by virtue of the church's evangelizing mission of liberation and other special privileges she enjoys in the country. Meanwhile, another question comes up here: how far has the Nigerian church wrestled with this burning issue? An answer was given about twenty-three years ago by Obiora Ike, a one-time Coordinator of Justice, Development and Peace Commission (JDPC) in Enugu diocese, Nigeria: "...the Nigerian Church and Christians have not done enough in the implications of working towards justice and peace, linking faith with concrete pastoral action. This is a new task, and a new challenge in our mission".[340]

I cannot deny the fact that the Nigerian church has done so much since then (as I mentioned in the last chapter), especially in the area of social human rights. I see a tendency of the church towards adopting Karl Marx's position in this connection, in her special attention to social human rights. The church in Nigeria has remained a champion of the cause for social rights. The roles of the JDPC and other similar religious organizations scattered in many parts of the country are eloquent examples in this case. I feel very proud to be associated with the church on this ground. On the other hand, I feel very uncomfortable with the extent of allegations leveled on the church on human rights violations charges. The church in Nigeria is not an exception in this regard. And these allegations come from the same world/ people the church advocates for from the perspective of social human rights. In most cases, the church's critics emphasize that some of her instruments for enforcing human rights promotion and protection are found very limited.[341] The correlation between the attitudes towards the church and attitudes towards human rights indicated the spirit of a church the Nigerian young populace expects. This is also a pointer to the fact that the church has to face the challenges of addressing the question of her relevance to the folks if she has to make claims to integral liberation and development of the human person.

This last remark notwithstanding, I still allow some positive space in considering the allegations against the church. My attitude to them is that the

340 Ike, O., Christian *Understanding of Justice and the Challenges on Nigerian Church.* In: Justice (Proceedings of National Seminar, 11 –15 April, 1988), p. 64.

341 van der Helm, A., *Survey on Human Rights in the Church.* In: Stichele, V. C., et al, Ibid., p. 13.

world still repose some confidence in the church and looks unto her for more. This is where the challenge lies! It beckons on the church to look inwards and re-evaluate herself for a relative integral accomplishment of this task, which forms the central focus of her mission. The church needs to strike a balance between classical human rights and social human rights; and also a balance between orthodoxy and praxis. There are a number of ways the church can bring about this. These are summarized in the following section.

5.2.1 Carrier of Human Rights Culture

5.2.1.1 What is Human Rights Culture?

In the previous chapters, especially in chapters three and four, I mentioned human rights culture in passing. It suffices at this point to give brief information about its description for a better understanding of why the church could be a carrier of human rights culture in the Nigerian context.

A global representation of human rights culture[342] is summed up in part of a speech by the Secretary-General of UNESCO in 1997, entitled 'The Right to Peace':

> Human rights! At the dawn of the new millennium, our ideal must be to put them into practice, to add to them, live and breathe them, to relive them, to revive them with every new day! Human rights can neither be owned nor given, but must be won and deserved afresh with every passing day. Nor should they be regarded as an abstraction, but rather as practical guidelines for action which should be part of the lives of all men and women and enshrined in the laws of every country. Let us translate the declaration into all languages; let it be studied in every classroom and every home, all over the world! Today's ideal may thus become the happy reality of tomorrow! Learning to know, to do, to be and to live together.[343]

342 This aspect of Human Rights Culture consideration is greatly dependent on its treatment and development by: van der Ven, J.A., et al: Is there a God of Human Rights?, Ibid., Chapter Three. I consider it as a bold attempt towards the development of Human Rights specifically, as a Culture. The church is obliged to this assignment as a religious as well as a cultural institution.

343 In: van der Ven, J.A., et al, Ibid., p. 81.

Human rights culture implies the imbibing of human rights attitudes in peoples and onward transmission from one generation to another. The cultivation of this attitude should touch all aspects of life. It means more or less the formation of consciences and the gradual strengthening of ways of thinking and styles of behaviour.

The general understanding of human rights culture is directly linked to the Universal Declarations of Human Rights. These declarations highly emphasise the need for people to describe, understand, apply, analyse, evaluate and synthesise their problems as connected to human rights. Such problems like questions of life and death or violation of equality and others should form the contents of human rights agenda as a cultural element.

Further analysis of the concept[344] opens up four aspects of human rights culture: the *principle, the arena, the object*, and *the aim.*

The Principle is that of publicity, which calls for equal sharing and participation of all human beings in the society, irrespective of social status. There should be no hidden agenda whatsoever. This implies giving voice to the voiceless and strength or power to the weak. The article two of the International Covenant on Civil and Political Rights that was adopted by the UN Human Rights Committee on 28 July 1981, articulated its view on this issue of publicity:

> The Committee considers it necessary to draw the attention of States parties to the fact that the obligation under the Covenant is not confined to the respect of human rights, but that States parties have also undertaken to ensure the enjoyment of these rights to all individuals under their jurisdiction. This aspect calls for specific activities by the States parties to enable individuals to enjoy their rights.[345]

This Covenant stresses the need for people to know what their rights are and called on parties involved with its enforcement to play significant roles in this regard, making use of every available means to bring it about.

344 The result of this analysis is also the effort of: van der Ven, J.A., et al, Ibid. p. 82.
345 In: Lawson, Wiseberg, L.S., and Dargel, J.D.K., (eds.): Encyclopedia of Human Rights, Washington D.C., 1996. p.720.

The Arena must be a forum that can enhance a better and wider publicity of the human rights culture. It must be a public (neutral) ground where all is capable of gathering for equal participation. Ordinarily such a forum is referred to as a *marketplace.* In the African sense, a marketplace is generally understood as a 'no man's land'; a generally owned square, where members of a given society gather for communal issues. With globalisation and technological/ scientific progress, such open forums are located in the mass media, especially the press, radio and television programmes, and the internet of course. It is advocated that participants in this forum should be conscious of the so-called 'hermeneutics of suspicion' in order to follow up the ideological processes that are involved.[346] Nevertheless, it is good to note that such an arena is possible only in a free society where the ruling authorities have no control of same for legitimating their whims and caprices.

The Object of human rights culture has to do with themes raised by members of the public, be it an individual, a group or a community, that has to do with human rights. Such themes are further identified as *problems* and *conflicts*. Human rights *problems* have to do with real situations that appeal to human rights, which demands clarification with regard to their meaning and scope. Their meaning could be applicable to civil rights, political rights, judicial rights, socio-economic rights and different kinds of collective rights. So human rights culture in this dimension addresses these areas mentioned above and seeks a proper integration and assimilation. This aspcct also addresses *conflicts* that occur in human rights application. Such conflicts like: *conflicts about the right to life*, which questions the *permissibility* and *autonomy* to take or preserve human life; and the conflicts that arise with regard to *the right to the freedom of religion*, which come up with one's freedom of religious expression and the inhibition of one's other rights due to religious affiliation. Development of human rights culture from these aspects is meant to take into consideration these delicate themes and go for a good formation.

The Aim of human rights culture could be inferred from the first three aspects already considered. This *aim* is derived from the fact that a human rights culture should not be rigid, but lively and demonstrable since it remains on constant changes due to the problems and conflicts that arise as

346 Further reference to this could be found in: van der Ven, J.A., et al, Ibid. p. 83.

a result of their application to concrete situations. It entails three aspects: *analysis, evaluation* and *synthesis. Analysis* involves a continuous analysis of one's position and arguments and those of others, especially with regard to *democracy, rule of law, principles of human rights and relation between law and religion, church and state.* Developing this aspect gives one the opportunity to make a better judgment of situations and events. *Evaluation* means making a critical evaluation of one's perspectives and conceptions and those of others. It is very necessary to make evaluation since analysis cannot continue *ad infinitum*. One can employ the use of *internal criterion*, which involves the use of logic and *external criterion*, which flows from placing the area of human rights side by side with the religious sphere. It is however, good to note that evaluation does not hold true all the time because it is not infallible. It remains useful only in unchanged situations. *Fallibility* does not negate the usefulness of evaluation since human rights must be set on the daily lives of real people in concrete situations. *Synthesis* implies taking a personal position with the adequate arguments after doing the analysis and evaluation. It makes the decisions reached by analysis and evaluation rationally passable. A synthesis here makes it possible to make good application of human rights *to* and *in* various given concrete situations. It is however dependent on the eventuality of time since it does not hold good for all time. The *Pastoral Mediation* of Boff calls to mind here once again[347].

As a cultural element, human rights culture must be transmitted in practical means. And one of the eloquent means is through teaching the human rights culture at various levels in order to involve all classes of people in the society. Adopting *human rights teaching* as a veritable option, the United Nations Educational, Scientific and Cultural Organisation (UNESCO), extensively directed and advocated:

> … while it is recognised that in human rights teaching there is a conceptual aspect of the acquisition of knowledge…, it is nevertheless a fact that in this field emphasis should be placed on forming the intellectual and moral aptitudes required for observance of human rights. … For such education to be effective the very atmosphere of social and cultural institutions must reflect respect for human rights; such education should be founded on a

347 The *Pastoral Mediation* of Boff is the translation into concrete action of what has been seen and addressed or judged. In otherwords, it calls for pastoral action after a particular pastoral situation has been assessed. It flows from two preceding Mediations: Socio-analytical and Hermeneutical.

> basis of reciprocity, solidarity and justice. Educational action should take into account cultural diversity throughout the world, and be based on the cultural identity, social values, language, socialization and communication systems… Human rights education should be the basis of non-formal or mass education programmes, particularly in adult education.[348]

Such forms of education, both formal and non-formal are means through which human rights culture can be transmitted in a society. The teaching must be integral so that it can permeate the individuals in the society.

In the final analysis, for the human rights culture to be developed, taught and transmitted in a society, the structure of the society must be adjusted in such a way that this culture – which may be more or less new – may be introduced without involving conflicts of any kind. When this structural change is made, the carriers of this (new) culture can effectively play their roles. These carriers must invariably conduct their roles in conjunction with Lyotarr's *Five Pillars of Society: economy, politics, religion, environment and science.* These are the pillars that determine the culture of a given society, and as such they cannot be isolated in the development and transmission of the human rights culture. I earlier mentioned that the historical facts of the church and human rights give the impression that she is not an institution *of* human rights; however she can be an institution *for* human rights. This means that she can be a carrier of human rights culture in Nigeria. But how can the church perform this delicate task? The following suggestions are attempts towards an approach to the said task.

5.2.1.2. Self-examination

During and after the mission of Christ on earth, up until now, it was not and has not been observed that he was accused of any form of violations of human rights. But it is very disturbing that constant allegations are levelled on the church Christ founded, almost on daily basis against human rights violations within her fold. As I said earlier, these allegations should not be waved aside with sound logical defensive sentences. They call the church to self-examination. There is need for the church to open herself to honest and open self-criticism for her to be able to identify areas of her structural and ideological set-up that give latency to any form of human rights violations, either within her fold or without. In this regard, the church is advised

348 Lawson, E., et al, Ibid. pp. 721-722.

to "assess those values which are most highly prized today and to relate them to their divine source".[349] The assessment in question here equally ought to involve a critical analysis and synthesis of the relevance of her ideologies and structural arrangements. In this connection Pope Paul VI in his Post-Synodal Apostolic Exhortation Evangelii nuntiandi, on Evangelization in the Modern World[350], contributes his version of the often repeated maxim, ecclesia semper reformanda, clearly stating that the Church „has a constant need of being evangelized, if she wishes to retain freshness, vigor and strength in order to proclaim the Gospel" (15). In otherwords this is a call to the church to be faithful to her identity in order to better evangelize. It calls for constant change and renewal. Ottmar Fuchs gave this call a similar nuance by stating that this identity of the Church as an evangelising body is not only within herself, but she has to give meaning to this identity „by realising itself from the inside to the outside".[351] In the same dimension Ottmar presents a question as to where the church ought to focus her interest: converting people to the church or asking herself the pertinent question of what to do with the people she converts.[352]

By constant self-examination the church understands better the gospel and continues to evangelise herself by taking the criticisms against her very seriously and sincerely making critical analysis of same for her growth.

One of the strong criticisms against the church is that she uses the separation of church and state factor for the purpose of shielding herself from the State's influence in matters of human rights violations within the church.[353] This allegation is not very distant from the Nigerian church as well. She likes to be the watchdog over the State's enforcement of human rights protection. In the same way she ought to also open herself in an opposite direction, in order to perform that duty better. This view is unequivocally supported by the Association of Episcopal Conferences of Anglophone West Africa (AECAWA): "With the Special Assembly for Africa of the Synod of Bishops held in Rome last year, we realize that justice is not al-

349 G.S., no. 11.

350 Evangelii nuntiandi was issued by Pope Paul VI on December 8, 1975. The text quoted here is the translated version of the Publication office of the United States Catholic Bishops Conference, Washington D.C., 1976.

351 Ottma, F.: God's People: Instruments of Healing, p. 92.

352 Ottmar, F., Heilen und befrien, p. 80.

353 van der Helm, A., Ibid., p. 14.

ways respected even within the Church and that if the church is to give witness to justice, then whoever dares to speak to others about justice should also strive to be just in their eyes".[354] This admonition that was given more than a decade ago is still relevant today for the Nigerian church as a result of the *intrusive* tendencies embedded in her mission methods.

On a similar note, the church is known to have always decried the unjust practices and violations of the rights of peoples in various corners of the globe, even to the point of defending the right of the unborn child to live *(Humanae Vitae).* This is one of the indications that it is very intrinsic in her mission of liberation to free humankind from all kinds of bondage and deprivation. Meanwhile, she is criticised of being unrealistic about some of the steps she takes to promote and protect human rights. She is said to be far removed from her ‚utopian target'.[355] This gives us the impression that the incompatibility between some of the church's proposals for human rights promotion/ protection and their realization makes such proposals utopic.

Taking cognisance of my earlier remark for the openness demanded of the church towards the societal demands, I strongly opine that the church ought to critically analyse some of her ideologies and positions on certain matters she has been accused of, which provide latency for certain violations of human rights. She cannot neglect these voices of allegation/ demands both from within and without. The church has to bear in mind that "he who plays thc pipe, dictates the tune". This expected mutual openness and re-evaluation could boost a better collaboration between the church, the State and other institutions/ organisations in the cause for human rights promotion and protection. Meanwhile, this cause has to begin from within the church.

5.2.1.3. Liberation from Within

In the previous section, I touched once again on the church's mission of liberation as an essential part of her mission that is meant to achieve the integral salvation of the human person. As a follow up to the challenges fac-

354 Communique issued by the AECAWA Bishops' Conference, Enugu, 1995, p. 1.

355 Raming, I., *Women in the Structures of the Church,* in: Stichele, V. C., et al, Ibid., p. 55.

ing the church to examine herself, is the need for this liberation in question to start from the church herself. Dorr is of the opinion that this quest for liberation ought not to be directed to only political and economic 'powers', but also against religious agencies that engage in overtly spiritual oppression.[356] This is a very important remark because churches and church agencies can be oppressive even within their own internal organisation. Another explanation for this challenge is that an event or tradition may not be evil or oppressive by nature, but could become evil and oppressive in practice; hence such events or traditions cannot be beyond redemption.

Looking back to the establishment of the church by Christ, one has no doubt about the purpose for which Christ instituted this institution. I have already noted that Christ was not accused of any form of oppression, but today, the church is continuously being accused of allowing oppression and violations of human rights by means of her structures and ideologies. The history of such violations supports the allegations. This means that something is wrong somewhere.

In the spirit of self examination, the church needs to structure herself in such a way that her faithful can freely claim their fundamental rights in the dispensation of the modern constitutional State. Such rights as inviolability of the human person, equality as to race, sex and sexual orientation; carefulness in procedures, equality of rights, participation and co-responsibility, social justice, freedom of conscience and opinion, freedom of action, respect for privacy, ought to be put into serious consideration for implementation.[357] These rights are being advocated for by the church as indicated in the church's instruments of legitimation for involvement in human rights question. This forms part of the pastoral tasks of the church in the modern world, which is anticipated to be accomplished in the atmosphere of religious freedom.[358] To this liberation from within is the dimension of Ottmar Fuchs's call on the Church to put up structural opportunities for her lay members to tell their spiritual encounters with God, people and with the Church herself as a way of mutual *upbuild* of each other in their *diversity* and *partiality*.[359] It is however pertinent to note that this pastoral

356 Dorr, D., Ibid. p. 114.

357 Borgman, E., et al, Ibid., p. 38.

358 Onwubiko, O., The Church and Mission, in the Light of Ecclesia in Africa, Paulines Publications, Nairobi, 2001, p. 382.

359 Ottmar, F., God's People: Instruments of Healing, p. 173.

dimension of the life and mission of the church ought to be a combination of orthodoxy and orthopraxis.[360] Though they specifically belong to the arena of civil human rights, they can still be applied within the church in accordance with the church's norms. When this is in place, the church can then match her words with adequate actions.

5.2.1.4. Prophetic Option

An antecedent question can initiate this section: what is prophetic option or rather, what do prophets do? I attempt an answer by saying that prophets serve as mirrors to societies and individuals. The major characteristic of prophets is their concern for the concrete situations and events, which signal elements of injustice and oppression. From the religious perspective, prophets are spokesmen of God who prophesy on behalf of God. Hence the manner of their prophetic introductions: "Thus says the Lord". They are always at war with oppressive elements in the society, by consistently denouncing evil and given moral exhortations. This description offers us a link to the Old Testament and New Testament Scriptures, especially the prophetic roles of Moses (Exodus 5), Samuel (1 Samuel 13:10-14), Nathan (2 Samuel 12:19) and John the Baptist (Gospel of Mark 6:18), among others. The prophetic role of Christ in his mission is very outstanding and cannot be contested. I have already dealt elaborately on that in the third chapter.

It is to this prophetic mission that the church is called to as a pastoral option in her defence and promotion of human rights. By this calling she becomes the voice of the numerous voiceless victims of human rights violations. This task "demands courage, charity, prudence and firmness. Above all it must be a truly human and Christian testimony in sincere dialogue with the parties concerned, and based on justice and objectivity".[361]

The Nigerian church is very commited towards this role. The Catholic Bishops Conference of Nigeria (CBCN) is a very strong and influential body in this regard. The bishops have for the past forty-eight years discharged their prophetic role through their constant and vocal denouncia-

360 Ibid.

361 Cf. Document of the 1971 Synod of Bishops, *Justice in the World,* in: *Justitia et Pax,* no. 80.

tion of the evils and violations of human rights in Nigeria through communiqués and Pastoral letters. They also engage in social actions in their respective dioceses and States. One may not underrate the influence of most of their communiques and pastoral letters towards a better Nigeria. Significantly, some of their communiques and pastoral letters have been singled out on this ground: Their joint pastoral letter of October, 1985 – *Listen: the Church Speaks,* emphasised their insistence on the commitment towards their prophetic role in the Nigerian society.[362] This commitment is also made manifest in many of their other communiques and pastoral letters such as those of 27 July, 1993, *First Business: What Next?*[363]; the communique given after their meeting of 10 – 13 September, 1996, *Rays of Hope*[364]; and the communique given after their meeting of 6 – 10 September, 1999, *Sustaining the Hope of our People into the New Millennium* .[365] Their immense concern towards the protection of the weak and the poor and freedom of movement is expressed in their Communique, *A Nation Adrift,* after their plenary meeting of 13 -17 September, 1988.[366] Their desire for religious freedom is clearly expressed in their communique of 8 February, 2000, *Let there be Peace!*, issued with regard to religious disturbances caused by the "Sharia controversy"[367]; and the one issued after their meeting of 10 – 14 September, 2001, *Towards a Just and Peaceful Society.*[368]

A special mention needs to be made as regards their attention towards social action as indicated in their 2004 communiqué, which partly reads:

> … At same time, we continue to insist that government has the responsibility to provide basic education, health and other social services to the entire citizenry. … We direct every parish to begin a programme of basic education in the civic rights and responsibilities of its members… If one does not know his or her rights, it is all too easy for government and others to take them away.[369]

---

362 Schineller, P., The Voice of the Voiceless (Pastoral Letters and Communiques of the Catholic Bishops' Conference of Nigeria, 1960 – 2002), Ibadan, 2002, p. 165.
363 Ibid. p. 288.
364 Ibid. p. 332.
365 Ibid. p. 402.
366 Ibid. p. 221.
367 Ibid. p. 408.
368 Ibid. p. 429.
369 http://lists.peacelink.it/africa/msg00856.html

The church in Nigeria tries to combine her prophetic role with some necessary action, but this is felt most in the social aspect of human rights, as I mentioned earlier. Nonetheless, she needs to go beyond this point since the Nigerian government is adamant to some of her denunciations.

Going beyond these prophetic denunciations, which applies not only to the hierarchy but also to the laity[370] is the cogent need to analyse "the deep-rooted causes of such situations and a firm commitment to face up to them and resolve them correctly".[371] The implication of this instruction is that for this commitment to be relevant, the church has to go beyond mere verbal denunciations, when necessary, to practical and concrete protests for the cause of human rights. This approach is to come in form of "symbolic acts" or "acts of solidarity" with the poor and the oppressed when their human rights are injured".[372] This is very necessary because "it is more difficult to promote and protect the full range of human rights when the people have very limited resources. Getting the next meal or the week's rent or the term's school fees loom larger for *people* than trial by jury or the right to periodic paid holidays".[373] It implies that the development of peoples ought not to rely only on verbal expressions. It demands some sort of "revolution" by way of "constructive protests against the present conditions of man".[374] Words become the church's weakest resource[375]when they are not converted into concrete actions. And when they are converted into deeds thereby practicing what she preaches and believes in and what she is, then the less she worries about her continued existence (stability).[376]

It should not be forgotten that it is also by fulfilling her prophetic role that the church also exercises her moral authority in the world. To this effect, care must be taken to guard against extreme liberalism. This is one of the tendencies of some of the agitations and demands of the world from the church. I am totally opposed to this perspective. On one hand, the world

370 *Jusitia et Pax,* no. 84.

371 Cf. "Messsage to the UN on 25th Anniversary of the Universal Declaration of Human Rights", in:*Justitia et Pax*, Ibid., no. 87.

372 *Justitia et Pax,* no. 85.

373 Welch, C.E., Jr., Protecting Human Rights in Africa, U.S.A., 1995, pp. 291 –292.

374 Nyerere, J., *The Development of Peoples and the Meaning of Service.* In: Anderson, G.H., and Stransky, T.F., (eds.), Mission Trends No. 1, New York, 1974, p. 145.

375 Ottmar, F., God's People: Instruments of Healing. p. 106.

376 Ottmar, F., Heilen und befrien, p. 86.

needs the church for maintenance of good moral standard and control. The church must be given the space to play this important role effectively in accordance to the divine law and right reason. On the other hand, the church needs to collaborate with the world, especially on matters that directly involve the world's intervention or expertise. From this perspective, the church needs to accord some space to the latter for this to take effect. In other words, the two need each other, hence the need for mutual understanding and collaboration. The autonomy should not be relegated to the State; neither should the church absolutise it.

5.2.1.5. Commitment to the Marginalized

Generally speaking, the marginalized in the society are the victims of human rights violations who do not have the economic, political, social or cultural strength to defend themselves. These commonly fall under the category of the poor or powerless. Such are the people Julius Nyerere called creatures, not of God, but of their fellow men.[377] In other words their wretched conditions could not have been of God's making, but out of human greed and aggrandizement. The development of such people "demands that the world shall become one and that social justice shall replace the present oppressions and inequalities".[378] The church ought to be part of this group in order to assist them out of their 'slums'. Nyerere strongly advocated that the church should support the oppressed not by giving them arms, but by assisting them to fight against injustice and oppressive structures in the society.

Significant parts of this marginalized group are women and children. The church in Nigeria has been so much engaged in assisting these marginalized members, especially under the general category of the poor or powerless and children's care. Yet she still has a lot of work to do with regard to the emancipation and empowerment of women. This aspect has formed another major part of the criticisms and allegations levelled against the church as a violator of human rights. So I am going to address the women issue in an attempt to propose what the church in Nigeria could do towards their emancipation and empowerment.

377 Ibid. p. 146.
378 Ibid. p. 147.

5.2.1.5.1. Agenda for the Emancipation and Empowerment of Women

I have already mentioned aspects of discrimination against women in Nigeria in chapters one and two. However, suffice it to point out in a clearer way that most of such discriminations are basically influenced by the traditional cultures of the peoples of Nigeria. Generally, African culture is noted to be oriented towards dignity rather than rights[379], and this is also true of Nigerian cultures (as I earlier indicated). These traditional cultures allow patterns of sexual differentiation to be deeply rooted in their values, which give priority to males and regard females as subordinate to males.

This is the practice in the traditional institutions in Nigeria up to this day. It has invariably permeated all aspects of life in Nigeria and has as well formed a major part of ideologies in many quarters. So this is why it is no big surprise to many in Nigeria that women are discriminated against at certain levels in the church. For majority, it is not even discrimination, but a cultural phenomenon. Meanwhile, the wind of globalisation has blown open the side-effects of such discriminations on women and the whole issue of equality that also forms the core part of Christian message. It then behoves on the church in Nigeria to address the issue in an unequivocal terms.

First and foremost, the church has to engage herself in strong educational and awareness programmes for this goal. Over and above all, emphasis ought to bc placcd on the dignity and privileges of women, which make them equal with men in the society. This effort has to begin specifically with women themselves, by means of getting them to appreciate themselves as special people who should enjoy the same privileges of being human with their men counterparts. This is so because the culture has made it in such a way that women have accepted their position in accordance with the cultural orientations. A lot of damage has been done already towards their ideologies and orientations. For example, the practice of female genital mutilations meets a lot of problems, which part of them has to do with the women themselves. Women have been meant to believe that if their genitals are not mutilated, they are either going to die immaturely, will not be able to get married or may not procreate at all. These are the superstitions that colour their orientation towards such practices. This is where

379 Welch, C.E., Jr., Ibid.

I opine the church should start from. The women should be assisted by every possible means to abolish any feeling or expressions of inferiority that has gone as far as self-contempt.[380] This cultural basis for discrimination against women in Nigeria is a historical fact that the church ought to root out of the society first, bearing in mind the admonition of Paul that "in Christ there is neither male nor female". Having started with this sort of correcting measure by means of education, the church should not stop there. She ought then to look inwards and address issues of discrimination as far as cultural influence is concerned.

Further I want to clearly mention that the woman is a central 'sign' in the church and as such ought to occupy a primal place therein. The weight of the reference made to the church as "Mother Church" ought not to be neglected. But women are in most cases placed at the 'receiving end'. It is interesting to note the remark of a Jesuit priest, Heinrich Pesch, on the role or position of women in the church. He is of the opinion that

> …men and women are really equal as regards their fundamental human essence and the final purpose of human existence, the communion with God. But they are different because of their natural characteristics, a physical, intellectual and mental individuality which suits the natural sexual differences and the ensuing special roles of each sex. …this is not a value of judgment and does not suggest any inferiority of woman: woman is equal to, but by nature basically different from man.[381]

Whatever his intentions may be for making such a differentiation, the fact remains that he did not deny the equality of men and women. But it is obsessing to note that his observation on the female nature lead to vehement rejection of equal rights for women from other scholars.[382] This rather looks absurd and also incompatible with the example of Christ who showed himself first to a woman immediately after his resurrection. Let us take cognisance of the position of women in the Jewish cultural set-up. They are considered to be second class citizens who have no 'voice' in religious and other spheres. This for me is an indication that natural differences do not imply differences in quality or inferiority or superiority.

380 Raming, I., Ibid. p. 64.

381 Borgman, E., van Dijk, B., and Salemink, T., Ibid. p. 35.

382 Ibid. This position leads to the view that the intellectual potentiality of men is of superior character and as such points to some sort of inequality between men and women. This is a similar position in Islam and Judaism.

Natural differences must not entail functional differences, just as in the family where taking care of the children or cooking is no longer termed the function of the woman only. If functional differences are based on tradition, then that tradition could be amended or erased when it is no longer relevant to the society. In the spirit of Inculturation, I support the inculturation of the Gospel not only in the African, Asian or European cultures, but also in the thought and culture of modernity.[383] The ethos of human rights, especially in its secularity, which are dangerously opposed to the fundamental principles of the Gospel of Jesus Christ, ought to be reviewed and corrected to suit the basic moral standard of life. This enhances another need for mutual collaboration between the church and the world. Capability, ability and charism ought to determine roles in this regard instead of natural differences or sexual orientations. Nevertheless, equality does not mean sameness.

The role of women in the Nigerian church cannot be degraded taking cognisance of their supportive abilities. They are reckoned as a very strong beacon on which the Nigerian church stands, morally, economically and numerically, and without exaggerations, spiritually[384]. They finance a lot of projects in the church and outside the church. The Catholic Women Organization of Nigeria for instance, has branches in all the dioceses of Nigeria. They operate at National, provincial, diocesan, parish and station levels. They are eloquent example of the strong support I talk about. If this group could be this strong, isn't it enough reason for the church to throw her own support behind them towards elevating their dignity and lifting them from the dungeon of inferiority complex when it comes to active participation in leadership roles both within the church and outside the church. I tend to think that their wide spread ignorance and illiteracy is widely utilized to perpetuate this manipulation and exploitation of their potentials and resources. They are in the majority but have the minority voice; they contribute enormously to agricultural economy[385] but they receive so little in return at the end of the day.

In a similar vein within the church, women are more restricted from approaching the sanctuary than men. Ministries like *lector* and *acolyte* are

383 Merks, K.W., *Anthropocentrism and Faith,* in: Stichele, V. C., et al, Ibid., p. 180.
384 Oduyoye, M.A., Three *Cardinal Issues of Mission in Africa.* In: Schreiter, R., (ed.), Mission in the Third Millennium, New York, 2000, p. 46.
385 Welch, C.E., Jr., Ibid. pp. 90 - 91.

dominated by men as far as installations to these ministries are concerned. The Nigerian church allows women lay readers but not as installed lectors, but on the basis of "occasional" practices. The ministry of acolyte is not yet accorded any room for women in any form. Women are completely excluded in this regard. They are only allowed the decoration of the altar. There is need to include women also in these areas and more especially by means of proper installations as men are. This could then serve as a starting-point for the admission of women into other higher ministerial positions in the church as was the case in the early Church.[386]

I also opine, as a way of fighting ignorance and inclusion of women in active participation within the church, that the church ought to engage women also in further studies in theology and allied courses. One can count the number of female theologians in Nigeria at the moment. 99% of them are religious sisters (nuns), who were privileged because of their status. When women are prepared this way, they can get into the structural and administrative systems of the church such as formation of ministers for the church – both ordained and lay, and enhance their possibility of getting into leadership positions in the church. It will also boost their status within the church and invariably change the cultural attitudes towards them, even in the larger society. An effective practical way the church in Nigeria could bring about this is by liasing with the Federal, State or private universities for the establishment of theological faculties therein to support the limited space available at her only one university.

386 This allution gets a special attention from the Letter to the Romans 16:1-4, where St. Paul referred specially to a deaconess: "I commend to you our Sister Phoebe, a deaconess of the Church at Cenchrease; give her, in the Lord, a welcome worthy of God's holy people, and help her with whatever she needs from you – she herself has come to the help of many people, including myself. My Greetings to Prisca adn Aquila, my fellow-workers in Christ Jesus, who risked their own necks to save my life; to them, thanks not only from me, but from all the churches among the gentiles; and my greetings to the church at their house". (The New Jerusalem Bible, pocket edition, 1990). The latter names mentioned by Paul as his fellow-workers are also names of women, whom he did not make mention of their particular position, but it indicates that Paul had women as close collaborators in his ministry. Since the Apostles were the then Bishops of the early church, could it not be that these close (women) fellow-workers were priests?

Lastly, but not the least, a closer cooperation of men and women in the church is very necessary so that each can contribute positively towards building a new society and in the church, each according to their specific gifts and creative talents.[387]

5.2.1.6. Intercultural/ Interreligious Exchange

Nigeria, as I mentioned in chapter one is made up of 250 ethnic groups in which the three major religions – Christianity, Islam and African Traditional Religions dominate. Other minor religious communities could be found in these groups such as Hindu Krishna movements, Godianism, an emerging Christian denomination with a strong African background – African Independent Churches, and a number of other very minor religious cults.

This multicultural/ multireligious nature of Nigeria cannot be neglected due to the strong influence the phenomenon has over the various aspects of life in Nigeria. It is a fact that more than one religion or denomination exists in each of these ethnic groups. Among the Igbo ethnic group, for instance, are so many Christian denominations and many traditional religionists, and a handful of Islamic adherents. There are also atheists in this same tribe especially among the literates. This is also the case in the other ethnic groups in Nigeria. This is a situation that has come to be, and any efforts towards converting all to one religion or one denomination may not succeed.

Meanwhile, the Christian denominations are busy struggling among themselves for conversions to the point of antagonising each other's image, mostly as objects of sermons during worship periods. These Christian denominations also apply every available means to convert the remaining traditional religionists. In the same vein, the African Traditional Religionists, at one end, are accusing Christianity for doing big harm to their traditional values and asking for reparation. And Islam is on the other end,

387 Raming, I., Ibid. p. 59.

working both at the national and international levels to islamise the whole Nigeria.[388] Other minority groups like the ones mentioned above are striving by all possible means to register and legitimise their existence.

Dialogue was employed as a solution to the conflicts pictured above, but *ethnocentric* and *triumphalist* tendencies among these groups did not allow a fruitful dialogue yet. The case is that dialogue among them have only resulted into each trying to present her religion or denomination as the most authentic and privileged. There is less emphasis placed on mutual recognition and appreciation of each other in their differences and values.

The above picture gives us an idea of the state of things – religious- and cultural-wise, and indicates the big problem of *ethnocentrism* and *triumphalism*. These are one of the biggest problems the Catholic Church in Nigeria has to wade with. Unfortunately this is one of the negative mission legacies the Irish Missionaries left behind in the Nigerian church.[389] These tendencies in her attitudes have not helped matters with regard to her protection of human rights in Nigeria despite her numerous projects in this regard. In most cases, she has failed to recognize and appreciate the importance of other denominations and religions by seeing herself as the superior and privileged group. This sort of attitude tends to make her do everything possible to remain on top – avoiding any form of rivalry. One is put in doubt as to the sincerity or authenticity of her missionary endeavours most of the time. Accepting the truth about other faiths is very unlikely for the church due to these tendencies.

---

388 An attempt was made in 1985 by the then leader of Nigeria, General Ibrahim Babangida, to secretly enrol Nigeria into the Organisation for Islamic Countries (OIC). The Christian Association of Nigeria played a significant role in seing to the termination of the project.

389 The territorial struggle, which one of the Founders of the Holy Ghost Fathers (Spiritans) Francis Libermann introduced in his mission strategy, was also felt in Nigeria during the early missionary years. It was a struggle for "Souls" between Catholicism and Protestantism. Leading missionary Figures in the Southeastern Nigeria like Joseph Shanahan and Archbishop Charles Heerey underlined their missionary motivation on this basis. Establishment of Schools, for example became a very lucrative means of winning converts to the catholic faith. This missionary motivation left an indelible scandal, which impacts and hampers the progress of ecumenical dialogue what more of interreligious dialogue. More reading on this could be done in: Ebelebe, C., *Africa and the New Face of Mission: A critical assessment of the Legacy of the Irish Spiritans among the Igbo of Southeastern Nigeria.*University Press of America Inc. 2009. p. 67 and p. 97ff.

Another aspect of this attitude is *tribalism,* which has also left the church in Nigeria in very scandalous divisions among her members – clergy and lay. These problems have continued to be a cog in the wheel of her efforts to realise her mission of liberation, especially as it regards human rights promotion and protection. For her activities to be more fruitful there is need for a change of attitude from this perspective. An intercultural/ inter-religious exchange is very urgent in her evangelisation.

There are two dimensions to this intercultural/ interreligious perspective. One is linked to a direct protection of human rights, while the other fosters and enhances the promotion of human rights by mutual collaboration among different cultural and religious groups.

The first dimension of the idea of intercultural/ interreligious dialogue is basically rooted in the universal mission of Christ whose "proclamation and works is that he consistently embodies the breaking down of barriers between ingroup and outgroup and the conversion of from exclusion to inclusion.... God is a benevolent God who is opposed to humiliation, enslavement, oppression and exploitation; he is a God of salvation and reconciliation for everyone."[390] This direct link to human rights protection takes its bearing on the basis of non-discrimination of anybody irrespective of race, religion or culture. Supporting this intercultural/ interreligious exchange, Oliver Onwubiko suggested the use of *Ujamaa*, a Swahili concept that means *togetherness, familyhood, and brotherhood.*[391] In order to enhance intercultural/ interreligious exchange, Onwubiko stressed that *Ujamaa* could serve as a good common ground with Muslims and with other non-Christians. He further opines that it is a good tool for reconciliation[392] since it is opposed to all kinds of discrimination and at the same time respects and promotes differences, stability and equality.[393] In other-words it is a call to "inclusivism".

When exclusivism is replaced with inclusivism there is then the opportunity for an enhancement of an interaction between multiple cultural

390 van der Ven, J.A., et al, Ibid., pp. 203-204.
391 Onwubiko, O., Ibid. p. 34.
392 Ibid. p. 59.
393 Ibid., p. 33

and religious orientations,[394] meant to create an 'in-between' position for bridging the perceived gap between various cultures and religious orientations in Nigeria. This provides an explanation for the second dimension of intercultural/ interreligious perspective. At the same time it presupposes a responsible analysis of a mutual intercultural/ interreligious contact and dialogue, for a better understanding, recognition and appreciation of each other's values. This sort of bridge is very necessary in the Nigerian pluralistic situation – between the various cultures, religions/ denominations and between peoples of various faiths and cultures. Again this second dimension makes for a very close link to the African (Nigerian) concept of family, which "pushes us to accept others different from us, as the children of the same father and mother; children who often do not look alike, but who, in their differences of gifts/ talents or of colour, do recognise one another as participants in the same life."[395]

By practice of this intercultural/ interreligious exchange, the 'other' is safeguarded and counted, and will no longer be taken for granted. In this approach, the "participant perspective" and "observer perspective" in the implementation of this exchange become very useful. By means of participant perspective, people "perceive, interpret and evaluate their environment and the people, things and situations in it, *while by assuming observer perspective*, we adopt a more abstract perspective and, by comparing the other's ideas and customs with our own and those of people we know a little better, try to understand the reality confronting us".[396] It is said that an understanding of the 'other' begins with an understanding of oneself. Hence it becomes very necessary for one to critically interpret, evaluate and possibly re-evaluate one's group for the purpose of understanding and appreciating what the 'other' has to offer. What can be learnt from the 'other' should not be taken for granted. There is need to allow inclusivism if we accept that no religion has monopoly of virtue and divine revelation.[397]

---

394 Wijsen, F., *Intercultural Theology and the Mission of the Church,* At: www.sedos.org.

395 Lumbala, F.K., *African Contribution to Christian Mission*, In: Odozor, P.I., Amadi-Azuogu, C., and Uzukwu, E., Africa: Towards Priorities of Mission, SIST Publication, 2000, p. 239.

396 van der Ven, J.A., et al, Ibid., p. 511.

397 In *Ad Gentes Divinitus* – Decree on the Missionary Activity of the Church, the Council Fathers attributed to the presence of God before the coming of Christ: „the Holy

Moreover, accepting and recognising the 'other' and the 'other's' differences is almost tantamount to accepting and recognising that the 'other's' fundamental rights ought to be respected to the latter. It will lead to the emergence of a society "in which all people are truly equal and yet differences respected".[398] In other words what divides us or makes us different from each other should not define us, but we ought to be defined by the common humanity we share.[399] By so doing, a very good base will be formed for the promotion and protection of human rights in the Nigerian society – "a religio-moral basis of human rights".[400]

When this sort of foundation is solidly laid among the various denominations and religions in Nigeria, they can then open up another form of dialogue, which exposes the common interest they can combine forces to fight for. Top in the list of these interests could be the case for the numerous violations of human rights in Nigeria. When they merge to defend this just cause in various 'forms' and with various 'instruments', the perpetrators of these evils (especially those linked to political and economic powers) cannot but throw in the towel.

Dialogue at this level ought to transcend the traditional formula of knowing the identity, richness, depth, imperfections, uncritical assumptions and fallibility[401] of the other to dialogue for peace and solidarity among peoples. The cause for human rights promotion and protection can pave the way towards the goal of this proposed aspect of dialogue. In this direction, thc principles of human rights – dignity, freedom, equality and solidarity ought to influence such a dialogue. This is indeed an aspect of dialogue that "presents us with a non-threatening moment on both sides for prophetic confession of faith; it allows us to know other religions not as abstract system but as ways of life lived by persons with whom we can actually be-

---

Spirit was already at work in the world before Christ was glorified". (Ad Gentes 59-76). This same Spirit of God must have also directed the various peoples to the recognition of the Supreme God, even before their particular „re-evangelisation".

398 De Gruchy: 1995, 7, In: van der Ven, J.A., et al, Ibid., p. 526.

399 This thought is taking from the Speech of President Barack Obama of The United States of America, on 11. February 2011 after the historical dethronement of the long regime of Mr. Husseni Mubarak as the President of Egypt.

400 Van der Ven, J.A., et al, Ibid.

401 Ibid. p. 542.

come friends and partners; and it helps us to deepen our knowledge as such of other religions."[402] Bevans and Schroeder call this dialogue a *prophetic dialogue* since it "demands honesty, conviction, courage and faith."[403]

The impact of the church's efforts towards fighting violations of human rights in Nigeria could be more positively felt when she can allow such mutual recognition and appreciation of other faith communities and enhance support for each other, by way of accepting and cherishing the differences that exist, failures and limitations shared between her and these communities. By so doing she will also clearly promote each other's possibilities and opportunities, and bring about a wonderful collaboration with these others towards fighting for the common cause – instituting the human rights culture. Nyerere remarked beautifully on this matter:

> It is necessary to recognize, however, that others – non-Catholics and non-Christians – will also be working to promote social justice; ... we should welcome other workers for justice. It is not necessary to agree with everything a man believes or says in order to work with him on particular projects or in particular areas of activity.[404]

The mission of God, which finds its full expression in Christ will be better realised if the church could learn to respect the humanity of the 'other' as Jesus did. Jesus was seen as one who crosses the gender, racial, and social barriers.[405] Since the church upholds the dignity of the human person on the basis of *Imago Dei,* it is more reason why she should not allow any form of discrimination or antagonism towards other faith/ religious communities and cultural orientations. It is also expected of the church to expose her members to educational programmes and policies to the values of other faiths and cultural orientations in order to enhance this intercultural/ interreligious exchange, for a better understanding and appreciation of these 'others' who are not Catholics. This will promote a very apprecia-

402 Bevans, S.B., and Schroeder, R.P., Ibid. p. 380.

403 Ibid. p. 384.

404 Nyerere, J., Ibid. p. 151.

405 Ariarajah, W., *Interreligious Dialogue as an Intercultural Encounter*, in Frederiks, M., Dijkstra, M., and Houtepen, A., (eds.), Towards and Intercultural Theology, Netherlands, 2003, p. 64.

ble and fruitful intercultural formation among the members of the church, especially her young members who must interact with these 'others' at various situations and places in Nigeria.

5.2.1.6.1. Dialogue with Islam

With regard to interreligious exchange I want to draw a special attention to the dialogue between the church and Islam since the two are biggest religious groups in Nigeria. Dialogue between the church and Islam in Nigeria is basically done on the platform of the Christian Association of Nigeria (CAN). On this platform the church is expected, taking cognisance of the above analysis, carry other Christian denominations along to this dialogue.

Christian – Muslim dialogue in Nigeria has been wrought with difficulties over the years, and as such has not contributed concretely enough to a harmonious co-existence between the two groups. More and more religious tensions and violence still remain a frequent occasional occurence in some Northen States of Nigeria. Most relgious leaders of both sides are of the opinion that disgruntled politicians use religious emotions to achieve their political ends, thereby causing tensions and violence among folks and religious groups under the guise of religion.[406]

Fundamentally Islam and Christianity hold the same belief about the existence of one supreme God, the maker and ruler of all things. In the same vein the two religions promote peace and love and hold respect for life at high esteem.[407] But at any least provocation caused by some misunderstanding one sees to utter dismay how the fellowers of the two groups desend on each other like in a fight between two wild Lions. This attitude gives the impression that the religious practices of most Muslims and Christians are only hypocritical and superficial.[408] In otherwords under-

406 The Archbishop of Jos Diocese, Dr. Ignatious Kaigama and the Emir of Wase, Dr. Haruna Abdullahi, are among the leading religious leaders in Nigeria who are of the opinion that religion is being misused by monstrous politicians for achieving their political motives. Andre, G., and Simone, R., (eds.): *Christlich-islamische Partnerschaft für Gerechtigkeit und Frieden. (Impulse aus Afrika, Asien and Nahost).* Don Bosco 8, Muenchen 2006. p. 136.

407 Cf. The Koran (Sura 6, 51) and The Bible (Mt. 5, 21).

408 This is the view of Archibishop I. Kaigama as stated in his Article: *Dialog des Lebens: eine dringende Notwendigkeit für nigerianisch Muslime und Christen,* in Andre, G., and Simone, R., (eds), Ibid. p. 129ff.

standing a true worship of God as rooted in the Love of God and Neighbour together with respect for the religious convictions and practices of the other indeed ought to be a serious call to all Nigerians and should form the basis of the dialogue between Islam and Christianity. But why is it that this dialogue is not bearing the desired fruit?

Archbishop Ignatius Kaigama opined that the dialogue between Muslims and Christians in Nigeria is not successful because in most cases it only offers the privileged Muslims and Christians opportunity of coming together to exchange pleasantries, make friendship with each other and take pictures as if everything is alright.[409] This form of meetings often take place among the leading Figures of these religions, and in most cases do not contribute to minimising the constant religious conflicts and tensions in the regions because the real issues are not been brought to the forum, and as such the interest of the ‚commoners' are not respresented.

Kaigama therefore suggests a dialogue of Life between Muslims and Christians in Nigeria as an imperative, and must be done in full representation of the young and old members of the two groups.[410] Interreligious dialogue should begin on this basis, he stated. Further on he opined a true development of friendship between the two groups by ways of identifying with each other, especially at religious ceremonies and feasts of each of the groups.

This idea of establishing true friendship with Muslims is not acceptable by some Christian scholars. Such Christian scholars carry the propaganda that dialogue cannot bring any good relationship between Muslims and Christians since the Koran forbids Muslims from fraternising with Christians. It is actually so stated in the Holy Koran (Sura 5, 51):

> O ye who believe! Take not the Jews and the Christians for your friends and protectors. They are but friends and protectors to each other. And he amongst you that turns to them (for friendship) is of them. Verily Allah guideth not a people unjust.[411]

409 Ibid., p. 132

410 Ibid.

411 English Translation of the meanings and commentary. Revised and edited by the Presidency of Islamic Researches, IFTA, Call and Guidance. Al-Madinah AL-Munawar-

Sura 4,134+144 has similar admonition with the above quoted Sura. There are other passages of the Holy Koran that made mention of non-believers in Islam as Pagans, and ordered their extermination (Sura 2:191; 8:12-13 +17+39; 9:14+29+30). These are passages that legitimise persecution of non-believers. Even Sura 47:35 encourages Muslims not bother themselves calling for peace with their adverseries as long as they have upper hand.

It could really sound very absurd that 'God' could forbid friendship between peoples, or command the killing of fellow human beings, but let us not loose sight of the historical period in which the Holy Books were written. The Christian Holy Bible (the Old Testament), for instance also has passages where God commanded and empowered Israel to exterminate their enemies in order to reach the Promised Land. Thus some aspects of these books reflect the events of the epochs. The verses of Koran that command the killing of unbelievers could be understood in the context of persecution the Muslims of the time suffered in the hands of ‚Pagans' and christians.[412] The people of Israel of old also suffered similar persecution in the hands of other races who exploited them. The command of the 'Lord' to exterminate and humble their 'enemies' could also be understood in this context. Consequently they reflect in some cases aspects of conflicts with evil, and the overpowering of evil by Good.

However these two books also have passages that reflect the promotion of peace, love, equality and justice.[413] The two books have contrasts between each other in some aspects, but they have also common grounds in other aspects. In otherwords there are areas of agreement and disagreement, but this does not negate creating room for dialogue. These two aspects ought not to be overrated. The aspects of agreement can be a very useful starting point for a dialogue of life, which could eventually lead to another open-

ah.

412 Such words like those of Sura 2:191 suggest killing non-believers on account of persecution: "And slay them wherever ye catch them, and turn them out from where they have turned you out; for persecution is worse than slaughter".

413 Some of these passages in the two Holy Books have been mentioned in Chapter two.

ning in dialogue to the aspects of disagreement. Knowing what divides Muslims and Christians and respecting it could be another opening point for dialogue.[414]

In other words, re-writing the Holy Books of the two religions or abolishion of their dogmatic differences is not the solution rather a proper understanding and acceptance that religion is by its very nature unique and their morals, dogmas, histories and cultures have basis.[415] This calls for an understanding of the Books in some cases, and in other cases give indepth insight into the words of the Books for better understanding of their meaning. The Texts could be better interpreted by and with signs of the times.

Based on these suggestions I optimistically suggest a continuous dialogue between Islam and Christianity as the only peaceful way towards harmonious and peaceful co-existence with each other in Nigeria. In the course of this dialogue (of life) the two groups could develop common ground for a better evaluation and interpretation of the Holy Books according to the demands of the present era.

Summary

In this chapter, I exposed the relationship between the previous chapters. This exposition indicated that the church's mission is a must for the pro-motion and protection of human rights if she is to address the integral liberation of humankind. I went further to describe some challenges the church in Nigeria has to face if she it to be true to this mission. These include essentially the responsibility of being a carrier of human rights culture. Nonetheless, she can only play this role when she must have looked inwards into her own institution to address aspects of her ideolo-gies and doctrine that give latency to the violations of human rights, starting from within to without. When the church must have done this and allowed some positive changes can she be in a better position to dis-charge her prophetic role through which she can be a church for the poor, a church with the

414 *Die integrative Kraft des Glaubens: Anerkennen, was verbindet, respektieren, was trennt,* in der Zeitschrift:Image – *Gerechtigkeit kennt keine leeren Hände.* 12/10, März 2011, p. 4

415 Kaigama, I., *Dialog des Lebens: eine dringende Notwendigkeit für nigerianisch Muslime und Christen* , Ibid. p. 134.

poor, and a church of the poor in the real sense. Finally an intercultural/ interreligious approach is also another form of challenge the church in Nigeria has to contend with. With it focus on the mission of Christ, this approach as indicated is meant to break down all kinds of barriers that provide latency for the perpetration of human rights viola-tions; and ask for mutual collaboration among cultural and religious groups towards the promotion and protection of human rights in Nigeria. Narrowing this dialogue down to Islam as a major religious institution is very imminent since most religious tensions and violence in Nigeria have always existed between Muslims and Christians.

GENERAL CONCLUSION

This project has been an attempt to establish the mission of the church in the context of the human rights violations all over the world, with particular reference to the Nigerian context. It has become clear that the church's mission of liberation is obligatory enough for her to work for the integral liberation of humankind in the face of various violations of human rights. It is one of the ways the church has to prepare humankind for its eventual eschatological encounter.

The following establishments on the issue have been made:

That the human rights situation in Nigeria is not a good one. So many violations have been and are being recorded with regard to the three generations of human rights. It was also established that the church is not totally free of giving latency to some of these violations.

1. Those cultural and religious factors have also significant influence in the area of human rights protection and violation.

2. The church has a mission – to liberate humanity from these violations and oppressive and inhuman situations, based specifically on the dignity of the human person. This is the fundament of the mission of Christ, her founder.

3. The mission of the church is more actively felt in the arena of social aspect of human rights, as the church's instruments of legitimation indicate. Thus calling the attention of the church to a balanced approach between the social human rights and other aspects – judicial and political human rights. The questionnaire results indicate a call to the church to create a significant approach to, and relationship between the church and human rights question.

4. Even though history proved the church not to be an institution *of* human rights, by virtue of her mission and activities in the world, she is capable of being an institution *for* human rights. This means that the church has still a lot of work to do in order to enhance an

> integral liberation of humankind. The world needs the church and the church cannot do without the world, hence the need for mutual understanding and collaboration between the two.

I have to remark here that this project is not about the church praise-singing. Allusions have to be made to the church's efforts in improving her mission, and as well aimed at presenting other areas of urgent attention for the church's mission, strictly based on the mission of Christ. This approach is in response to the invitation of the President of the Pontifical Commission *Justitia et Pax,* Maurice Cadinal Roy, who among other issues, indicated that the document was also meant to raise questions, stimulate research, suggest activities and offer doctrinal and theological reflection on the question of human rights as it concerns the church.[416]

That notwithstanding, I cannot ignore to mention again the Nigerian church's current active involvement in all kinds of liberation activities: liberation from sickness, which is manifested by her engagement in hospital/ health care apostolate, liberation from ignorance, through her massive and impressive educational apostolate at various levels, liberation from physical pain such as hunger, manifested in her involvement in agricultural and commercial enterprises, liberation from oppression, made manifest by her condemnation of the unjust political and economic procedures. An eloquent example here is the results of her prisons apostolate, which I mentioned an aspect of it in chapter one.

These eloquent testimonies of the church's involvement in liberation activities could be better appreciated if she can make some critical and positive evaluation of herself and elicit possible adjustments regarding some of her ideologies and structures that have provided latency for human rights violations within her fold and without. The ethnocentric and triumphalist tendencies clouding around her is another threat to her missionary success. She can teach more effectively by good examples.

There is no doubt that the church is constantly shifting her position on certain issues relating to her mission in and to the world. In most cases, she is slower in handling 'sensitive' issues, mainly matters that are deeply rooted in her traditions. Her slow pace of movement notwithstanding, the church

416 Cf. Foward to Justitia et Pax, p. 2.

inevitably shifts and reforms herselt. Some of the sensitive matters have been mentioned already in this project: abortion, women emancipation and empowerment for a more active participation, enhancing the atmosphere for freedom of expression among her members, etc. It is expected that the church will make more shifts on these issues.

This project is however, one of the ways of keeping the church constantly awake and on the shifting mood to steadily maintain reasonable reforms of her structures and ideologies, in order to respond positively to the demands of the world she claims to liberate and salvage. This fact is made clearer by the 1974 Synod of Bishops:

> From her own experience the Church knows that her ministry of fostering human rights in the world requires continued scrutiny and purification of her own life, her laws, institutions and policies.... purification is needed in internal practices and procedures, and in relationships with social structures and systems whose violations of human rights deserve censure.[417]

Issues of human rights form the backbone of human existence and dignity has to be taken very seriously by the church. It is one of the means the church has to legitimise the relevance of her mission to the world. This has to start with a stimulation of internal recognition of human rights, and will invariably help to avoid dramatic factionalism and loss of social relevance. For the church to accomplish this feat, the assumed separation between the church and human rights issues, as indicated by the questionnaire results, ought to be bridged in order to enable the church consciously identify in all ramifications with human rights question.

417 Document of the 1974 Synod of Bishops, In: *Justitia et Pax,* Ibid., no. 62.

EPILOGUE: Agents of 'Hope'

The above scenario of human rights situation in Nigeria seems hopeless, but it is not helpless at the long run. It is interesting to know that there are Nigerians who have defied the fears of the unknown and uncertainties of survival to advance their own particularistic life ideals and conceptions of democracy. These individuals and organizations have formed the backbone and energizer of democracy in the country.

Professional groups like the Nigerian Bar Association, the Nigerian Medical Association and some of the Labour Unions have frequently challenged the government on human rights violations, by means of press conferences, press releases and organized strike actions. Along side these groups are the pro-human rights and pro-democracy NGOs who have continually contributed to creating the atmosphere that all is not well with the nation. Through their instrumentality, some measures are readdressed. The case of Amina Lawal who was sentenced to death for adultery by Shari'a Law, was eventually settled through their protests, which attracted international support. Some of the northern states have been also pressurized to lessen the severe practices of the Shar'ia by means of their continuous opposition.

The roles of the "Women's Rights Watch, Nigeria" founded by Ngozi Imoukhuede, cannot be overlooked. They are poised to fight against most of the violence against women in Nigeria. One of their success stories was recorded in Edo State in 1999, when they pressurized the Edo State House of Assembly to pass a bill prohibiting the practice of Female Genital Mutilation in that part of the country.[418]

Another strong agency is the "Justice, Development and Peace Commission" (JDPC), a Catholic church's organ for fighting against human rights violations and other social ills in Nigeria. Among others, this organ has played a more significant role in the area of *Prisons Apostolate*. They have at so many occasions initiated and effected the trial of detainees awaiting trial, and release of innocent prisoners and detainees. Statistics has it that

418 Imoukhuede, N., *Presentation on Female Genital Mutilation in Edo State, Nigeria*: www.rufarm.kabissa.org/articles/fgm.htm.

through the efforts of the JDPC of the Catholic Diocese of Ondo, 256 detainees were released between 1998 and 2003 from the Akure Medium Security Prison.[419]

The church in Nigeria has also employed other avenues of addressing human rights issues, but those notwithstanding; she still has a lot of work to do towards the promotion and protection of human rights in Nigeria. We therefore have every reason to heave a sigh of relieve and direct our view towards a future of hope knowing that there are 'Agents of Hope', who are not giving up effort to restoring promotion and protection of human rights in Nigeria.

419 JDPC, Catholic Diocese of Ondo, Nigeria. Human Rights Department, *2003 Updated Statistics of Released Prisoners from Akure Medium Security Prison.*

EINE DEUTSCHE ZUSAMMENFASSUNG

(A Summary in German)

Einführung:

Nigeria ist, das ist wohlbekannt, eines der reichsten Länder Afrikas und hat rund 150 Millionen Einwohner. Nigeria gehört zu den fünf größten Erdöllieferanten der Welt. Leider gehört es auch zu den fünf korruptesten Ländern der Erde. Die Korruption ist einer der Gründe, warum 75% der Einwohner dieses an sich „reichen“ Landes in Armut leben und rund 65% von ihnen weder lesen noch schreiben können. Es ist keine Überraschung, dass Armut und Analphabetismus zu den Hauptfolgen der Korruption in Nigeria zählen, denn eine Bevölkerung, die sich keine angemessene Schulbildung leisten kann, bleibt naturgemäß unwissend und folglich unterdrückt.

Eine Verbesserung der Menschenrechte wäre unter diesen Umständen nicht mehr als ein kleiner Beitrag. Die Menschenrechte, das ist altbekannt, sind eines der immer wiederkehren Themen, denen im Verlauf der Geschichte immer wieder besondere Aufmerksamkeit gewidmet wurde. Allgemein kann man sagen, dass die Menschenrechte jene Rechte sind, die allen Menschen allein durch ihr Menschsein zustehen. Ein „Recht“ kann man als Anspruch ansehen, der berechtigt erhoben wird. „Menschenrechte“ sind daher Ansprüche mit einem kleinen Unterschied, da sie nicht von der Zusicherung oder Gewährung Anderer abhängen. Erkennt man die Menschenrechte als legitim an, so muss man im gleichen Zug anerkennen, dass jeder Mensch auf Grund seines Menschseins diese Ansprüche stellen kann. Menschenrechte wohnen allen Menschen inne und müssen respektiert, gefördert und geschützt werden.

Über die vergangenen Jahrhunderte hat es in bestimmten Teilen der Welt bemerkenswerte Fortschritte bei der Förderung und beim Schutz der Menschenrechte gegeben. Leider haben sich noch nicht alle Teile der Welt diesem guten Weg vorbehaltlos angeschlossen. An dieser Stelle muss ich auf die blutigen Ereignisse zu sprechen kommen, die durch die Übertretung von Menschenrechten in den vergangenen Jahrzehnten und in der gegenwärtigen Ära der menschlichen Geschichte bedingt sind: die abschreckenden Ereignisse des Apartheid-Regimes in Südafrika, die schockierenden Vorfälle, in denen die menschliche Persönlichkeit im Zeitalter des Kommunismus erschüttert und vernichtet wurde, die schrecklichen Situationen, in denen sich Menschen in Diktaturen befanden und immer noch befinden, die Verweigerung der Religionsfreiheit in vielen Ländern der Welt, die Ungerechtigkeit der Globalisierung und des Neokolonialismus, unter denen die meisten Dritte-Welt-Länder leiden. Die Lage der Menschenrechte in Nigeria ergibt auch kein anderes Bild: Verletzung von Redefreiheit, Versammlungsfreiheit, fehlende Beschäftigungsmöglichkeiten, das Aufstöhnen der immer zahlreicher werdenden Massen, der Niedergeschlagenen und Unterdrückten, sowie der bizarre Anblick der eklatanten sozialen Ungerechtigkeit, die in den meisten Bereichen des Lebens im Land an der Tagesordnung ist.

Gleichwohl ist die Situation der Menschenrechte in Nigeria nicht hoffnungslos. Einen Schimmer der Hoffnung auf eine bessere Zukunft kann man in den privaten Sektoren erkennen, in den religiösen Institutionen (besonders den christlichen) und in den Nichtregierungsorganisationen (NGOs). Diese Seiten führen einen ständigen Kampf gegen die Korruption, für die Förderung und den Schutz der Menschenrechte und für die Verbesserung der Lebensbedingungen der Menschen.

Motivation:

Dieses Engagement für ein besseres Nigeria hat mich persönlich dazu motiviert, mich diesen „Guten Samaritern" anzuschließen, auf ihrer Suche und bei ihrem Einsatz für mögliche Lösungen im Interesse einer besseren Zukunft für Nigeria und die Nigerianer. Aus der Perspektive der Kirche in Nigeria konnte ich mir unmittelbar vorstellen, als katholischer Priester einen eigenen Beitrag zu leisten.

Naturgemäß stellen die Verletzungen der Menschenrechte ein lebenswichtiges Band zwischen den Menschenrechten und der Mission der Kirche dar, und verpflichten sie daher, eine umfassende Befreiung der Menschheit anzustreben. Daraus folgt, dass die Betroffenen der traurigen und bedauerlichen Verletzung der Menschenrechte in der ganzen Welt (und vor allem in Nigeria) ständig Zuflucht und Trost im tiefsten Herzen der Kirche suchen und von ihr erwarten, im Geist des Evangeliums den prophetischen

Krieg zur Förderung und zum Schutz der Menschenrechte in Wort und Tat zu führen. Durch das Erbe des Evangeliums ist diese Mission der Kirche direkt in der prophetischen und befreienden Mission des Herrn Jesus Christus verankert, „dessen Worte und Taten alle dem Wohl der *Menschen* dienen, um sie zu retten, heilen, befreien und ihnen beizustehen." (*Kirche und Menschenrechte: Päpstliche Kommission „Justitia et Pax", Vatikanstadt, 1978, Nr. 56).* Aus dieser Perspektive wird die Kirche als eine Art Allheilmittel wahrgenommen, als Ergebnis der sozialpolitischen Dimension ihrer heilbringenden Mission, zu der, unter anderem, die Anerkennung, Förderung und der Schutz der Menschenrechte gehören sollte.

Ziel:

Ziel dieser Arbeit ist die Untersuchung, wie die Katholische Kirche in Nigeria ihre Missionstätigkeit auf die Verbesserung der erbärmlichen Situation der Menschenrechte im nigerianischen Kontext ausrichten kann. Im Verlauf der Untersuchung möchte ich unterstreichen, dass sich dieser Aspekt der kirchlichen Mission als sehr schwierig und wahrscheinlich unmöglich herausstellen wird, wenn sich die Kirche nicht von den *intrusiven, ethnozentrischen* und *triumphalistischen* Tendenzen befreit, die manchen ihrer Methoden, Normen und Ideologien innewohnen. Diese Tendenzen setzen die Kirche einem stetigen Strom der Beschuldigungen wegen Menschenrechtsverletzungen aus.

Es scheint übertrieben und respektlos von Menschenrechtsverletzungen innerhalb der Kirche zu sprechen, besonders wenn man berücksichtigt, wie schwer die Menschenrechtsverletzungen in vielen Teilen der Erde sind. Gleichwohl lautet der allgemeine Tenor dieser Anschuldigungen, dass die Kirche wohl in vorderster Front stehe, wenn es darum geht, die fundamentalen Rechte zu fördern, die es Menschen erlauben, ein menschenwürdiges Leben zu führen, andererseits ihre Strukturen aber ein Hindernis bei der Umsetzung ebendieses Bestrebens darstellen (Stichele, V.C., *Disciples and Discipline (European Debate on Human Rights violations in the Roman Catholic Church), 1993, Leuven, S. 8).* Wie kann also die Kirche im Angesicht dieser Anschuldigungen ihrer Befreiungsmission gerecht werden? Es liegt mir am Herzen, nach den verfügbaren Möglichkeiten zu suchen. Diese Suche gliedert sich in fünf an Länge und Umfang unterschiedliche Kapitel.

Kapitel Eins:

Kapitel 1 liefert einen Überblick der vorkolonialen, kolonialen und postkolonialen Geschichte Nigerias. Darin wurde Bilder des „Fortschritts" bei der Entwicklung der Menschenrechte im nigerianischen Kontext in Vergangenheit und Gegenwart dargestellt. Es ist ein Versuch, eine Antwort darauf zu finden, wie die Menschenrechtsfrage in Nigeria aufs Tapet kam, welches Verständnis der Menschenrechte im nigerianischen Kontext vorherrscht und in welchem Maß die Menschenrechte in Nigeria respektiert, gefördert oder aber vernachlässigt oder verletzt werden. Durch die Beschreibung der strukturellen Probleme der Menschenrechte in Nigeria zeichnet dieses Kapitel ein Bild der Menschenrechtssituation in diesem Land. Man gewinnt stark den Eindruck, dass die umfassende Einbeziehung der Menschenrechte in die nigerianische Verfassung keine oder nahezu keine Auswirkung auf die Umsetzung der Menschenrechte in der Praxis hat. Der Einfluss der African Commission on Human Rights und der National Commission on Human Rights wurde nicht übersehen, soweit er die nigerianische Verfassung betrifft.

Es wurde in diesem Kapitel auch sehr deutlich gemacht, dass die Verletzung der Menschenrechte in Nigeria fast allen Institutionen zugeschrieben werden kann - seien sie ziviler, religiöser, wirtschaftlicher oder kultureller Art. Es ist auch überraschend, feststellen zu müssen, mit welcher Verzögerung und Nachlässigkeit die Religionen auf die fortgesetzte Verletzung von Menschenrechten in Nigeria reagieren. Dies ist in Zusammenhang mit Religionsfreiheit, Nicht-Diskriminierung, Meinungsfreiheit und sozioökonomischen Rechten beobachtbar, besonders wo das Prinzip der Gleichberechtigung beim Zugang zu Erwerbstätigkeiten betroffen ist. Ich schätze diesen Aspekt als einen Bereich ein, in dem die Aufmerksamkeit der Kirche dringend gefordert ist. Das bedeutet auch, dass alle, da sie ja in der ein oder anderen Art an der Verletzung von Menschenrechten in Nigeria beteiligt sind, sich auf der anderen Seite auch am Kampf für eine Verbesserung der aktuellen Lage beteiligen sollten.

Kapitel Zwei:

Kapitel 2 und seine Unterteilungen stellten den Reichtum und die Schönheit der kulturellen und religiösen Traditionen Nigerias dar, mit besonderer

Betonung der drei größten kulturellen und religiösen Traditionen. Die kulturelle und religiöse Vielfalt Nigerias wurde hier deutlich zum Ausdruck gebracht. Es gibt über 250 Ethnien und Sprachen in Nigeria. Von diesen widmet sich die Darstellung aus Gründen der Zweckmäßigkeit und Präzision vorrangig den drei wichtigsten kulturellen und ethnischen Gruppen der Hausa, Yourba und Igbo (Ibo). In ähnlicher Weise wurde mit den drei wichtigsten religiösen Gruppen verfahren, dem Islam, dem Christentum und der Naturreligion. Die Darstellung konzentriert sich auf die Frage, in welchem Ausmaß die kulturellen und religiösen Traditionen die Menschenrechte in Nigeria fördern, schützen oder verletzen.

Eine vertiefte Untersuchung der Ideologien und Prinzipien dieser Traditionen legt den Eindruck nahe, dass diese Ideologien und Prinzipien die Menschenrechte fördern und schützen. In der praktischen Anwendung der Werte dieser Traditionen treten allerdings widersprüchliche Anzeichen zutage, die auf das Vorhandensein von gegenteiligen Tendenzen schließen lassen. Gelegentlich sind es die Prinzipien und Ideologien selbst, die in offenem Widerspruch zu den international anerkannten Maßstäben in Menschenrechtsangelegenheiten stehen. In den meisten Fällen liegt das Problem jedoch in der Schnittstelle zwischen Theorie und Praxis auf Grundlage der authentischen Prinzipien und Ideologien dieser Traditionen. Die gelebte Praxis entspricht, anders gesagt, ihren theoretischen Vorgaben nicht. Ein Konsens setzt voraus, dass jede dieser Traditionen nach innen blickt und, wo erforderlich, eine Neubewertung ihrer Ideologien und Prinzipien vornimmt und die eigenen Methoden überprüft. Die gemeinsame Teilnahme an einem Dialog zur Klärung der Konfliktfragen bietet auch die Möglichkeit, einen Konsens zu erzielen.

Kapitel Drei:

Kapitel 3 stellte ausführlich die verschiedenen Aspekte der Missionstätigkeit der Kirche dar. All diesen Aspekten zentral ist die Mission des Herrn Jesus Christus, dem Gründer der Kirche. Das Kapitel konzentriert sich außerdem auf die befreienden Aspekte der Mission Christi als zentralem Aspekt seiner Mission, sofern die Unterprivilegierten der Gesellschaft betroffen sind. Es wurde vorgeschlagen, dass sich die Befreiungsmission der Kirche auf dieser Grundlage den Anforderungen des modernen Zeitalters stellt, das hier in seinen die Menschenrechte betreffenden Aspekten dargestellt wird. Durch die Diskussion der Frage, inwiefern der Beschäftigung der Kirche mit Menschenrechten legitim ist, berücksichtigte dieses Kapitel auch die kirchlichen Dokumente, die den „Kontext der Legitimation“ bilden, im Interesse einer besseren Reaktion auf die Menschenrechtsforderungen der Kirche.

In dem ich die obigen Aspekte der Legitimation der Kirche für Ihre Beschäftigung mit Menschenrechtsfragen zur Kenntnis nehme, bin ich gezwungen, mir die drei *Mediationen* zur Befreiungstheologie von Leonardo Boff ins Gedächtnis zu rufen: *die sozioanalytische, hermeneutische und pastorale Praxis.* Es kann keinen Zweifel geben, das die Kirche in den ersten beiden Mediationen noch nicht sehr erfolgreich war. Was die Realität der Menschen betrifft, so hat die Kirche auch was die dritte Mediation betrifft, noch eine Menge Hindernisse zu überwinden. Das ist der Zeitpunkt, an dem allerlei Probleme und Konflikte mit der Welt auftreten, die sie bekehren will. Es sind, in diesem Zusammenhang, die Missstände unserer Zeit, besonders die Menschenrechtsverletzungen, die Anlass für die Entwicklung der obigen Gedanken waren, die immer noch eine Herausforderung für die Kirche darstellen, sich noch weiter in die „Tiefe“ ihres Inneren zu begeben, um die Suche nach gerechteren und menschlicheren Gesellschaftsstrukturen zu stimulieren und den stetigen Kampf gegen die aktuellen *Gegenkräfte und destruktiven Tendenzen der Entfremdung und menschlichen Rebellion zu führen. (Boff, L. 1983:16, In: Bosch, David. Transforming Mission: Paradigm Shifts in Theology of Mission, Orbis Books, Maryknoll, N.Y., 1991, S. 49).* Die Kirche hingegen muss diese Mission unter der Führung des Heiligen Geistes und dem Licht der Welt weiterführen, um aus ihren eigenen Grenzen heraus als sichtbare historische Realität in Erscheinung treten zu können, bis hin zur vollständigen Kommunion der menschlichen Familie beim Festmahl im Reich des Herrn (s. Jesaja 25,6; Matthäus 8,11).

Mit besonderer Berücksichtigung der Rolle des Heiligen Geistes wurde in diesem Kapitel die Dialogmission der Kirche diskutiert. Dem Beispiel ihres Herrn folgend, öffnet sich die Kirche für die Werte und Traditionen der Völker, die einen anderen Glauben und andere Gebräuche haben. Sie kann diesen Aspekt ihrer Mission nur dann erfolgreich durchführen, wenn sie keinen Anspruch auf absolute Wahrheit oder Alleingültigkeit der Interpretation ihrer religiösen Praxis erhebt. Dies verlangt nach der Umsetzbarkeit der Forderungen und Vorschläge des Zweiten Vatikanischen Konzils. Sie ist dazu aufgerufen, der Tugend der Bescheidenheit Reverenz zu erweisen.

Doch auch wenn die Bekehrung und Verkündung der frohen Botschaft die Grundlage der Befreiungsmission der Kirche bleiben, so sind die Bewahrung und Anwendung der Menschenrechte zweifellos ein unverzichtbarer Bestandteil dieser großen Aufgabe. Sie stellen eine der wirksamen Möglichkeiten dar, die der Kirche zur Verfügung stehen, um in engem Kontakt zu den Realitäten der Menschenrechtsverletzungen zu bleiben und sich eine relevante Rolle in der modernen Welt zu bewahren, in der sie das Evangelium verbreiten möchte. Dazu ist es allerdings auch erforderlich, das die genannten Mittel, mit denen sich die Kirche in der Menschenrechtsfrage engagieren kann, auch wirksam in Taten umgesetzt werden, denn ansonsten, (wie es gelegentlich der Fall ist), riskiert das Engagement für die Befreiung ein Papiertiger zu bleiben. Ruft man sich beispielsweise die *Mulieris Dignitatem* von Johannes Paul II ins Gedächtnis, so ist man unmittelbar geneigt, die sofortige Anwendung dieser dritten Mediation durch die Kirche zu erwarten, sofern dies die Stellung der Frauen in der Kirche in großen Teilen der Welt betrifft.

Das führt uns zur nächsten Frage: In welchem Maß trägt die Kirche tatsächlich zur praktischen Anwendung der Menschenrechte bei?

Kapitel Vier:

Der Versuch von Kapitel 4, diese Frage zu beantworten, führt zu sowohl theoretischen als auch empirischen Erörterungen. Von besonderem Interesse sind in diesem Zusammenhang: religiöse Einstellungen und religiöses Verhalten, Einstellungen zu den Menschenrechten und die Auswirkungen der religiösen Einstellungen und Verhalten auf die Einstellungen zu Menschenrechten. Im Interesse einer fruchtbaren Verbindung von Theorie und Empirie wurde hier stark auf die Ergebnisse einer empirischen Untersuchung zurückgegriffen, die mit Hilfe eines Fragebogens unter Schülern der Real Schulen in drei der wichtigsten geographischen Zonen Nigerias (Südosten, Westen und Norden) durchgeführt wurde. Dabei ist es von besonderem Interesse zu erfahren, wie die nigerianische Jugend (als zukünftige Führungspersonen) die Kirche einschätzt und welche Erwartungen sie an die Kirche stellt, besonders was deren Einstellung zur Frage der Menschenrechte betrifft.

Im Allgemeinen ist die Korrelation zwischen der religiösen Einstellung und der Einstellung zu Menschenrechten positiv, außer bei einigem die Euthanasie betreffenden Aspekte. In diesem Bereich finden sich gemischte Reaktionen und Tendenzen. Die in diesem Zusammenhang gegebene Interpretation lässt auf eine zukünftige Generation hoffen, die der Kirche wohlgesonnen ist. Die „Null"-Korrelationen fallen im Vergleich zu den zahlreichen positiven Korrelationen zwischen den beiden Einstellungen nicht signifikant ins Gewicht. Die Teilnehmer an der Umfrage, unter denen sich die zukünftigen Führungskräfte Nigerias befinden, haben ihre Position klar artikuliert, nicht nur was die Rolle der Kirche in Nigeria betrifft, sondern auch die der zivilen Institutionen. Im Allgemeinen haben sie sich zu Gunsten von Wandel und Fortschritt im Interesse der Etablierung einer Menschenrechtskultur in Nigeria ausgesprochen. Sie erwarten von der Kirche eine auf Wandel und Fortschritt ausgerichtete Mission und Struktur.

Diese Tatsache bringt mich zurück zu Kapitel 3, in dem ich die unterschiedlichen Meinungen zum Engagement der Kirche in der Menschenrechtsfrage dargestellt habe. Ein Denkrichtung vertritt die Ansicht, die Kirche sei eine strikt eschatologische Organisation, die sich in gesellschaftspolitische und rechtliche Angelegenheiten, wie es die Menschenrechte sind, nicht einzumischen habe. Eine andere Denkrichtung vertritt das Gegenteil dieser Position. Unabhängig von dieser Meinungsverschiedenheit artikulieren die Teilnehmer an der Umfrage ein brennendes Verlangen nach einer Kirche, die die frohe Botschaft nicht nur verkündet, sondern auch praktisch vorlebt, indem sie relevante und realistische Antworten und Lösungen zu den Fragen und Anforderungen des 21. Jahrhunderts anbieten kann. Die Teilnehmer bringen damit, in anderen Worten, zum Ausdruck, dass das spirituelle Wohlergehen der Menschheit nicht von seinem gesellschaftlichen, politischen und wirtschaftlichen Wohlergehen trennbar ist. Erst der angemessene Umgang mit dem temporalen Aspekt führt zu einer fruchtbaren Umsetzung des spirituellen. Dies trägt zur Diskussion über die integrale Natur der Befreiungsmission der Kirche bei, (wie bereits in Kap. 3 dargelegt).

Die strukturelle Beschaffenheit der Kirche ist ein weiterer Bereich, über den die Teilnehmer Besorgnis artikuliert haben. Die Struktur der Kirche ist sehr hierarchisch. In den meisten Fällen ist diese Struktur durch eine starke Zentralisierung gekennzeichnet, die zur Autokratie führt. In manchen Fällen neigt diese starke Zentralisierung dazu, die Kirche hinter den Schatten der Menschenrechtsfrage zu positionieren, wo sie von der Wirklichkeit ausgeschlossen ist. Das impliziert, dass diese Struktur es als Bedrohung empfindet, wenn die Realität bloßgelegt wird. Einige Aspekte der Menschenrechtsthematik, wie Gleichheit, Meinungsfreiheit, Religionsfreiheit und Freiheit der Lebensweise können als sehr bedrohlich für die Integration der Kirchenhierarchie wahrgenommen werden.

Die Umfrageteilnehmer bringen hier daher, statistisch betrachtet, ihre Erwartung zum Ausdruck, dass die Kirche offener und zugänglicher für Kritik und konstruktive Beiträge wird. Das ist nicht neu oder abwegig, wenn man an die offiziellen Kirchendokumente denkt, (die bereits im vorigen Kapitel zitiert wurden), die dazu aufrufen, sich der konstruktiven Kritik mehr zu öffnen. Dieser Aufruf ermahnt die Kirche, sich darauf zu konzentrieren, was sie auf konkrete Weise vorweisen kann, um ihrer Aufgabe als Heilung (Hoffnung) der Welt gerecht zu werden. (Fuchs, O., Heilen und befreien: Der Dienst am Nächsten als Ernstfall von Kirche und Pastoral. 1990, Patmos Düsseldorf. S. 82. (Wort in Klammern von mir hinzugefügt).

Es ist nicht verwunderlich, dass die Ergebnisse der Umfrage eher auf Wandel und Fortschritt abzielende Einstellungen zur Menschenrechtsfrage erkennen lassen. Das in Nigeria anzutreffende Maß an Ungerechtigkeit und die Häufigkeit und Schwere der Menschenrechtsverletzungen reichen aus, um aus jedem wohlgesinnten Nigerianer einen Verfechter einer besseren Gesellschaft zu machen. Unsere Jugend verlangt einen Generationenwechsel.

Zusammenfassend möchte diese Untersuchung die Kirche in Nigeria dazu aufrufen, sich zu öffnen und die Menschenrechtsfrage in ihre missionarische Tagesordnung aufzunehmen, wenn sie vermeiden will, dass ihr Streben nach umfassender Befreiung der Menschen eine Utopie bleibt und vor ihrer Missionstätigkeit ein großes Fragezeichen steht bleibt, wenn die Frage nach deren Relevanz gestellt wird. Was kann getan werden, um diese Lücke zu füllen? Das folgende und abschließende Kapitel dieser

Forschungsarbeit ist ein Versuch, diese Frage zu beantworten und einige Vorschläge hinsichtlich der möglichen, für die Kirche gangbaren Wege in Menschenrechtsangelegenheiten in Nigeria zu unterbreiten.

Kapitel Fünf:

In diesem letzten Kapitel wurde daher Beziehungen zwischen den vorangegangenen Kapiteln hergestellt. Aus der Darstellung geht hervor, dass die Förderung und der Schutz der Menschenrechte ein notwendiger Bestandteil der Missionstätigkeit der Kirche sind, wenn die Kirche eine umfassende Befreiung der Menschheit anstrebt. In der Folge habe ich einige der Herausforderungen beschrieben, denen sich die Kirche in Nigeria gegenübergestellt sieht, wenn sie diese Mission erfüllen möchte. Dazu gehört vor allem ihre Verantwortung als Trägerin einer Kultur der Menschenrechte. Diese Rolle kann nur dann glaubhaft wahrgenommen werden, wenn ihr ein von innen nach außen fortschreitender Prozess der Introspektion vorangeht, der jene ideologischen und doktrinären Aspekte anspricht, die dazu neigen, Menschenrechtsverletzungen außer Acht zu lassen oder zu verschleiern. Nur wenn die Kirche diesen Prozess durchschritten und einige positive Veränderungen zugelassen hat, wird sie in einer geeigneteren Lage sein, ihre prophetische Rolle zu erfüllen, durch die sie eine Kirche *für* die Armen, eine Kirche *mit* den Armen und eine Kirche *der* Armen im wahren Sinn des Wortes sein kann.

Schließlich ist der interkulturelle und interreligiöse Ansatz eine weitere Herausforderung, der sich die Kirche in Nigeria zu stellen hat. Mit einer Konzentration auf die Mission Jesus Christus, versucht dieser Ansatz die bestehenden Barrieren zu durchbrechen, mit denen Menschenrechtsverletzungen gerechtfertigt oder verschleiert werden und ruft zu diesem Zweck zur Zusammenarbeit unter den kulturellen und religiösen Gruppen auf. Die Einengung dieses Dialogs auf den Islam als große religiöse Institution ist prioritär, da es in Nigeria seit jeher religiöse Spannungen und Gewalt zwischen Muslimen und Christen gibt.

Die Menschenrechte stellen das Rückgrat menschlicher Existenz und Würde dar und sollten als solche von der Kirche sehr ernst genommen werden. Sie stellen eine der Möglichkeiten dar, die sich der Kirche bieten, um die Relevanz ihrer Mission in der Welt zu legitimieren. Am Anfang muss eine Stimulation der inneren Anerkennung der Menschenrechte stehen, die Konsequenz wird helfen, innere Zerspaltenheit zu vermeiden und gesellschaftliche Relevanz zu verlieren. Damit die Kirche diese Großtat vollbringen kann, muss die angeblich zwischen der Kirche und der Menschenrechtsfrage existierende Trennung, wie sie aus den Umfrageergebnissen hervorgeht, überbrückt werden, damit sich die Kirche bewusst und in aller Konsequenz mit der Menschenrechtsfrage identifizieren kann. Nur dadurch kann sie die Reihen der Institutionen verstärken, die als „Agenten der Hoffnung" an der Verbesserung der Menschenrechtslage in Nigeria arbeiten.

BIBLIOGRAPHY

BOOKS

Agbakoba, O., et al., Travesty of Justice: An Advocacy Manual against the Holding of Charge, Hurilaws Publication, Lagos, 2004.

Akumadu, T.U., Repudiating Repugnant Customs; Supra, 2000

Andre, G., et al., Christlich-islamische Partnerschaft für Gerechtigkeit und Frieden. (Impulse aus Afrika, Asien and Nahost). Don Bosco 8, Muenchen 2006.

Bevans, S.B., and Schroeder, R.P., Constants in Context. A Theology of Mission Today, Orbis Books, Maryknoll, New York, 2004.

Boff, L., Jesus Christ Liberator: A Critical Christology for our Time, Orbis Books, Maryknoll, New York, 1978.

Boff, L., and Boff, C., Salvation and Liberation, Orbis Books, Maryknoll, New York, 1985.

Bosch, D.J., Transforming Mission: *Paradigm Shifts in Theology of Mission,* Orbis Books, Maryknoll, New York, 1991.

Buhlman, W., The Coming of the Third Church, Orbis Books, St. Paul Publications, New York, 1976.

David, L., et al., Human Rights and the Conflict of Cultures: Western and Islamic Perspectives on Religious Liberty, (Columbia, 1988).

Dorr, D., Mission Today, Orbis Books, Maryknoll, New York, 2000.

Ebelebe, C.: *Africa and the New Face of Mission: A critical assessment of the Legacy of the Irish Spiritans among the Igbo of Southeastern Nigeria.* University Press of America Inc. 2009.

Effah-Chukwuma, J., and Osarenren, N., Beyond Boundaries (Violence Against Women in Nigeria), Mbeyi Associates Press, Lagos, 2000.

Ellacuria, I., Freedom Made Flesh, Orbis Books, Maryknoll, New York, 1976.

Fredericks, M., et al.: Towards and Intercultrual Theology, Uitgeverij Meinema, Zoetermeer, 2003.

Gachiri, E.W.; Female Circumcision, Paulines Publication Africa, 2000

Guity, N., (ed.): Women and Revolution in Iran, ed. (Westview Pres, 1983).

Halama, Jindrich (ed.): The Idea of Human Rights: Traditions and Presence, Prague, UK: ETF, 2003.

Hallaq, W.B., Sharia: Theory, Practice and Transformations. Cambridge University Press. 2009.

Heckel, Roger: Social Teaching of John Paul II, Vatican City, 1980.

Ibhawoh, B.: Imperialism and Human Rights. State University of New York, 2007.

Idowu, E.B.; Oludumare – God in Yoruba Belief. London Longman, 1962.

Ishay, M.R., The History of Human Rights: *From Ancient Times to the Globalization era.* University of California Press, London, 2004.

Lynn, H.: Inventing Human Rights. W.W. Norton & Comp., New York. 2008.

Mayer, A.E.,, Islam and Human RIghts: Tradition and Politics (Third Ed.); Westview Press, U.S.A., 1999.

Obi, A. C., (ed.): Hunderd Years of the Catholic Church in Eastern Nigeria (1885 – 1995), Africana-Fep Publishers, Lagos, Nigeria, 1985.

Odozor, P.I. et al.: Africa: Towards Priorities of Mission, SIST Publication, 2000.

Onwubiko, O., The Church and Mission (In the Light of Ecclesia in Africa), Paulines Publications, Nairobi, 2001.

Onwubiko, O., African Thought, Religion and Culture, (Snaap Press Ltd. Enugu, 1991.

Ottmar, F., God's People: Instruments of Healing. Peter Lang, Berne, 1993.

Ottmar, F., Heilen und befrien: *Der Dienst am Nächsten als Ernstfall von Kirche und Pastoral.* Patmos Düsseldorf, 1990.

Roland, O.: Africa since 1800, London, 1978.

Schillebeeckx, E.: The Mission of the Church, Orbis Books, Maryknoll, New York, U.S.A. 1973.

Schinneller, P., The Voice of the Voiceless (Pastoral Letters and Communiques of the Catholic Bishops' Conference of Nigeria, 1960 – 2002), Ibadan, 2002.

Schreiter, R.: Mission in the Third Millennium. Orbis Books, Maryknoll, New York, U.S.A. 2000.

Stichele, V.C. et al.: Disciples and Discipline (European Debate on Human Rights Violations in the Roman Catholic Church), Leuven, Beligium. 1993.

Tarimo, A., Human Rights, Cultural Differences and the Church in Africa, Salvatorianum Publications, Tanzania, 2004.

Udo, J.I.: *The Rope: Country Report on death penalty application in Nigeria.* HURILAWS Lagos Nigeria, 2004.

Ven van der, A.J.: Ecclesiology in Context. Wm B. Eerdmans Publishing Co., Cambridge, U.K. 1996.

Ven van der, A.J.: Is there a God of Human Rights. Brill, Leiden, 2004.

Wafi, A.A.W. Humn Rights in Islam (Translated by Derar Saleh Derar), Riyadh, 1998.

Walbert, B.: The Coming of the Third Church, Orbis Books, Maryknoll, New York, U.S.A. 1976.

Welch, E. C. Jr.: Protection of Human Rights in Africa. University of Pennsylvania Press, U.S.A. 1995.

Wijsen, F., *Intercultural Theology and the Mission of the Church,* at: www.sedos.org.

Wilson, B., How Jesus became Christian.Orion Books, United Kingdom, 2009.

SACRED SCRIPTURES

The New Jerusalem Bible (Pocket Edition), Darton, Longman & Todd, London. 1990.

Christian Community Bible (Catholic Pastoral Edition), Claratian Publication, Philippines, 1994.

The Holy Qurán: English Translation of the meanings and commentary. Revised and edited by the Presidency of Islamic Researches, IFTA, Call and Guidance. Al-Madinah AL-Munawarah.

CODE OF CANON LAW AND CATECHISM OF THE CHURCH

The Code of Canon Law**:** (New Revised English Edition), 2004. Theological Publications, Bangalore, India.

The Catechism of the Catholic Church: Paulines, 1994.

VATICAN COUNCIL II DOCUMENTS

Flannery, A., (General Editor): Vatican Council II. The Conciliar and Post Conciliar Documents, Pauline Publishers, India, 1975.

Dignitatis Humanae

Gaudum et Spes

Lumen Gentium

Nostra Aetate

Ad Gentes Divinitus

PAPAL ENCYCLICALS AND APOSTOLIC LETTERS

Pius XI: Quadragesimo Anno: AAS 1931.

Paul VI: Evangelii Nuntiandi. Vatican City, 1975.

John Paul II: Redemptoris Missio, Vatican City, 1990.

Benedict XVI: Charity in Truth (Caritas in Veritate), Published in Washington by the USA Conference of Catholic Bishops, July 2009.

CURIAL DOCUMENTS

The Church and Human Rights: Pontifical Commission Justitia et Pax. Vatican City, 1978.

Sacred Congregation for the Doctrine of the Faith: Instruction on Christian Freedom and Liberation, Boston: Daughters of St. Paul Publications, U.S.A. 1986.

Congregation for Catholic Education, *Guidelines for t he Study and Teaching of t he* Church's *Social Doctrine in the Formation of Priests,* 20, Vatican Polyglot Press, Rome 1988.

Compendium of the Social Doctrine of t he Church, *Compendium of the Social Doctrine of the Church,* Paulines Publications, Africa, 2005.

EPISCOPAL CONFERENCE DOCUMENTS

Communiques issued by the AECAWA Bishops Conference, Enugu Nigeria, 1995.

JOURNALS AND NEWSPAPERS

Anderson, H. G. et al.: Mission Trends *No. 1*, 1974, Paulist Press, New York, U.S.A.

African Journal XXII Ed., 1982, Cambridge University Press Ltd. London.

The International Journal of Not-for-Profit Law, Volume 8, Issue 4, August 2006.

Forum Weltkitche, No. 4. (July/August 2009).

The Guardian Newspapers, *Nigeria,* Wednesday, 7 September, 2005.

Jahrbuch Mission

Image – *Gerechtigkeit kennt keine leeren Hände.* 12/10, März 2011.

ENCYCLOPEDIA

Lawson, Edward; Wiseberg, S. Laurie and Dargel, D.K. Jan (eds.): Encyclopedia of Human Rights, 1996. Washington D.C., U.S.A.

DECLARATIONS AND CONSTITUTION

Universal Declaration on Human Rights

Universal Declaration and the International Convention on Economic, Social, and Cultural Rights.

African Charter on Human and Peoples' Rights

African Commission on Human and Peoples' Rights

National Commission on Human Rights

1999 Consitution of the Federeal Republic of Nigeria.

UNPUBLISHED DOCUMENTS AND PAPERS

Ike, O., *Christian Understanding of Justice and the Challenge on Nigerian Church,* In: Justice: (Proceedings of National Seminar on Justice and Peace) 11 – 15 April, 1998. Enugu, Nigeria.

Catholic Diosese of Ondo, Nigeria; Human Rights Department: 2003 Updated Statistics of Released Prisoners from Akure Medium Security Prison.

Odoeme, P.: Isa Ahu rite of purification in Uturu; unpublished paper at Bigard Memorial Seminary, Enugu, 1995.

World Mission Sunday 2009 under the Motto: „Peace and Reconciliation"; MISSIO, Aachen, Germany, 2009.

INTERNET SOURCES

www.nigeria-law.org/ConstitutionOfTheFederalRepublicOfNigeria.htm#Chapter_4

http://www.historycentral.com/nationbynation/Nigeria/Index.html

www.amnesty.org.nz/web/chogm.nsf/opendocument

www.globalpolicy.org/socecon.tncs/2004/1109amnestynigeria.pdf

www.hrw.org/legacy/english/doc/2004/09/21/nigeria9364_txt.htm

www.ecoi.net/doc/en/NG/content/4/941_961

www.dec.org/pdf_docs/PNACX553.pdf

www.rufarm.kabissa.org/articles/fgm.htm

http://lists.peacelink.it/africa/msg00856.html

www.sedos.org

www.historycooperative.org/journals/ahr/109.1/cmiel.html

www.photius.com/countries/nigeria/national_security/nigeria_national_security_human_rights.html.

www.waado.org/nigerian_schlolars/archive/contents.html.

www.infoplease.com/ce6/world/A086005.html.

www.org/english_info/history_en.html.

http://en.wikipedia.org/wiki/african_commission.

www.dfa.gov.za/foreign/multicultural/african/afrhr.html.

www.nigeriarights.gov.ng/mission-vision.htm

www.hrw.org/doc/?t=africa&c=nigeria

www.extrajudicialexecutions.org/law

www.allafrica.com/stories.

www.ngrguardiannews.com

www.nigeriaworld.com

www.lists.mayfirst.org/pipermail/friends/2006-May

www.zenit.org.vwww.icnl.org/knowledge/ijnl/vol8iss4/art_2.htm

www.afrol.com/articles

www.state.gov/g/drl/rls/hrrpt/2005

http://hdr.undp.org/statistics/data/cty/cty_f_NGA.html

http://web.amnesty.org/library/index/engafr

www.amnestyusa.org/annualreport.php?id=ar&yr=2006&c=N

www.unhcr.org/home/RSDCOI/45aca2a316.html

www.cia.gov/cia/publications/factbook/geos/ni.html

http://www.scienceinafrica.co.za/2001/nov/Nigeria.html

http://www.mertonai.org/amina/amina.asp

http://www.ksg.harvard.edu/cchrp/pdf/Amadi.pdf

www.sanford.edu/lilyhumanrights/papers.html

Tübinger Perspektiven zur Pastoraltheologie und Religionspädagogik

hrsg. von Ottmar Fuchs, Albert Biesinger, Reinhold Boschki

Matthias Gronover
Katechese als Übung
Eine Grundlegung. Mit einem Geleitwort von Christian Bauer und Ottmar Fuchs
Die Übung gehört zum religionspädagogischen Inventar. Sie soll Gelerntes verfestigen und ermöglichen, darauf aufbauend Weiteres dazu zu lernen. Aber die Übung hat auch eine grundlegende Bedeutung, die über ihren methodischen Aspekt hinaus auf das Christsein selbst verweist: Im Horizont der Reich Gottes-Botschaft sind Christen Übende, die in Zeiten des gesellschaftlich entsicherten Glaubens ihre christliche Haltung bewahren wollen. Katechese zielt dann darauf ab, auch die Gesellschaft zu gestalten. Katechese als Übung ist die Funktion der Differenz von Kirche und Gesellschaft.
Bd. 48, 2012, 176 S., 19,90 €, br.,
ISBN 978-3-643-11785-4

Michael Pflaum
Die aktive und die kontemplative Seite der Freiheit
Freiheit kann nur in der Differenz von Aktivität und Kontemplation gedacht und gestaltet werden. Dies wird sowohl philosophisch, insbesondere anhand von Karl Popper und Henri Bergson, dargestellt, als auch durch die Analyse verschiedener therapeutischer und spiritueller Wege, wie zum Beispiel: Rational-emotive Verhaltenstherapie, Logotherapie, lösungsorientiertes Arbeiten, Tetralemma-Arbeit, Gewaltfreie Kommunikation, Eckhart Tolle, Enneagramm, Qigong, Homöopathie, Naikan, Focusing, das Jesusgebet und die stille christliche Meditation. Das Buch soll gerade auch für Seelsorger eine Hilfe und Bereicherung sein.
Bd. 47, 2012, 488 S., 49,90 €, br.,
ISBN 978-3-643-11732-8

LIT Verlag Berlin – Münster – Wien – Zürich – London
Auslieferung Deutschland / Österreich / Schweiz: siehe Impressumsseite